E.T.A. HOFFMANN AND MUSIC

R. MURRAY SCHAFER

E.T.A. Hoffmann and Music

UNIVERSITY OF TORONTO PRESS
TORONTO AND BUFFALO

© University of Toronto Press 1975
Toronto and Buffalo
Printed in Canada

Library of Congress Cataloging in Publication Data

Schafer, R Murray.
    E.T.A. Hoffmann and music.

    Includes bibliographical references and index.
    1. Hoffmann, Ernst Theodor Amadeus, 1776-1822.
    2. Romanticism in music. I. Title.
    ML410.H7S3   780'.9034   73-93502
    ISBN 0-8020-5310-6

To John Beckwith, for many kindnesses

Contents

Preface

Music history books always mention the importance of E.T.A. Hoffmann's musical writings in shaping the ideas of musical romanticism. But curiously, while Hoffmann's *Tales* have often been rendered into English, few of the musical writings have ever been translated, leaving the English reader in a somewhat embarrassed position in accounting for this importance.

The format this book has taken seemed the only logical one, as obviously a body of Hoffmann's writings about music would have to be translated before they could be commented on. The book thus consists of my translations of writings by Hoffmann alternating with essays on aspects of his life and work. For all translations I used the edition of Georg Ellinger (*E.T.A. Hoffmanns Werke*, 15 vols, Berlin 1912, subsequently referred to as *Werke*).

The selection of passages for translation has necessarily been arbitrary. The selected extracts have served as points around which circles are made to vibrate. If the reader may not always feel that his sympathies are concentric with these points and circles, it may be, as I shall be suggesting in a moment, that it is because we are losing touch with the romantic era to a greater extent than is generally realized. If there are difficulties with the texts, they will be on the affective and philosophical levels. Obviously it is my hope that the commentaries will help to remove these difficulties. I hope none of the problems will be due to Hoffmann's language, for I have tried to render it as simply as possible, bearing in mind the intricate nature of nineteenth-century German style.

This work was originally written between the years 1960 and 1963, but it lay on the shelf for several years as more pressing matters engaged my attention. When I opened the typescript in December 1971, I discovered that it was not so much Hoffmann's prose which required the services of a translator, but my own. For help in defoliating the jungle of Schafer's prose, grateful thanks are offered to many people. Phyllis Mailing Schafer assisted greatly in gathering the source material. Beverly Matsu assisted in the final research and typed out the final draft of the manuscript. Joan Henderson and Jean Reed corrected my grammar. Professor John Beckwith of the University of Toronto read the manuscript in its first form and made numerous suggestions, helpful as always. Dr Herbert Jackson of Memorial University, Newfoundland, kindly read many of the translations, and Mrs William Aide read them all. R.M. Schoeffel was encouraging and kind as the manuscript approached publication. But, of course, all these people remain guiltless of any errors or unattractivenesses still remaining in these pages.

This book has been published with the help of a grant from the Humanities Research Council of Canada, using funds provided by the Canada Council, and a grant to the University of Toronto Press from the Andrew W. Mellon Foundation.

Vancouver, September 1973

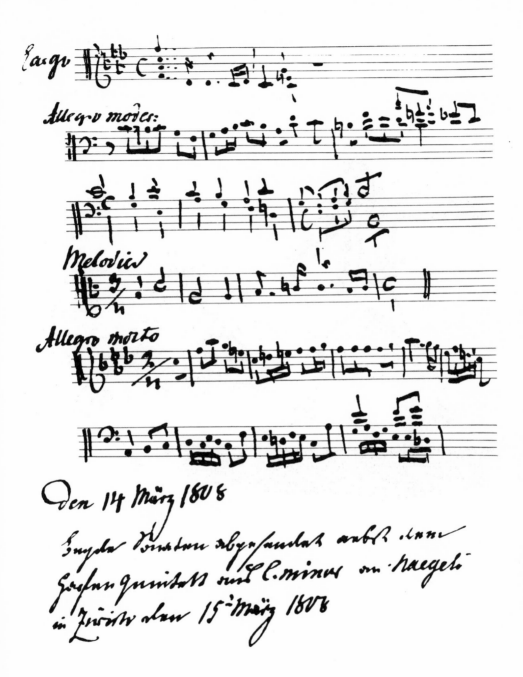

Musical sketches in E.T.A. Hoffmann's hand, from a letter to the music publisher, Hans Georg Nägeli, 15 March 1808 (from *E.T.A. Hoffmann: Briefwechsel 1794-1814* by permission of Winkler Verlag, Munich)

Drawing by Hoffmann to illustrate his story 'Der Musikfeind'
(Sächsische Landesbibliothek, Dresden)

Ernst Theodor Amadeus Hoffmann

Self-portrait by Hoffmann (Sächsische Landesbibliothek, Dresden)

Hoffmann in an engraving by Wilhelm Hensel, 1821
(Öffentliche Bibliothek der Universität Basel)

Kapellmeister Johannes Kreisler in his dressing gown.
The score is that of Hoffmann's own opera *Undine*.
(Sächsische Landesbibliothek, Dresden)

The mad Johannes Kreisler, in a sketch by Hoffmann
(Sächsische Landesbibliothek, Dresden)

E.T. A. HOFFMANN AND MUSIC

ONE

Introduction

This book is about romanticism as it affects music. It is not a book about romantic music strictly speaking, but rather about the artistic and social climate that surrounded the birth of the music to which we now give that name.

Anyone writing about romantic music today has a right to feel vaguely uncomfortable about it; for there is much ambivalence in our general attitude towards the music of the century preceding our own. Although romantic music has been attacked and denounced a great deal in recent times, it can by no means be said to have gone down to defeat. Despite the inadequate critical defence it has received, it is apparently surviving the attackers. One might be tempted to agree with the statements of many philosophers and historians – mostly German – that the nineteenth century really did represent some pinnacle of musical expression never again to be attained.

As a result, romantic music has become institutionalized in conservatories, opera theatres, and concert halls. This institutionalization has assured it a consistent place on musical programs, perhaps more consistent than might otherwise have been the case; for certainly other important musical styles have declined in popularity because today they lack sufficient patronage to secure a continuity of tradition in performance (one thinks, for example, of medieval and renaissance church music). Vehicles for the presentation of romantic music survive intact. The grandest, the symphony orchestra, reached its maturity during the nineteenth century with additions to the wind and brass sections, the elimination of the harpsichord, and the strengthening of the strings both in construction and in numbers, and this same symphony orchestra is still the complement of men and instruments that performs regularly today in every fair-sized city in the Western world.

The movement against romantic music was strongest during the early decades of the twentieth century. The reaction against rationalism, which characterized the late-eighteenth century *Sturm und Drang* epoch of German literature and the music it eventually inspired, appeared alien to an age which had traded its faith in poetry for faith in technology. Composers too, ceased to employ the borrowed forms of the past, such as the sonata and the *Lied*; they sought greater control over their material; they revived classicism and developed mathematical techniques which eventually led to serial and computer music. In their works the symphony orchestra was broken up into chamber music groups of varying dimensions with unorthodox instrumentation. Their music was more austere, created for the broadcasting or recording studio rather than for the mellow assembly of the formal evening concert.

Did romantic music survive these vicissitudes merely because it had strong institutions behind it, or was it consciously maintained by the public as an antidote to the anxieties of modern life? These are difficult questions to answer. The fact is that today, late into the century, its major figures still remain upright and their music is still performed. Moreover, among many of today's younger composers there is a detectable return to romantic idioms: longer lines, bigger shapes, more opulent orchestrations – even melodies!

Nevertheless, something has changed. We have lived through different experiences than our ancestors of a hundred and fifty years ago and these experiences have affected our attitudes. Today many romantic sentiments elicit self-consciousness and diffidence; the more temperament and abandon the interpreter of romantic art brings to his subject the more embarrassed his audience becomes. Who today, for example, would confess readily to having wept at a concert? Who has ever wept at music? Today we are dispassionate; weeping is sentimental. Yet in 1805 people bragged about it:

> If music has the ability to overpower the quiet heart, how much more may it be
> expected to affect the energetic breast? As the full tree of harmony rushed over
> him, a strange new spirit descended to him, and it said but one word: weep!
> (Jean Paul)[1]

The spectacle of Beethoven playing C-sharp minor *arpeggios* by moonlight on the Danube is difficult to bring into view now that moonlight has been replaced by neon and all the rivers are polluted. We try to draw the experience into focus but it eludes us. We are looking through a Claude-glass covered with the varnish of intervening traditions. We wish to see

Beethoven, but in most cases *our* Beethoven would seem to be more accurately described as Romain Rolland's or Gustav Mahler's Beethoven; that is, Beethoven seen against the backdrop of Wagner, Brahms, and all that passed between the birth of romanticism and its last flicker of expression. And all these interpretations have deflected what Beethoven originally was. Liaison figures often provide interesting interpretations, but their interpretations are ultimately more helpful in understanding *them* and their own times than in clarifying original issues. Each age needs its own liaison figures: performers, conductors, musicologists. Since musicologists today are more concerned with remoter periods, there seems to be a sizable and growing vacuum of literature relating the philosophies and practices of musical romanticism to our own time, with the result that interpretive artists and music lovers are driven back to many superannuated and often spurious volumes in their quest for a relationship with the subject.

For history is our way of looking at it. The moment a new generation opens its eyes to the past, a new light is revealed and the illumination of the preceding generation passes into shadow. No generation is privileged to look at history from all angles; each discovers its own private and uninheritable view. To observe history is to touch it, to dislocate it, to change it.

One of the most troublesome words in any language, romanticism is a word open at both ends. In the past it has been used in a variety of ways and it is still being used in new ways. As a result it has become one of the most untrustworthy words in the critical repertoire. Even setting chronological limits on it has met with much opposition. Some people would rather not regard romanticism as a special period in intellectual and artistic history at all, but as an attitude of mind which anyone may possess at any time. There is no such thing as romanticism, they argue, there are only romantics. Thus, Shakespeare may be a romantic, or Plato, or Calderón; and such men, indeed, were often considered romantics by the writers and thinkers living within the confines of the narrower nineteenth-century movement which assumed the (frequently capitalized) title of Romanticism.

This is not the place to reform whatever notions the reader may already attach to this word. Rather the intention is to provide a little source material on the subject against which these notions may be measured. But since this source material originates particularly with one man, it is necessary to focus attention on romanticism in its more limited historical sense.

A student of the romantic movement in Germany would probably isolate literary romanticism between the dates 1795 and 1830, that is, roughly from the time Ludwig Tieck and Novalis started writing until the death of Hoffmann in 1822. However, a critic of French literature would place the first date considerably later and let the period run until 1848, when Gautier and Hugo began to talk about their youthful romanticism retrospectively. Again other critics, interested in a more panoramic view, are inclined to move the beginnings back considerably, to 1770 or earlier, to include the gathering influence of Jean-Jacques Rousseau and the *Sturm und Drang* movement in Germany.

In music the dates are different again. Beethoven is not usually called a romantic composer, though he certainly brought music to the very threshold of the movement now given the name. For some special reason, known to critics alone, Schubert and Weber are usually considered the first romantics, though one scarcely outlived Beethoven and the other despised what he stood for. These are quickly followed by Berlioz and Schumann and then the whole wave of later composers. This places the date of the first romantic outbursts shortly after 1800. And romanticism in music continues at least until the deaths of Wagner (1883) and Verdi (1901) – in other words, nearly a century. This lengthy attenuation of the romantic movement in music contrasts sharply with the packed vitality of the literary movement.

It is interesting also, as we shall see, that Hoffmann should have referred to Haydn and Mozart as romantic composers, while today we usually place them in the classical era. In other words, for Hoffmann musical and literary romanticism were much more nearly contemporaneous than they have since become in popular usage. But then Hoffmann was unaware of Nietzsche's dictum that music is supposed to consummate an era after the other arts have begun to grow stale.

There are several underlying principles of romantic philosophy that will, through our interpreter, concern us. The romanticists deliberately cultivated a turning-away from everyday life towards a world of illusion and nostalgic *Träumerei*. The romanticist seems either unwilling or unable to face everyday reality squarely. At worst the dichotomy between these two existences created unbearable pressure and led to madness or suicide: Hölderlin went mad, as did Schumann, Lenau, and Büchner; Kleist and Nerval committed suicide; many others, such as Brentano, Zacharias Werner, and Wackenroder fled to the protective breast of the Roman Catholic Church. At best it led to the fantastic world of the *Märchen*, in which the dividing line between reality and illusion is dissolved completely. This is illustrated beautifully in one of Hoffmann's best tales, 'The Golden Pot,' where the student Anselmus straddles two worlds, unable to decide to which he really belongs, and yet is completely content to remain hovering between them, leading a contradictory but hypersensitized existence. The romanticists deliberately created this dual world, though by disclosing the impor-

tance of the world of dreams they were acknowledging the value of something to which we should give a different name today – the unconscious.
Thus, there ought to be something deeply informative for us when the
romanticists use the dream to describe their sensations of listening to or
composing music, provided we can read their symbolism.

Another aspect of romanticism has bearing on our theme – the pan-
theism of nature. This divine spirit existed everywhere; it was unseen, but
it could be heard. For those who wished to describe nature, her acoustics
became vitally important:

> Suddenly it was moonlight. As if evoked by the lovely, shimmering light, there
> sounded down from all the silver treetops a sweet, melodious sound. All fear was
> lost. The forest blazed gently with the most beautiful glow, and nightingales
> awakened and flew close past him, singing with sweet voices, and always in time
> to the music of the moonlight. (Ludwig Tieck)[2]

The descriptive prose and poetry of many romanticists is alive with
natural sounds: the howling of the wind, the tossing of the sea, the whispering of the leaves – friendly sounds, or sounds of terror heard in the stillness of night. At this time, instruments which captured something of the
acoustic spirit of nature were very popular – the aeolian, or wind harp, for
example:

> The poetry ... of romanticism is an aeolian harp, through which the tempest of
> reality sweeps in melodies, its howlings resolved in tones; but melancholy trem-
> bles on these strings, sometimes even a grief rends its way in. (Jean Paul)[3]

Nature was like an enormous orchestral score, respirating mysteriously.

> There is about the imperceptible beginning, the swelling and the dying of the
> tones of nature, something which has a most powerful and indescribable effect
> on us; and any instrument which could be capable of reproducing this would
> undoubtedly affect us in a similar way.[4]

This is Hoffmann speaking, in an essay in which he is criticizing the mechanical reproduction of music by pointing out its opposition to nature,
its *unnaturalness*. Music speaks in tones of the secrets of nature. In nature
one hears the great song of the trees, flowers, animals, stones, waterfalls,
and winds, unified into a brilliantly instrumented composition. One finds
these ideas not only in the three writers I have quoted, but also in Wackenroder, Schelling, the Schlegels, and Novalis as well; and they are passed
along to Schopenhauer and Wagner.

This fusion of music and nature is made explicit through the medium of language and the liberal use of visual imagery. Thus, the romanticists often disclosed their deepest convictions about *music* by means of *language*, used in a provocatively *visual* manner, a means which may strike the contemporary reader as bewildering or artificial. The romanticists were extremely concerned with breaking down the barriers that kept the arts apart. The elder Schlegel voiced a general credo when he wrote:

> We should strive to bring the arts closer together and search for bridges from one to the other. Statues will come alive to become perhaps paintings; paintings will become poems; poems will become music; and who knows, perhaps solemn religious music will rise up again as a temple in the sky.[5]

Romanticists were forever longing to transform one art form into another, and because of this there was something unsatisfactory about the repose of the self-contained art form. The writer Hoffmann longed to be a composer, the composer Weber attempted all his life to write a romantic novel, and these are examples of the romantic longing not only to invade the other arts, but to take them over completely. There was something keenly synaesthetic about romantic aesthetics, something which made it possible to see the closest relationships between different works or media where few would see it today. The relationship of Hoffmann's prose to music was extremely close in the minds of the nineteenth-century composers; and Schumann and Wagner were by no means the only composers to have found it inspirational.

Of all the arts, music became, for the romanticists, the highest; and all the arts were in one way or another aspiring towards the condition of music long before Schopenhauer pointed this out explicitly. There were two main reasons for this. The first has already been suggested: the abstract and invisible substance of music made it an ideal metaphor for the mysterious spirit of nature, the divine essence which pervaded all things. The second reason lay in the timely emancipation of music from the church and state so that it was now free to develop new associations in an independent manner.

All the arts have at one time or another been held prisoner by the church or state. Although music was at first mistrusted by the early Christian fathers, when it was eventually accepted, it was quickly accorded a high place in the exercises of worship. With the church as its guardian, music became influential to a seldom-experienced degree. Clearly purposive, with high moral duties, it achieved great prestige. But it was by no means a free art and its dignity was insecure outside the church. The fact that we do not possess any purely instrumental music until the thirteenth century does not indicate that none existed before this time, but it does show that secular music was felt in some way to be inferior and not worth collecting and preserving.

Music was the last art form to break away from the church and play a part in the secular movements which, over time, had come to challenge the church's sovereignty. Religious music remained strong right up until the eighteenth century. Bach was still a servant of the church. The ultimate liberation and secularization of music is a nineteenth-century achievement – probably the greatest single artistic achievement of that century. It is in the triumph of pure instrumental music over vocal music (where the music was to some extent still governed by the text) that this achievement was celebrated, in the symphonies and quartets of Haydn, Mozart, and Beethoven; and Hoffmann, in his championing of instrumental music, is exulting in this emancipation.

As the youngest of the liberated arts, music seduced the age. She cast a spell over all the other arts; none could remain untouched by her. The whole aesthetic of the age was melted down to comply with music's fluid condition. Even architecture was talked about as 'petrified music.'[6] Kleist believed music to be the root or fundamental formula of all the arts.[7] Ludwig Tieck objected to language because words rendered vague and misty emotions too definite, and in his *Sternbald* he suggests the idea that one might even devise conversation musically.[8] Novalis, too, in his *Fragments* attests to the gravitational attraction of music: 'Compositions of speech; musical handling of the art of writing; one should write as the composer composes.'[9] Aestheticians no longer talked of materials – of cross-hatchings or minor thirds or trochees – but were bewitched by speculation about the spirit rather than the substance of a work of art. Witness Friedrich von Schelling in his *Philosophie der Kunst*:

> Beauty exists when the particular (the real) is so adequate to its conception that the latter, as infinite, enters the finite and presents itself to our contemplation in concrete form. With the appearance of the concept, the real becomes truly similar and equal to the idea, wherein the universal and the particular find their absolute identity.[10]

Elsewhere Schelling had maintained: 'There is but one sole and absolute work of art.'[11] Now he saw in music 'the very ideal rhythm of Nature and the Universe, which by means of this art makes itself felt in the derivative world.'[12] Such transcendental ideas were attractive to Hoffmann, and he too conceived of music as the most romantic of all the arts. To an extent this explains why he calls Haydn and Mozart romantic composers, since for him music is in itself the apotheosis of romanticism. As Schumann later wrote: 'It is scarcely credible that a distinct romantic school could be found in music, which is itself romantic.'[13]

Later Schopenhauer paid music the ultimate tribute. For him music is 'just as much the immediate objectivication and image of the collective will as the world itself is.' While the other arts 'are concerned only with phantoms of things ... music is concerned with their essence.' And if music is as much an image of the collective will as the world itself, music would continue to exist even if the world did not.[14]

The starting point of this book is the assumption that many of these themes have passed or are now quickly passing into shadow, and therefore require forceful restatement if we are to comprehend romantic music properly. Direct oral heritage connects no more than two generations before it gives way to fiction. How can we appreciate the nascent outburst of enthusiasm that characterized the birth of romantic music? The only way to block out spurious intermediary traditions is to go directly to source material. If we could see the birth of romantic music through the eyes of an observant and articulate participant, we might then begin to fix our own relationship to it.

Such an eye-witness is E.T.A. Hoffmann. Most celebrated in the English-speaking world as the author of *The Tales* and the subject of an opera by Offenbach, E.T.A. Hoffmann was, in reality, a much more valuable figure, active as a composer, stage designer, conductor, and, for our purposes most importantly, an early pamphleteer of the gospel of romanticism through his music criticism. Hoffmann was almost an exact contemporary of Beethoven, and with his combined gifts for music and literature was in an excellent position to describe the musical philosophy he saw taking shape around him.

This he did with eloquence and passion. There is no doubt that he would have preferred to make his statements directly in the composition of romantic pieces of music. I have discussed his strengths and weaknesses as a composer in an essay at the conclusion of the book, but it might as well be stated at the beginning that the latter outweighed the former. His awareness of this resulted in a more or less deliberate curtailment of composition for literature in mid-life. But this is no indictment of his abilities as a propagandist for the music of his time; in fact, as all historians agree, the age produced none finer.

TWO

E.T.A. Hoffmann: Life and Credentials

Eighteenth-century Germany was a land possessing neither the uniform texture of life nor the patriotic spirit that it later developed. Its provincial capitals were pinpoints separated from one another by many days' uncomfortable journey by coach, each with its own local colour and its own political and cultural life. To see our informant clearly we will want to fix a number of locales in Germany and those parts of eighteenth-century Prussia now belonging to Poland and Russia: to begin with, Königsberg. Lying on the shore of the Baltic Sea, Königsberg is described by its most illustrious citizen, the philosopher Immanuel Kant:

> A large city in the middle of a realm, home of the provincial government, with a university for the cultivation of learning, together with a maritime commercial industry; a city favoured by the mixture of different languages and customs from our own and neighbouring lands, brought down to it by the inland tributaries – such a city is Königsberg on the Pregel river; and it serves as a good place for broadening the study of human knowledge and understanding, even if one is unable to travel abroad.[1]

Ernst Theodor Wilhelm Hoffmann was born in Königsberg in 1776. Christened Wilhelm, he later changed his name to Amadeus out of love for Mozart, who was twenty years his senior. In 1776 Beethoven and Hegel were six years old, Napoleon was seven, Goethe was twenty-one, and Kant was fifty-two.

Ernst was the youngest of three sons born of the marriage of Christoph Ludwig Hoffmann to Luise Albertine Doerffer, his cousin. The father was a brash and unstable man, and the numerous temperamental differences between him and his nervous, reserved wife led to an early dissolution of their marriage. Ernst was between two and three years old when his father departed from Königsberg and the boy and his mother returned to the shelter of the Doerffer family household.

Hoffmann's association with music dates from his early youth. His father had played the viola da gamba enthusiastically, if none too accurately. His uncle Otto, who, as his mother's brother, now assumed many of the responsibilities of father to the boy, also loved music and could 'handle the spinet with barbaric virtuosity.' Musical evenings were common in the Doerffer household. The friends and relatives gathered with their instruments and attacked the music of Stamitz, Hiller, or Benda with more vigour than sensitivity. The tortured sounds produced by this grimacing group are described by Hoffmann in his story 'Der Musikfeind' (The Music Hater), where the author makes a case for the impressionable person being driven away from music as a result of having to listen to such recitals. Hoffmann himself, however, does not appear to have been uncooperative about studying music and he received instruction in piano, organ, and music theory from a local organist. An early facility enabled him to transpose at sight by the time he was eight. His enthusiasm for Mozart may also date from these early years, for in 1788 Mozart's *Entführung aus dem Serail* was performed in Königsberg, and in 1793, *Don Giovanni*. To gather from contemporary newspaper clippings, the musical life of eighteenth-century Königsberg must have been spirited and entertaining.

Mr Christian Seelig would like to make it known that on October 25 the first winter concert will be given at his home, and that they will be continued every Tuesday at five o'clock. He is making every effort to locate all those who appreciate fine music, and promises that though the charge is modest, the refreshments will always be the finest. (Advertisement in the Königsberger *Gelehrten und politischen Zeitung*, 1774)

We should like to inform the public at large, and particularly lovers of music, that the concerts which were given in the Junker's court in the old city will be resumed and will take place every Sunday until Easter 1777. Immediately following each concert there will be a ball. Subscription tickets for the concert and the ball: 8 thalers – for the ball alone: 5 thalers. (Advertisement in the same paper, 1776)

I should like to inform all lovers of music that next Friday, February 4, the cantata *Der Sieg der Maurerey* by Türk will be repeated once again. However, since the practice of attending concerts without a ticket has increased so sharply that not only the audience but even the musicians are being crowded out, I beg every gentleman with a ticket to restrict himself to accompanying not more than two ladies. (Newspaper announcement, 1785)[2]

Although talented at music and art, the young Hoffmann was a poor student at school. He appears also to have been friendless until the age of eleven, when he met a youth his own age who was to become a lifelong friend. Theodor Gottlieb Hippel, like Hoffmann, had been brought up largely in the company of adults. His mother was dead; his father was indulgent and kind but from the outset had planned a career in statesmanship for his son and began preparing him for this career early. The friendship between the two persisted throughout their lives despite their contrasting careers, and Hoffmann's correspondence with Hippel is a major source of information concerning his thoughts, activities, and feelings. Hippel appears in many of Hoffmann's stories as a devoted friend of differing temperament, and is most fully developed in the dialogue 'The Poet and The Composer.'

It was suggested that Hippel, who was an exemplary scholar, might tutor Ernst in his poorer subjects, and thus on Wednesday and Saturday afternoons the two boys were left alone together in the Doerffer house. Although the studies began faithfully with Latin and Greek homework, they invariably developed with the discovery on uncle Otto's bookshelf of volumes such as Goethe's *Sorrows of Young Werther*, or Rousseau's *Confessions*, and the afternoon would pass in reading and discussion.

Hoffmann's interest in musical composition appears to have received an initial impetus from Rousseau's *Confessions*. Reading there how the author had composed one of the greatest operas revealed to man while lying in bed (though unfortunately out of reach of a pencil with which to write it down), Hoffmann resolved to imitate his idol. Unfortunately he fell asleep and somehow set fire to the curtains of his room, thus depriving the world of yet another masterpiece.

At the age of sixteen Hoffmann entered the University of Königsberg to study law, the traditional profession of his family. He was personally opposed to this choice of professions as his own inclinations still lay firmly with music. He wrote to his friend Hippel in May 1795: 'You can have no idea how it tortures me to go against my resolution and desire. My studies proceed slowly and sadly. I must force myself to become a lawyer.'[3] Contrary to his own expectations Hoffmann developed an interest in his legal studies, and although his career at the university was unexceptional, by the age of nineteen he had passed his preliminary examination for admission to the bar. He was now required to serve a probationary term at the law court of Königsberg without receiving a salary. It was during this period that Hoffmann, whose artistic interests were still uppermost in his mind, began the serious study of painting in an effort to win some portrait commissions; he also made himself available as a teacher of piano.

Among his piano pupils was an attractive married woman in her late twenties, Johanna Dorothea Hatt. Apparently Frau Hatt's husband, a prosperous businessman well over sixty, was incapable of gratifying his young wife, with the result that, not unnaturally, she found the feverish artistic sensitivity of her young music teacher a source of fascination. Hoffmann, for his part, had begun referring to Frau Hatt as Cora, after the heroine of a popular play who violates her marital vows for the sake of love. Of course the affair was doomed from the outset, but for the moment Hoffmann saw in Cora the radiant ideal of womanhood, despite the despair and frustration caused by her inaccessibility. His friend Hippel writes of Hoffmann at this time:

> A new world had arisen before him, but at the same time he had fallen into an ocean whose waves cast him anchorless this way and that. He had won a heart that he could call his own, but still not possess; in daily visits lay the daily separation, and with fullness of happiness the certainty of inevitable loss was mingled. With the goblet of love's joy the bitterest of torments were meted out to him.[4]

When Hoffmann's attentions had grown conspicuous to a point of public scandal, Frau Hatt's husband asserted himself and the affair ended abruptly.

Hoffmann distracted himself now by applying himself feverishly to art and it is from this time that his first works of fiction date. He also wrote some music to Goethe's *Faust*. However, a further number of disturbing events – the death of his mother, news of his father's serious illness, and a visit from his prodigal elder brother, together with the generally irritating environment at home – forced Hoffmann to contemplate leaving his native Königsberg. In May 1796 he departed for Glogau in Silesia.

While waiting to try his second or 'referendary' examination for the bar, Hoffmann was to serve a vague apprenticeship in Glogau with his mother's brother, Johann Ludwig Doerffer, a prominent court official. Johann Ludwig and his wife had two daughters and a son. They seem to have welcomed young Hoffmann into their social circle and although he was at first critical of the daughters, he later found their company amiable and, in fact, actually became engaged to one of them for a time. In 1798 he passed his 'referendary' examination. Shortly afterwards Johann Ludwig received an appointment at the higher court of Berlin, and the family prepared for the removal there. It was only natural that the talented younger lawyer, who was now betrothed to one of the daughters, should accompany them.

Berlin offered Hoffmann theatre, concerts, opera, and art galleries. It was an exciting world for the young man. Under these forces his own interest in the arts could not remain exclusively passive and he composed a *Singspiel* or music drama entitled *Die Maske*, which he dedicated, somewhat naïvely, to the Prussian Queen, sending her the score. It was rejected. At the same time he composed a group of six songs which he sent to a publisher. They were also rejected.

In 1799 Hoffmann took his third and final examination, the 'assessor' examination, which he passed with high honours, and soon after he received a position in the administration of Prussian Poland at the city of Posen.

Posen, a gloomy provincial town, had little to commend itself to Hoffmann, but it did provide him with the opportunity for the first time in his life to arrange his affairs without the supervision or intervention of his elders. Although he continued to be scrupulous in his legal affairs, after hours he gave himself over to questionable forms of physical relaxation. Hippel recalls his shock at meeting his old friend after his first year in Posen:

> An unusual merriment which degenerated almost into buffoonery and a delight in the obscene caused one to suspect that some sort of change which had come over his heart had turned him to the vulgar and especially to a certain lasciviousness, which could not help being so much the more ruinous for him since the southern violence of his temperament always led him to extremes.[5]

Despite these outward changes, Hoffmann continued to produce; he wrote some quite successful music for Goethe's *Scherz, List und Rache*. The degeneration of his outward life may have been partly a conscious rebellion against the unconscious desire to give up law entirely and obey what he regarded as the higher calling of a creative artist. But with which art lay his destiny? About this time he wrote Hippel:

> Some work of art must be born out of the chaos! But whether it will be a book, an opera or a painting – *quod diis placebit*. Don't you think I should ask the High Chancellor once again whether I am supposed to be a painter or a musician?[6]

Breaking his engagement with the Doerffer girl sometime about 1802, Hoffmann shortly after married Michalina Rohrer, a Polish girl about nineteen years of age, dark, slender, and attractive, but possessing no particular accomplishments. Hoffmann says little about her other than that she 'strengthens my spirit.' Nevertheless Michalina remained faithful to him throughout his turbulent and frequently impoverished career.

About this time Hoffmann drew a series of caricatures of local officials and military leaders, which some friends distributed in jest at a ball. They created an immediate uproar and as punishment the offending civil servant was transferred to Plock, a dreary Slavic village at what, from the German point of view, was the very edge of the civilized world.

'Were I only out of this damned hole!' Hoffmann writes from Plock, and fills whole blocks of days in his diary with the single comment 'Dies tristes et miserables.' It seemed as if Plock had nothing to offer him. Yet the very absence of social and artistic life left him with much free time, and he spent it in studying musical theory and in writing. In response to a competition for a piano composition by the Zurich music publisher Nägeli, Hoffmann sent in a 'Grosse Fantasie für das Klavier,' signing himself 'Giuseppo Dori aus Warschau.' Nägeli's comments were unfavourable, but Hoffmann replied by sending a further sonata as proof 'that just censure does not offend me.' He also wrote an essay on the use of the classical chorus in drama, which, thanks to Hippel's assistance, was published, becoming Hoffmann's first printed work.[7] 'Twenty times I gazed upon the magazine with sweet loving glances of paternal joy,' he writes. Nevertheless, life in Plock was stultifying and Hoffmann longed to be rid of it. Eventually, through the efforts of friend Hippel, he obtained a transfer to Warsaw.

The Hoffmanns arrived in Warsaw in April 1804. Ernst liked Warsaw, a city of colourful extremes, full of Turks, Greeks, Russians, Italians, and Frenchmen in addition to Germans and Poles, and possessing an 'inconceivably tolerant police, who never interfered to prevent any popular enjoyment, so that the streets and squares were always swarming with punch-and-judy shows, dancing bears, camels, and apes.'[8] Here Hoffmann met congenial and inspiring companions: Julius Eduard Hitzig, who later became his first biographer, had just come recently from Berlin where he had been an intimate of the Schlegels' circle; and Zacharias Werner, a dramatist of considerable though erratic genius, whose mother had been a close acquaintance of Hoffmann's mother in Königsberg. For Werner's play *Das Kreuz an der Ostsee* Hoffmann produced incidental music.

At the instigation of a group of young noblemen, Hoffmann was induced to assist in the establishment of an academy of music in Warsaw, of which he became musical director, supervising the successful, if brief, career of the institution. He now found himself conducting performances of Mozart and Gluck in addition to composing a considerable quantity of music of his own. In April 1805, Hoffmann's musical setting of Brentano's

Die lustigen Musikanten was performed by the German theatre in Warsaw. Another *Singspiel, Der Kanonikus von Mailand*, and a mass for orchestra and chorus were composed in the same year. Things were beginning to prosper for Hoffmann when news reached Warsaw of the disastrous battle of Jena. Napoleon's soldiers had occupied Berlin already, and on 28 November 1806 they entered Warsaw. Immediately the Prussian civil service was disbanded.

Hoffmann, who never showed the slightest interest in politics, was nevertheless out of work. He sent his wife and daughter back to her relatives in Posen. Shortly after this his funds gave out and he became seriously ill with a fever. On recovering he wrote an opera, *Liebe und Eifersucht*, and hoped to be able to go to Vienna in order to devote himself fully to a career in music; but he was unable to raise the funds for such an extended trip, and in June 1807 he returned to Berlin.

The following year spent in Berlin was bleak and tragic. Almost as soon as he arrived there he received word that his little daughter had died and his wife was seriously ill. In impoverished Berlin it was not easy to find employment and Hoffmann desperately trod the streets trying to get commissions for portraits or even caricatures. At one point he wrote to Hippel asking with embarrassment for a loan; he had had nothing to eat for five days but bread. He inserted an advertisement in the *Allgemeine Reichsanzeiger* offering his services as a theatre music director. Replies came in from Lucerne and Bamberg. At length an acceptable offer was made and Hoffmann was appointed musical director of the theatre at Bamberg. His appointment was commented on approvingly by the *Allgemeine Musikalische Zeitung* in July 1808:

> Music director Hoffmann, who until recently was employed in Warsaw and since the altered political situation there has been residing in Berlin, has been engaged by Count Soden to become music director of the Bamberg Theatre. We wish this theatre well on the appointment of this thoroughly trained composer, experienced singing master, and generally talented, discriminating, and noteworthy person.
>
> Three large characteristic piano sonatas by him are soon to be published by Nägeli of Zurich, and we should like to assume that before long an opera may appear with libretto by Count Soden and music by Hoffmann. It would be an enrichment to the stage.

On 1 September 1808 the Hoffmanns arrived in the medieval city of Bamberg. Cut by the river Regnitz, with a Romanesque cathedral and numerous Gothic monuments and baroque churches, Bamberg was then the seat of the prince-bishop and residence of the Bavarian duke.

In many ways the four-and-a-half years Hoffmann spent in Bamberg were the most significant in his life – certainly as far as his musical career is concerned. He wrote at this time: 'How well the life of the artist suits me! For the first time in my life I am absolutely convinced that my earlier career was the wrong one.'[9] It was about this time that Hoffmann began substituting Amadeus for Wilhelm in his name, in reverence for Mozart. Although his spirits were high when he arrived in Bamberg, they did not remain in this state for long, and on the whole the Bamberg years must be reckoned as both artistically and personally disastrous for him, though they continued to vibrate throughout his life and conditioned much of his philosophy of aesthetics. For this reason, the Bamberg period of his life deserves detailed examination.

Hoffmann's almost immediate failure with the musicians at the Bamberg Theatre was probably largely his own fault, for although he had conducted in Warsaw he could scarcely have been regarded as an experienced conductor. Conducting in 1810, of course, was not done with a baton; this was a refinement brought about only gradually by Carl Maria von Weber and others. Previously the conductor had given the time with a long pole which was struck audibly on the ground. Later the conducting was usually managed by the first violinist or the pianist. The orchestra at Bamberg had been accustomed to taking their cues from Anton Dittmaier, the first violinist. When Hoffmann arrived, usurping Dittmaier's position and conducting from the keyboard, the orchestra responded sluggishly to the unaccustomed arrangement. For his part, Hoffmann described the bassoons as 'combs,' the horns as 'jews-harps,' and the recently appointed director of the theatre as an 'ignorant, conceited windbag.'

Within two months Hoffmann had relinquished his position (though not his title) as director of music at the theatre, and while he continued to write incidental music for the productions, 'for which I receive thirty florins per month,' he had ceased to conduct the musical productions. Again he was forced to teach music privately and although he found many pupils (in a letter to Hitzig he says he is teaching five countesses, and reinforces the remark with an exclamation mark) the inevitable stream of ungifted students had a frustrating effect on the music teacher. He describes the situation with much bitter humour in 'Reflections on the High Value of Music,' a translation of which appears in chapter seventeen.

In another effort to make a living, Hoffmann wrote to Friedrich Rochlitz, the general music director of the publishing firm of Breitkopf und Härtel, offering his services as a music critic for the *Allgemeine Musikalische Zeitung*, the leading musical periodical of its time, then edited by Rochlitz.

Thus he wrote the editor of the Leipzig music magazine, and in those days I was that editor – though I had never heard of Hoffmann. His letter was ingenious and witty, and at the same time as lucid and glowing as anything he ever wrote. He explained how necessary he felt it was to dissociate himself from his earlier life; he told of his latest adventures and then in a most comical manner of his present difficulties – how he had nothing, was nothing, wanted everything, though specifically he knew not what. He hoped to learn that from the editor. But he had to know as soon as possible, for his stomach was aching with hunger, and if not exactly *his* stomach, certainly that of his wife. The only thing that would cause him more pain would be to receive money without working for it. He would gladly work. He could write, either the kind of nonsense that pleased the public, or musical criticism and things related to it.[10]

Rochlitz accepted the invitation and Hoffmann now began to produce for the paper a continuous stream of reviews and works of fiction on musical themes, many of which are included in this volume.

In the fall of 1810 a friend of Hoffmann's from Berlin, Franz von Holbein, was appointed director of the Bamberg Theatre, and he at once re-engaged Hoffmann, not only as musician, but also as scenic designer and stage manager. Holbein's productions were brilliant; it was a golden age for the Bamberg Theatre and one commemorated by German theatrical history books. About this time Hoffmann made the acquaintance of Carl Maria von Weber, then still an obscure itinerant musician. Max Maria von Weber, the composer's son, later described Weber's impressions of the encounter:

He sat one evening in the 'Rose,' sipping his cool Franconian wine, when he fell into conversation with two men, seated at a neighbouring table. The one was a somewhat savage-looking individual, a certain Hoffmann, then musical director, and, at the same time, scene painter at the theatre under Holbein's management. Young Weber did not then foresee that this strange personage was thereafter to become one of Germany's most celebrated authors; that his 'Phantasie-Stücke nach Callot's Manier' [*sic*] would soon fly through the whole land like wild-fire; that the name of Hoffmann would soon be spread far and wide throughout the civilized world; but the young fellow was, then and there, dazed and enchanted with the delightful flashes of lightning wit, which sparkled in unceasing coruscation from the mouth of this singular but genial companion. When both, in later years, came together on the same field of wild romance, although by different paths, a nearer intimacy, almost friendship, as far as their widely contrasting characters would allow, was formed between the two artistic natures, and worked influentially on the tendencies of their reciprocal careers.[11]

Let us consider Hoffmann the man and his personality at this decisive point in his career. As a conversationalist he was, by all accounts, brilliant, with a witty, often stinging sense of humour. He was an especially convivial companion when around a table in the 'Rose' (his favourite Bamberg pub) where he spent many long afternoons and evenings entertaining his friends. He was not a handsome man, but short, with a low forehead and an overlong nose. Hitzig describes him in greater detail:

Hoffmann was very short of stature, of yellowish complexion, with dark, almost black hair, growing down low upon his forehead, and he had grey eyes, which had nothing remarkable about them when they were at rest, but which assumed an uncommonly humourous and cunning expression when he blinked them, as he often did. His nose was thin and of the Roman type, and his mouth was tightly closed.

During the earlier part of his life his dress was sufficiently elegant, without falling into foppery. The only thing about which he took great and special care was his whiskers; these he carefully cut so as to form a point against the corners of his mouth ...

What particularly struck the eye in his exterior was his extraordinary vivacity of movement, which rose to the highest pitch when he began to narrate stories. His manners at receiving and parting from people – repeated quick short bendings of the neck without moving the head – had the appearance of caricature, and might very readily have been taken for irony had not the impression made by his singular gestures on such occasions been softened by his cordial warmth of manner.[12]

One of Hoffmann's Bamberg neighbours recalls their first meeting:

'Herr Hoffmann!' cried one of the actors with a fine, sonorous voice; 'Herr Hoffmann!' The little man made a malicious face and through the tightly-pinched lips slipped a soft, though accented remark: 'Damn scoundrel!' I was the only one who heard. Turning quickly, he approached the actor and the latter whispered something in his ear.

'Aha!' I thought to myself, 'that ominous little man is our music director of whom the whole town is talking.' Everyone talks of him and few understand him, though all are respectful of his talent.

Scarcely had I thought this when Hoffmann stood before me on the arm of the retired theatre director Cuno, and was presented with the words 'Music director Hoffmann!'

I muttered a few polite words to the effect, 'I am very pleased to meet you; I have waited a long time for the pleasure,' and so forth, during which Hoffmann, smiling bowed his head – or rather his neck – at least a dozen times in rapid succession, without replying.

At last he began. 'I notice by your speech that you are no Bamberger either, but a half-compatriot of mine – I'm delighted – splendid region – many people but few humans ...' and so on. And at my invitation he sat down with me.[13]

What else can we add to fill out this picture of Hoffmann?[14]

How did he dress? Brown overcoat, a long buttoned brown dress coat, yellow nankeen stockings, and a flowery vest. At home he wore a dressing gown and a red night cap.

How did he speak? Very rapidly with a somewhat hoarse and high-pitched voice. Later in life, after he had lost a few front teeth, he was difficult to understand. His normal conversation was in short and clipped sentences; but when he narrated stories his sentences were long and beautifully turned.

Did he sing? He had a pleasant tenor voice and must have sung some of his own songs, for instance, his duets for tenor and soprano.

What instruments did he play? The piano, the harp, and the guitar. As a performer he was in no way outstanding, though Rochlitz says he was a good pianist. Above all he liked to improvise, and Hitzig says he used to improvise every night.[15]

How was his musical ear? We may assume he had a relative sense of pitch, for after hearing Weber's *Freischütz* he speaks of the first chorus as being in E-flat. It is in D. Similarly, Agatha's *cavatina* is not in A, as he says, but in A-flat.

Was he a healthy individual? No, rather sickly. He suffered from nose bleeds, fevers, chills, and, above all, frequent headaches. Once or twice in his life he was critically ill with fever.

Did he ever cry? Infrequently. His contemporaries remarked on it as unusual.

Did he confide in his friends? He seems to have enjoyed talking over his affairs of the heart with close friends.

Did he have many close friends? Not many, despite his own warm and sociable nature. He used the intimate *Du* form in speech with relatively few people.

Would we characterize Hoffmann as an egoist or an altruist? Undoubtedly an egoist, and his Bamberg associate, Carl Friedrich Kunz, used this word to describe his character. Throughout his life Hoffmann placed his own affairs before those of all others.

Was he an energetic worker? He was energetic and indefatigable. He seems to have belonged to that group of people who require little sleep, despite exacting and intense work. If he stopped work at one in the morning he was ready to begin again by eight. It is said that at times he worked all night without sleep at all, though this may be exaggeration.

Did he work systematically or unsystematically? His work for the courts was always systematic and painstaking. His creative work was unsystematic and often careless. He had no particular hours of work but let these be dictated for him by his inspirations. These seem to have been numerous, for Hoffmann underwent no arid periods; but he often seemed to have depended on stimulants. He found women a great source of inspiration; in particular the 'ideal woman' or muse, who remained inaccessible. He also drank and smoked a great deal. As one of those individuals whose faculties are not dulled by alcohol, but rather heightened and sensitized by it, Hoffmann once commented on the relationship of alcohol to inspiration in his life:

> There is a good deal of talk about the inspiration that artists derive from the use of strong drink; musicians and poets are named who can work only in this way ... I don't believe it; but it is certain that strong drink promotes the more active transformation of one's ideas in the pleasant mood, I might say, in the fortunate constellation, when the mind passes over from reflection to creative work.[16]

This comment is frequently quoted in accounting for Hoffmann's inspirations, and to substantiate it further biographers have pointed to the diaries, where entry after entry displays the little symbol of the goblet ♈, employed by Hoffmann to denote drinking:

> 21 January 1811: Morning lessons – afternoon composed – feebly – Cassino – evening ♈
> 22 January 1811: Morning lessons with Mark and Stepf – afternoon with Kunz ♈ very heavy ♈

We should notice the order of the activities.

> 13 January 1809: ... worked on the *Miserere* – Nulla dies sine linea!! – ♈[17]

A close examination of the diaries shows that almost invariably the alcohol followed the periods of work. On those days when Hoffmann worked hardest there is no goblet sign. On those days when he drank at noon or in the early evening there is seldom any work noted. Hoffmann occasionally mentions being in a 'poetical' mood after drinking, but almost never is there a notation of actual creative work being done. More caution must be exercised in discussing the relationship between alcohol and inspiration in Hoffmann's work than has been displayed by some commentators.

Hoffmann experienced the one shattering emotional experience of his life while in Bamberg. In his mid-thirties, he fell desperately in love with one of his singing pupils, the fourteen-year-old Julia Marc. Julia Marc, pretty, inexperienced, with an attractive – perhaps outstanding – singing voice, began to appear on every page of Hoffmann's diary, in one of the numerous pseudonyms he had devised for her to deceive his wife. He calls her Käthchen in reference to the heroine of Kleist's drama *Käthchen von Heilbronn*, and later abbreviates this to 'Ktchn' or 'Ktch,' often repeated emphatically: 'Ktch – Ktch – Ktch!' At first the diary entries record the moods of elation her presence created in him:

'AM Lesson at Marc's – PM at Kunz's – then to Holbein's – at home – to the children's ball – Ktch: plus belle que jamais et moi – amoureux comme quatre vingt diables – excited – to Kunz as invited ♉ at night – very good humour – completed the sextet.'

But soon he has premonitions and writes (using characters of the Greek alphabet, again in order to veil the entry from his wife): 'This romantic mood is becoming more and more possessive and I fear a disaster will result – Ktch.' He imagines he may be going mad: 'Why do I spend so much time either asleep or awake in thinking of madness?' Again: 'Ktch – Ktch – Ktch!!!! exalted to madness.' Rising: 'Ktch crescendo.' And falling in desperation: 'Ktch – not in the theatre – hope shattered.'[18]

Quite aside from the obvious intensity of Hoffmann's affection, there is a certain bravura in these remarks; this is evident also in an account of the affair by Carl Friedrich Kunz:

With the most vivid descriptions he complained to me every day of his sorrows and joys in music, which recently had all been directed towards one house, in which lived the object of his adoration and the one person who links all his writings like a golden thread – Julia. He taught her in singing. She was what he lived for. During his whole stay here she strengthened him, led him, ennobled him, mesmerized him, and in the end flung him aside.

Every day he described to me in glowing words the rapture of his relationship with her. She was his greatest pleasure, his sweetest consolation; and he assured me that nothing made him happier than when his tear-stained eye detected in me an attentive and indefatigable listener.[19]

Hoffmann saw in Julia the same vision of the 'ideal woman' he had seen in Cora Hatt, though much more intensely this time; and the extravagances

of self-pity and fits of alcoholic debauchery in which he indulged helped
him fashion an image of her so strong that it would never be lost from his
mind or his work again. Julia was his muse. Inasmuch as he gave her the
romantic pseudonym of Käthchen in his diaries, and frequently signified
her also by a drawing of a butterfly, we gather that she was more an abstract symbol to him than real flesh and blood: 'Ktch – in her we live and
have our being.'[20] In the manuscript the *c* of the word Ktch seems to be
distorted to read *s*, perhaps implying that the word *Kunst* (art) was in
some way subconsciously intended; and a later annotation in the margin
reading *der Kunst* undoubtedly indicates that this suggestion was carried
forward to the conscious mind, giving us: 'Art – in her we live and have
our being.' It is worth drawing attention to this detail because it provides
a key to the whole Hoffmannesque aesthetic; for with him the muse not
only inspires art, but *is* that art, becoming its very shape and presence.

It is possible that Julia Marc remained totally ignorant of her music
master's frustrated affection, though Julia's mother appears not to have
misinterpreted his ardour, and Hoffmann records in his diary that he had
an 'infamous, murderously vexatious quarrel' with her. The inevitable en-
sued. Julia's mother arranged for her daughter to marry a merchant from
Hamburg and towards the end of December 1812 Julia left with her husband, never to be seen again.

While Hoffmann's emotional life was thus stretched to the breaking
point, Holbein left the Bamberg Theatre, a move which deprived the musician of this valuable and invigorating source of employment. Another
period of poverty followed and Hoffmann was forced to sell his coat to
get enough money to eat. However, the timely arrival of a small but welcome legacy from his uncle Otto enabled him to exist comfortably for a
brief period and he planned to begin work on what has subsequently
become his most accomplished composition, the opera *Undine*, inspired
by de la Motte Fouqué's tale. Fouqué himself agreed to provide the libretto.

About this time Friedrich Rochlitz recommended Hoffmann as a conductor to Joseph Seconda, the manager of an opera company in Dresden.
When approached, Hoffmann agreed willingly, glad to leave Bamberg, and
in April 1813 the Hoffmanns left Bamberg for Dresden.

Dresden was at this time in a state of extreme political unrest. Occupied
by the Prussian and Russian forces, it had just been besieged by Napoleon's
army, and although the allied troops had abandoned it, the Russian forces
still occupied the opposite bank of the Elba at Dresden-Neustadt, so that
the city was frequently under fire. Hoffmann reports that the atmosphere
was of 'the most horrible disquiet and anxiety.' Almost daily he saw sol-

diers and citizens killed. The privations of war had made food scarce and disease had broken out among the wounded soldiers. Hoffmann had received an advance from Seconda, who was in Leipzig with the company; and while he awaited a pass to join them there he scurried about, a fascinated spectator of the confusion about him:

> Rather uneventful night – but from four o'clock on continual shooting. The French were in the tower and the gallery of the Catholic church – I stood close to the gate and was almost hit when five or six bullets struck the wall and rebounded back.[21]

At length he obtained the necessary visa and Seconda greeted him warmly on his arrival in Leipzig. There he also met Friedrich Rochlitz, who had been an encouragement to him in correspondence, and had, indeed, been the first to recognize his literary gifts. Beginning work at once, Hoffmann was pleasantly surprised by the quality of the orchestra he was to conduct and felt immediately at home, 'like a fish in the water, moving joyous and free in the right element.'

Rochlitz, however, had warned him about Seconda, calling him 'a nice, honest, stupid man.' Hoffmann soon discovered this to his own misfortune and described him scurrilously as 'an uncouth ass.' Despite the difficulties with Seconda, Hoffmann conducted in Leipzig and Dresden (since the company was itinerant between the two cities) performances of Mozart's *Don Giovanni*, *Die Zauberflöte*, *Die Entführung aus dem Serail*; Gluck's *Iphigenie in Tauris*; Weber's *Silvana*, and Cherubini's *Wasserträger* and *Faniska*.

Moreover, his own creative work was prospering. On 1 July 1813 he noted in his diary: 'Composition of *Undine* begun,' and on 23 February 1815 he noted: 'Finished writing *Undine*.' But little by little his writing was taking precedence over his composition. During the Dresden-Leipzig period he wrote 'Der goldene Topf' (The Golden Pot), one of his greatest tales, and concluded the first part of *Die Elixiere des Teufels* (The Devil's Elixirs), together with a large quantity of further miscellaneous fiction. His first book, *Fantasiestücke in Callots Manier* (Fantasy Pieces in the Style of Callot), containing many of the musical writings he had first prepared for Rochlitz's magazine, was in the press and was shortly to appear with a foreword by Jean Paul. Hoffmann wanted the book to come out anonymously, still convinced that his true vocation was music and fearful that the volume might deflect interest from his accomplishments in this field: 'I do not want to be named, for my name should become known to the world by means of a successful musical composition and not otherwise.'[22]

The disagreements with Seconda, however, had multiplied to a point where an acrimonious remark by Hoffmann had brought about his dismissal. Just at this time his friend Hippel passed through Leipzig following a holiday in Switzerland. Hippel was now president of the court at Marienwerder, and had many influential friends in the Prussian capital. Hoffmann begged his friend to use his influence to secure him a position in the musical world there. When he was contacted two months later, he was offered a position as assistant at the *Kammergericht*, the Supreme Court of Judicature. On the brink of poverty, with no alternative prospects, and in spite of a resolve never again to return to law, in the autumn of 1814 he set out for Berlin.

Shortly after his arrival, his friend and biographer-to-be, Hitzig, arranged a party to welcome the successful author to Berlin – for the *Fantasiestücke* had brought him immediate acclaim. The guests included Ludwig Tieck, Fouqué, Chamisso, and a number of other illustrious authors. In a sense this literary party set the scene for what was to follow, for during the remaining years of Hoffmann's life, writing became the principal creative activity and almost completely excluded his activities in the other arts.

But if his active involvement with music had ceased, music nevertheless continued to have an ineluctable influence over much of his creative fiction and, in fact, it formed the leitmotif of his long and unfinished novel, *Lebensansichten des Katers Murr* (Tom-cat Murr's Opinions on Life). In Kater Murr Hoffmann developed the impressive figure of Johannes Kreisler, the mad Kapellmeister, so brilliantly that when Oswald Spengler was later searching out the archetypal characters of history, he put Kreisler in a class with Faust and Don Juan as figures who dominate whole epochs of artistic thought. In addition to *Kater Murr*, Hoffmann's output was crowded with stories in which music played a smaller or larger role, many of which cast light on contemporary social attitudes towards the art; stories such as *Rat Krespel* (Councillor Krespel), *Das Majorat* (The Legacy), *Die Fermate* (The Fermata), and *Der Kampf der Sänger* (The Singing Contest) – later to be taken by Wagner as a basis of his *Tannhäuser*.

One musical event of importance in Hoffmann's life occurred in Berlin: on 3 August 1816 his opera *Undine* received its *première* at the Royal Theatre. It had been chosen for an auspicious occasion, the king's birthday, and was well received by public and critics. Carl Maria von Weber, whom Hoffmann had met previously in Bamberg, was most impressed with the work and wrote an extremely favourable review. *Undine* was performed fourteen times before a disastrous fire, which burned down the theatre together with all the costumes and sets for the production, forced it to be dropped from the repertoire. By the time it might have been revived, Weber had already written his immensely popular *Der Freischütz*, and had thereby usurped the distinction, previously granted to Hoffmann, as the author of the first truly romantic German opera.

Hoffmann's work at the law courts was exemplary and he eventually obtained an appointment as chairman of the court, presiding in the absence of the president, a position which brought social distinction as well as a comfortable salary. The position also left much free time for writing and pubbing – at places like the 'Lutter and Wegner,' the 'Klaus and Weber' of the 'Ritter Gluck' story that follows in chapter three.

Whether as a result of living too hard or working too hard, Hoffmann's health began to fail while he was still in his early forties. In the spring of 1818 he was dangerously ill for weeks, and the following spring he was so ill again that he was forced to take a leave of absence from the courts. In 1821 a paralysis began spreading up his body, crippling first his legs, then his hands, so that he was forced to dictate his stories to his wife or his nurse. On 24 January 1822, when his friends Hippel and Hitzig visited him to celebrate his forty-sixth birthday, he was confined to his chair. On 25 June 1822 he was dead. The epitaph on his gravestone in Berlin reads:

E.T.A. HOFFMANN
BORN KÖNIGSBERG IN PRUSSIA
ON JANUARY 24, 1776
DIED BERLIN, JUNE 25, 1822
DISTINGUISHED
IN LAW
AS WRITER
AS MUSICIAN
AS PAINTER
DEDICATED BY HIS FRIENDS

Although Hoffmann made his name as a writer, he was actively involved in two other arts in which his contemporaries praised his distinction, with the result that some German critics have been inclined to see him as a kind of renaissance hero, a composite, portmanteau man, capable of consummate expression in whatever medium he desired. But this is an exaggeration. Until past his thirty-fifth year, when he moved solidly into the field of literature, Hoffmann had an indecisive talent, imperfect and uncontrolled. One may certainly believe in Carlyle's idea of the adaptability of talent, though eventually the question of skill or *métier* has to be faced; and this means professional dedication and concentrated work over a substantial portion of a lifetime. Hoffmann, whose legal activities kept him from being a totally free agent, had neither the time nor the energy to fashion a *métier* for himself in three arts.

Throughout the first part of his life, music stood uncontradicted as his foremost interest, and he confessed on numerous occasions that he wished to make his mark only as a composer. In several of his tales he has his characters sing or discuss his own compositions along with those of Mozart or Rossini – a sign of the high hopes he had for success. After he gave up his career in law to become a professional musician, he worked hard at this vocation and made every effort to master the techniques of the art. A few consecutive passages from the diary bear witness:

> January 20: Worked some at the *Miserere* ... It's beginning to take a direction.
> January 21: Splendid day! Worked hard at the *Miserere*.
> January 22: Remained at home the whole day and worked industriously at the *Miserere*.
> January 23: Terrible day! Practically nothing accomplished on the *Miserere*. Alas! Alas![23]

In the Bamberg diaries, work at composition is carried on simultaneously with literary and critical work. One is impressed with the intense interweaving of these activities; the transfer of creative energies seems neat and effortless. If we could draw the curve of activities in the different arts through Hoffmann's lifetime, those in literature would be shown to ascend slowly but imperturbably, while those in the graphic arts oscillated irregularly and musical activities declined. But if we drew the curve of *interest* in the different arts, the evidence of music criticism and the incorporation of this art into so much of the late fiction, including *Kater Murr*, would show us that music remained ascendant with literature growing to meet it.

Hoffmann's association with the graphic arts need attract little attention. On the evidence of his diaries and his reported conversations, the graphic arts never occupied his thoughts as did music and literature. His artistic talent was for caricature, rapid and spontaneous outbursts, not for obsessive and premeditated undertakings.

The relationship between music and literature is alone of real interest to us, for it is only here that truly synaesthetic interpenetrations come about. In this relationship, it is the music which penetrates the literature and not the other way around. And it is primarily the subject matter of the literature that is affected by the introduction of musical characters and discussions. Hoffmann was not principally a lyric writer, but his prose did at times take on a musical cadence, for example, in the onomatopoeic song of the three serpents in 'Der goldene Topf':

Zwischendurch – zwischenein – zwischen Zweigen, zwischen schwellenden
Blüten, schwingen, schlängeln, schlingen wir uns – Schwesterlein – Schwesterlein,
schwinge dich im Schimmer, schnell, schnell herauf, herab – Abendsonne schiesst
Strahlen, zischelt der Abendwind ...

Thomas Carlyle, a vigorous Hoffmann admirer, managed a translation of
this, which preserves much of the musicality of the original:

'Twixt this way, 'twixt that; 'twixt branches, 'twixt blossoms, come shoot, come
twist and twirl we! Sisterkin, sisterkin! up to the shine; up, down, through and
through, quick! Sunrays yellow; evening wind whispering ...[24]

Hoffmann's activity as a musician was threefold: as a performer and
conductor, as a composer, and as a music critic. Although he was never a
virtuoso performer, he was apparently a skilled accompanist and impro-
viser on the piano. It is difficult to determine the extent of his abilities
as a conductor. Certainly the evidence we have of his difficulties with performers would seem to lead to the conclusion that he was at best tempera-
mentally unsuited to that kind of work. Although Hoffmann's abilities as
a composer were by no means inconsiderable, it is as a critic of music and
musical society that we will be studying him; for it is in this activity only
that he opens a window on the forces of musical romanticism. All his
other accomplishments might be regarded merely as his credentials for
speaking to us about the musical life of his time.

To fix this time we should recall that following the deaths of Gluck
(1787) and Mozart (1791), the young musicians, under the impress of the
romantic movement in literature, were just beginning to demand that
music, too, should display a comparable intensity and drama of emotion.
It was an age of revolution, and Hoffmann participated in this revolution.
Frequently, however, he detached himself from it in order to study it
more carefully. In several of his musical stories he characterized himself
as a 'travelling enthusiast,' a mere observer, sympathetically reporting the
events taking place around him. It is as such that he approaches us now
in the year 1809 ...

THREE

Ritter Gluck: A Recollection from the Year 1809[1]

Usually late fall in Berlin still holds a few beautiful days. The sun emerges amiably from the clouds evaporating the dampness from the lukewarm air which drifts along the streets. It is then that one sees a motley spectacle: dandies, families with their governesses and children all dressed in their Sunday best, clergymen, Jewesses, barristers, prostitutes, professors, milliners, dancers, officers – everyone, in fact, strolling down the main avenue on their way to the Zoo. Soon all the seats at the 'Klaus and Weber' are occupied. The coffee steams; the dandies light up their cigars; and everyone argues about peace and war, or whether Miss Bethmann's shoes were grey or green the last time she was seen, or about the closed economy of the country and the bad state of the currency – in short, about anything and everything. At length all this dissolves into an aria from *Fanchon*[2] played in a tortured fashion by an out-of-tune harp, a pair of untuned violins, a short-winded flautist, and a practical-joking bassoonist. Many small, round garden tables and stools stand close to the fence which separates the Weber establishment from the street. Here one can breathe fresh air and observe the comings and goings undisturbed by the cacophonies of the cursed orchestra. I sit down and turn myself over to the free play of my imagination, to those friendly apparitions with whom I would speak about science and art, about everything that is dearest to man. Livelier and livelier moves the mass of pedestrians before me, but nothing disturbs me, nothing can drive away my imaginary company. Only a request for the trio of a most vile waltz tears me away from my dream world. The stridulating upper voice of the violin and the flute together with the buzzing ground bass of the bassoon is all I can hear; up and down they go, clinging to one another in parallel octaves that pierce the ear until, like one stricken with a burning pain, I am instinctively driven to cry out: 'What abhorrent music! Parallel octaves!'

Near me someone murmurs: 'What a happy coincidence, another octave hunter!'

Looking up I suddenly notice that a man has seated himself at the same table and is now staring at me. I cannot take my eyes off him. Never have I seen a head or figure that made such a deep, instantaneous impression on me. A delicately hooked nose, joined to a broad, open forehead with noticeable swellings over the bushy, greying eyebrows, under which the eyes shone with a wild, almost youthful fire – though the man could have been over fifty. His underdeveloped chin formed a curious contrast with the tightly closed mouth and mocking smile, brought about by an unusual play of muscles in the sunken cheeks, and seemed to resist the deep melancholy earnestness that rested in the brow. Only a few locks of hair lay beneath the large ears which stood out from his head. The meagre figure was muffled up in a large, new overcoat. As soon as my glance met the stranger's he lowered his eyes and returned to the business that my outcry had evidently interrupted. With noticeable enjoyment he was shaking tobacco from numerous tiny packages into a large tin which stood before him, and was dampening it with red wine from a carafe. The music had stopped. I felt like speaking to him.

'Thank goodness the music has stopped,' I said. 'That was terrible to put up with.' The old man glanced at me fleetingly and shook out the last package. 'It would be better if they didn't play at all,' I began again, 'don't you agree?'

'I have no opinion,' he said. 'You are a musician by profession and a connoisseur ...'

'You are mistaken; I am neither. I once learned to play the piano and to read figured bass, for that was all part of a good education. I was told then, among other things, that nothing creates such a bad effect as when the bass and the treble move in parallel octaves. I accepted it then as a rule but since I have found it holds true.'

'Really?' he broke in suddenly, and standing up he walked slowly over to the musicians, frequently striking his brow with the flat of his hand like someone trying to recall something. I watched him speak with the musicians, whom he treated with the respect due them. He turned back and scarcely had seated himself when they began to play the overture to *Iphigenia in Aulis* by Gluck.

With dreamy eyes, his shrivelled arms propped on the table, he listened to the *andante*, his left foot moving gently to indicate the entries of the voices. Now he raised his head, his left hand moving with spread fingers on the table-top as if he were playing a chord on the piano, while he lifted his right hand in the air. He was a Kapellmeister, cuing the change of tempo to the orchestra. His right hand fell and the *allegro* began. A burning crimson spread over his pale cheeks; his eyebrows contracted on his wrinkled brow and he seemed aflame with a wild inner fire which dispersed the trace of smile that had hovered till now in his half-open mouth. Now he leaned back, his eyebrows arching, the muscle-play in his cheeks returning, his eyes flashing; a deep, inner pain dissolved into pleasure that gripped all fibres in convulsive jerks. He breathed in deep gasps and drops of perspiration appeared on his brow. He signaled the tuttis and climaxes, his right hand never missing a beat while with his left he drew out a handkerchief and mopped his brow. How he enlivened that skeleton of an orchestra with fresh colour! I heard the soft melting figure with which the flute ascends after the storm of the violins and basses has abated and the thunder of the timpani is silenced. I heard the gentle, rippling tones of the violoncelli and bassoons and my heart was filled with inexpressible melancholy. The tutti returned like a giant and the unison cried out majestically, overwhelming the musty sounds with its crushing climax.

The overture had ended. The man let both arms sink and sat there with closed eyes, like a person weakened by excessive strain. His carafe was empty. I filled his glass with Burgundy which I had in the meantime procured. He sighed deeply as if waking from a dream. I urged him to drink and he did so without hesitation, downing his glass with one gulp and crying out, 'I am satisfied with the performance; the orchestra performed well!'

'Nevertheless,' I added, 'it was only a pale sketch of the original vivid masterpiece.'

'Do I judge correctly? You are not from Berlin!'

'Quite correctly; I am only here intermittently.'

'The Burgundy is good. But it is getting cold.'

'Then let us go inside and finish the bottle.'

'A good suggestion. I don't know who you are – for that matter, you don't know who I am either – but we won't ask each other's names; names are often troublesome. I am drinking Burgundy for which I am paying nothing. We are enjoying each other's company. That's enough.'

He spoke all this with good-natured joviality. We had entered the room and as he sat down his overcoat fell open and I noticed with astonishment that under it he wore an embroidered vest with long lapels, black velvet trousers, and a small silver dagger. He carefully buttoned his coat up again.

'Why did you ask me whether I was from Berlin?' I began.

'Because if that had been the case I would have been forced to leave you.'

'That sounds like a riddle.'

'Not in the least, when I tell you that I am a composer.'

'I still don't follow you.'

'I see that you understand absolutely nothing about Berlin and the Berliners.'

He stood up and strode about boldly, then he went to the window where he began to sing the chorus of the priestesses from *Iphigenia in Tauris* in scarcely audible tones, striking the windowpane now and then with the entrances of the tuttis. I noticed with amazement that he took certain original turns of melody which were strikingly unique and powerful. I let him be. He concluded and returned to his seat. Quite shaken by the man's peculiar behaviour and the fantastic expression of his odd musical talent, I was silent. After a while he began:

'Have you ever composed?'

'I've given it a try, but I found that everything I wrote down in what I thought were moments of inspiration later proved to be feeble and insipid, so I let it go.'

'You made a mistake. Just because a few attempts should not win your favour is no bad sign for your talent. One learns music as a boy because Mama and Papa wish it, and one hacks and strums away; but the mind is imperceptibly being initiated to melody. Perhaps that half-forgotten theme of a song which affected one so indifferently then was the first true thought, and this embryo was slowly nourished by strange powers until it grew to gigantic proportions and consumed everything about it, transforming it completely. Ah! how is it possible to indicate the thousand ways in which one can be led to composition? It is like a broad highway full of people bustling about rejoicing and crying 'We are the chosen; we have reached the goal!' Through the Ivory Gate one enters the land of dreams. Few even notice the Gate; fewer still pass through! What an adventure! Behind the Gate intoxicating shapes sway back and forth. Some more rapidly, others slowly; all are oblivious of the highway. They exist only behind the Ivory Gate. Once entered it is difficult to leave this realm, for just as monsters blocked the way to Alzinen's castle, the shapes whirl about threateningly. Many are those who dream away the dream of this dream-world – dissolving into dreams. No longer do they cast a shadow, or they would be aware of it by the ray that passes through this realm. Only a few awake from this dream to pass through the dream-world and advance on high to the moment of truth, the highest moment there is, contact with the eternal, the inexpressible! Look at the sun! It is the triad from which the chords of the stars shower down at our feet to wrap us in their threads of crystallized fire! A chrysalis in flames, we await Psyche to carry us on high to the sun!'

With the last words he sprang up and threw his arms and his eyes heaven-wards. Then he sat down again and quickly emptied his glass. A stillness arose that I did not dare break in order not to throw this unique man off the track. At length he began again more calmly:

'As I was in the realm of dreams a thousand fears and pains tormented me. It was night and I was terrified of the leering masks of the monsters who dragged me one moment into the abyss of the sea and the next raised me on high. Rays of light came through the night, and the rays of light were tones which surrounded me with their serene purity. I awoke from my pains and saw a great, clear eye which stared into an organ; and as it stared, tones arose and wound themselves into more shimmering and majes-tical chords than I had ever thought possible. Melodies poured up and down and I swam in their current and wanted to drown. Then the eye looked at me and raised me up over the raging waves. It was night again. At length two giants stepped up to me in shining armour; the Tonic and the Domi-nant. They bore me on high with them and the giant eye smiled. "I know the reason for the longing which fills thy breast. It is the longing for the Third, that tender youth, who now steps up between the two giants. May you hear his sweet voice and until we meet again, may all my melodies be thine."'

He paused.

'And you saw the eye again?'

'Yes, I saw it again! For years I lingered on in the world of dreams. Yes, I lingered – lingered! I sat in a magnificent valley and listened to the flow-ers singing to one another. But one sunflower was silent and bent its un-opened petals sadly to the earth. An invisible force drew me to it. It raised its head, its bloom opened, and from it the eye beamed towards me. Now tones, like beams of light, flowed from my head to the flowers which eagerly absorbed them. The sunflower's leaves grew larger and larger, liquid fire poured from them, they flooded me; the eye had disappeared and I was the bloom!'

With the last words he sprang up and rushed out of the room. In vain I waited for him to return, and at length decided to return to the city. Just as I was nearing the Brandenburg Gate, I saw a thin figure walking along in the darkness and immediately recognized him to be my odd acquaint-ance. I spoke to him.

'Why did you leave me so quickly?'

'It was hot and the euphony had begun to sound.'

'I don't understand you.'

'All the better.'

'All the worse, for I would very much like to understand you completely.'

'Don't you hear anything then?'

'No.'

'It's passed. Let's go. Generally I don't care for company, but since you are neither a composer nor a Berliner ...'

'I don't understand why you are so against the Berliners. I should think a person of your artistic sensibilities would feel right at home here where art is so cultivated and respected.'

'You are wrong! Here I am condemned to misery, like a lost spirit wandering aimlessly in a desert.'

'A desert? – Berlin?'

'Yes, a desert, for I can find no kindred spirit. I stand alone.'

'But the artists! The composers!'

'To hell with them! They're always ready with their petty criticisms. They refine everything down to the smallest detail. They rummage through everything only to come up with frivolous thoughts. They'll never learn how to create simply by chattering about artistic matters, and even if they do chance to prompt the odd idea into the light of day, it just emphasizes the great distance that separates their glacial frigidity from the sun. They are in the arctic circle of art.'

'Your verdict seems to me to be far too severe. At least the splendid performances in the theatre must satisfy you.'

'I was once persuaded to go to the theatre again to see an opera by a young friend of mine – what was it called now? Ah, the whole world was at this opera! The spirits of Orcus strolled through the bustling crowd of well-dressed people. Everyone was speaking noisily, omnipotently. Damn it, of course, it was called *Don Giovanni*! But I couldn't even tolerate the overture, which was quite misunderstood and tossed off in a meaningless *prestissimo*. And I had prepared for it by fasting and praying, for I knew that the voice of the euphony would be far too disturbed by this multitude to be heard with purity.'

'I'll grant you that Mozart's masterpieces are, for the most part, quite inexplicably neglected, but fortunately Gluck's works have been well produced.'

'Do you think so? Once I wanted to hear *Iphigenia in Tauris*. As I entered the theatre I noticed they were playing the overture to *Iphigenia in Aulis*. H'm, I thought, my mistake; they are playing *that* Iphigenia. I was astonished when this was followed by the opening *andante* from *Iphigenia in Tauris*. Twenty years lie between the two works! The whole effect, the carefully wrought exposition of tragedy was lost. A calm sea, a storm, the Greeks cast up on the shore – here is the opera! Eh? Has the composer thrown the overture into the banquet scene to be treated as a little piece for trumpet and played when and where one wishes?'

'I admit my blunder. Nevertheless, they are doing all they can to revive Gluck's works.'

'No doubt,' he said abruptly and smiled bitterly, then more bitterly still. Suddenly he darted off and nothing could have stopped him. In scarcely a moment he had disappeared. During the succeeding days I looked for him at the Zoo – in vain.

Several months passed. Then one cold, wet night after I had been delayed in a remote part of town and was hurrying to my home in Friedrich Street, I happened to pass the theatre. The roaring sounds of trumpets and drums served to remind me that Gluck's *Armida* was being given. I was tempted to go in when my attention was attracted to a curious monologue being spoken close to the window where the music could be heard almost perfectly.

'Now the king comes – they play the march – oh beat, beat it together! – it's supposed to be bright! – yes, yes you must play it eleven times tonight, otherwise the procession can't process properly. Ah ha! – *maestoso* – don't drag it, you children. Watch it, that character with his shoe-laces dragging. Right, a twelfth time and always returning to the dominant. Good grief, this mighty array will never end! Now he pays his compliments. Armida thanks him graciously. Once again? Right, two soldiers are still missing! Now the opening of the recitative is botched! What evil demon banished me to this place?'

'The curse is broken,' I cried. 'Come with me!'

I grabbed my odd acquaintance from the Zoo by the arm – for the soliloquist was none other – and drew him away with me. He appeared taken by surprise and followed me without protest. We were already in Friedrich Street when he suddenly stopped still.

'I know you,' he said. 'You were at the Zoo – we spoke a great deal – I drank wine – became overheated – after that the euphony sounded for two days running. I had to endure a great deal – but it's passed!'

'I'm glad chance has brought us together once more. Let us get to know each other better still. I live not far from here. How about ...?'

'I can't and don't dare visit anyone.'

'No, you can't escape me so easily. I'll go with you then.'

'You'll have to walk a bit if you want to come with me. But you were on your way to the theatre.'

'I wanted to hear *Armida*, but now ...'

'You *will* hear *Armida*. Come with me!'

Silently we went up Friedrich Street. He turned swiftly into a crossstreet. Scarcely was I able to follow him, so quickly did he go up the street, until at last he stood still before a modest house. He rapped at the door for quite a while before someone came and opened it. Groping in the dark we reached the staircase and a room in the upper floor, the door of which my guide carefully shut and locked. I heard another door open and soon after he entered with a lighted candle. The sight of the unusual furnishings of the room quite surprised me. Antique, richly-decorated chairs, a wall clock in a golden case, and a large, heavily ornamented mirror gave the whole room the mournful appearance of bygone splendour. In the middle stood a small piano; on it a large porcelain inkstand and a few sheets of manuscript paper. A longer look at this arrangement convinced me that nothing could have been written in recent times for the paper had turned quite yellow and the inkstand was covered with spiders' webs. My friend stepped up to a case at the end of the room which I had not noticed before, and as he drew back the curtain, I perceived a line of beautifully bound books with gilt titles: *Orfeo*, *Armida*, *Alceste*, *Iphigenia*, and so forth – in short, I saw all Gluck's masterpieces standing side by side.

'You possess Gluck's entire works!' I cried.

He made no reply but for just a moment his smile was distorted by the muscle-play of his sunken cheeks into a frightening mask. He fixed a mournful look on me and grasped one of the volumes – it was *Armida* – and stepped solemnly over to the piano. I opened it quickly and fixed the music stand. He appeared obliged, and opening up the volume – how can I describe my astonishment! – I was looking at blank manuscript paper without a single note written on it!

He began: 'First I'll play the overture. You turn the pages, and mind, at the right time!'

I promised to do so and he began to play the majestic *tempo di marcia* with which the overture begins. He played magnificently with full, resonant chords, almost completely true to the original. But with the *allegro* he brought in so many new and ingenious turns of expression that my astonishment grew continually in spite of the fact that it only approximated Gluck's thoughts. His modulations, though striking, were tasteful and never strident; and he knew how to join up the principal ideas with tuneful melismas which were given new, rejuvenated shapes each time they appeared. His face glowed; his eyebrows drew together as if an uncontrollable passion wanted to break free from him. Then his eyes swam with tears of deep melancholy. From time to time, when both his hands were occupied with the embellishments, he sang the theme with a pleasant tenor voice. He also knew how to use it to imitate the muffled tones of the timpani. I turned the pages industriously, always in pursuit of his glances. The overture was at an end, and with closed eyes he fell exhausted into the armchair. But soon he collected himself and, turning over several pages of the volume, said in a muffled voice:

'All this, Sir, I have written as I came out of the realm of dreams. But I betrayed the sacred to the profane and an ice-cold hand laid hold of my heart. It wouldn't break and thus I was damned to walk among the condemned, a solitary soul, formless, unrecognized by all, until the sunflower again bears me up to the eternal. Ah well – now let us sing Armida's scene!'

Now he sang the final scene of *Armida* with an expressiveness that surged through my whole being. Here too he departed noticeably from the original, but his changes seemed, as it were, to capture a higher essence of Gluck's music. In the most forceful manner he linked together love, hate, madness, despair – everything that it is possible to express in tone. His voice became that of a youth; out of deep gloom it swelled up with penetrating strength. My whole being trembled; I was transfixed. As he ended I threw myself in his arms and cried with choked voice: 'How is it possible? Who are you?'

Standing up, he fixed an earnest, penetrating look on me; then as I was about to ask him again, he vanished through the door with the candle, leaving me in darkness. After nearly a quarter of an hour had passed I despaired of seeing him again and attempted to make my way to the door, feeling my way along the piano. Suddenly the door opened and he appeared in full dress – court dress – with an opulent waistcoat, his dagger at his side. He approached me with the light. I was motionless with fright. Solemnly he came up to me and gently taking my hand he said, smiling strangely, 'I am Gluck.'

FOUR

Five Romantic Concepts

'Ritter Gluck' is worked around a configuration of at least five concepts: night, mystery, dreams, madness, and music. Individually they are by no means unique to the spirit of romanticism; but they become uniquely romantic by the chemistry of their interaction.

It is noteworthy that this story about music is shrouded in mystery and lacks resolution, for when the encounter is alleged to take place Gluck had already been dead twenty-two years. The significant events of the story take place at night, when they gain further ambiguity and terror. Writing to his editor, Friedrich Rochlitz, Hoffmann claimed he was writing about 'a real event.' But does this mean he had really met the ghost of Gluck, or merely a madman cleverly impersonating the composer? Imperceptible is the line separating the great musician from an ostensible lunatic; for here we meet a man whose life no longer has any social meaning, a man who has withdrawn into an embellishment of dreams.

Like many of his contemporaries, Hoffmann was in revolt. Each of the above concepts had its significance for the attuned romanticist, and their association was still excitingly novel, perhaps even a little audacious. The eighteenth-century Age of Reason – which the Germans called the *Aufklärung* – had proved an unsatisfactory formula for life. In the course of time its high rationalistic principles had degenerated into drab utilitarianism, and its ethics into eudemonism. It had suffered the fate of most ideological movements; its ideals had slipped from the highest minds to the lowest. It was, therefore, to be mistrusted and held in contempt; and the *Sturm und Drang* of the 1770s and 1780s sharply attacked the philosophical principles of the *Aufklärung*. Kant opened the way to a new vision by subjecting this complacent 'enlightenment' to a revealing scrutiny in his *Critique of Pure Reason* (1781). And German artists, in their habit of pausing until the critical principles of a new creed had been formulated, now sprang to the attack by vigorously and somewhat thoughtlessly opposing everything that had previously seemed valuable. Write down the more or less antipodal concepts of the five around which Hoffmann tells his story and you have the pillars of the Age of Enlightenment – of the *Aufklärung*.

Romanticism	*Aufklärung*
Night: darkness; ineffability	Day: clarity; explicitness
Mystery: the incommensurability of things; delight in the unresolved	Solution: faith in penetrability by thought; deduction
Dreams: the unconscious	Thoughts: the conscious
Madness: desirability of social protest and maladjustment	Sanity: integrated social behaviour
Music: the language of the emotions	Literature and Philosophy: the language of the intellect

These were diametrically opposed philosophies of life. Novalis led the re-action against rationalism when he wrote: 'Inasmuch as I give the lowly a higher meaning, the common a hidden aspect, the known the dignity of the unknown, the finite an infinite appearance, thus I romanticize them.'[1] Night, mystery, dreams, madness, music; each was a rebellious thought at the close of the eighteenth century, each a powerful intoxicant.

'I turn aside to the sacred, ineffable, mysterious night.' This is Novalis again, in the first of his *Hymns to the Night*, after he has found the blinding light of day unsatisfactory. The disenchantment with the light of day is symbolic of a renunciation of clarity and precision in exchange for the excitement of the unknown. For Novalis night is 'the queen of the world,' 'the prophetess of sacred realms,' and 'the guardian of sweet love.' Significantly, night is feminine. She is the container into which are poured mysteries, dreams, and music, allowing them to mix freely, blurring their outlines, destroying their private existences.

Lighting effects have always been important to the artist. Greek and Roman art, created under a brilliant sun, is firm in outline and solid in shape. The art of Northern Europe, where the light is less intense and more unpredictable, began to be created indoors after dark; that is, it was created in small pools of illumination beyond which lurked vast mysterious forces in the drapery of shadows. The underworld creatures of Northern mythology are always nocturnal. It may not be mere coincidence that romanticism died after the invention of the electric light in 1879. The electric light eliminates the shadow, and the consequences of this may be observed by looking at contemporary painting with its hard edges and brilliant colours.

Romanticism begins at twilight. In 1809 Berlin was a dark city at night, for it was not until 1826 that an English firm installed an adequate system of gas street lamps. Indoors the soft flickering of candles was still common, and often preferred to the less hesitant illumination of the recently invented oil lamp. By candlelight the powers of sight are sharply reduced; the ear is supersensitized and the air stands poised to beat with the subtle vibrations of music. In Jean Paul's *Hesperus* a concert by the celebrated harmonica player, Franz Koch, is listened to in a room especially darkened for the occasion.[2] The very sounds favoured by lovers of music had some of the smudged and shadowy qualities of night – the aeolian harp with its weird chromatic lamentations, and the glass harmonica from which the tones poured forth like drops of dew, shimmering unevenly and dying reluctantly as if at a great distance:

> Romanticism is beauty without bounds, or the beautiful infinite ... It is more than a simile to call romanticism the wavelike ringing of a string or bell, in which the tone-wave fades into ever further distances, finally to lose itself in us so that, while already silent without, it still resounds within. In the same way the moonlight is at once a romantic image and a romantic example. (Jean Paul)[3]

With the setting sun the whole of Europe became a *mondbeglänzte Zaubernacht* – an enchanted moonlit night; the phrase is Ludwig Tieck's. For that specific accumulation of minds living before the invention of the electric light, night was a cult. It was the time when the mysterious workings of the underworld and the heavens were manifest. It was boundless, formless, unresolved, terrible. When the protagonist of 'Ritter Gluck' leaves the room with the candle before returning to announce his identity, he prepares us for a sinister revelation. Suspense flies to the end of the story, and the last three words quiver strangely in the limitless space of night.

Night opens the mind out to speculations about the supernatural, reducing the upright mind to the insensibility of narcosis. This is evident in the marked growth of secret societies during the late eighteenth century. Occultist groups such as those around Lavater and Jung-Stilling sought to give mystical experience the dignity of a religion. For the philosopher G.H. Schubert, dawn was equated with death. Day focused its harsh light on singulars; with night all singulars slipped into the ocean of universals – universals unbounded by placement in time or space. Night released the unconscious mind to dream in a realm where stars may weep, waves may fly, flowers may sing. Only when one is prepared to accept the synaesthesia of the romantic cosmology can one get to the heart of Hoffmann's writings. Otherwise, how whimsical the descriptions will seem, the equation of the perfect fifth with two giants, for instance, or the personification of the major third as a tender youth.

I shall be discussing the symbolism of Hoffmann's dream-descriptions of music later, after the reader has had a better opportunity to become acquainted with them. But our immediate attention must be focused on the symbolic description of the composer's creative process as it appears in 'Ritter Gluck.' From an outward turbulence of language, which at times may appear quite uncontrolled, emerges a resolute description of the compositional process, which, we may suppose, is a fair account of how the romantic composer pictured himself at work.

When the artist contemplates a new work he is cast into the realm of dreams. Unconsciously, like the fledgling who has read the master's book, he calls forth the wonderful visions and they dance and play for him. But he dares not remain forever in this realm of dreams. He can only become a true musician when he grasps the unconscious inspiration firmly and carries it forth. An impression is mere self-gratification until it becomes an expression. Little patience is accorded those who 'dream away the dream of this dream-world.' A supreme effort must be made to 'advance on high to the moment of truth,' and this moment of truth is the art of giving explicit formulation to the thoughts and intuitions experienced in the dream-world. If the inspiration is perfect the work will achieve undying life and 'contact with the eternal' will have been made. Since the discovery of truth, unlike the contemplation of beauty, demands an intellectual commitment, it becomes obvious that true genius is inseparable from absolute presence of mind. Hoffmann frequently used the word *Besonnenheit* in his critical writings to describe this state of intellectual composure and reflectivity. To prove that great art is never dreamed or improvised, he once attacked a current story to the effect that Mozart, having put off writing the overture to *Don Giovanni* until the very last moment, dashed it off effortlessly a few hours before the first performance. Hoffmann demonstrated that such a highly integrated composition could only have been the product of conscious and unconscious thinking, extending back to the moment the opera was begun.[4]

It is true that the shortcoming of Hoffmann's fictitious composer, Kapellmeister Johannes Kreisler – who will be encountered in full force later – was his inability to control the demon of art that had taken hold of him, and as a result he hovered constantly on the verge of insanity. But this is by no means the case with Gluck. To the public at large Gluck may appear to be mad, for the violence with which he describes his dreams places him in the category of the neurotic; but from this neurosis are produced works of great originality and beauty.

The violence of Gluck's dreams constitutes the nerve of the story, beside which the physical circumstances of sitting in the coffeehouse, or even attending an inferior performance at the opera, pale to unimportance. While normal people talk about politics, the state of the economy, or the colour of Miss Bethmann's shoes, two pathetic lunatics discuss music.

There is no doubt that Gluck's relative unpopularity in Berlin further isolates him and his confidant from society. We may ask whether Hoffmann could have achieved the same effect had 'the travelling enthusiast' interviewed one of Berlin's current idols. It is important that the general public should not be interested in Gluck's disclosures, for this keeps it well in the background, and the secrets of music can be retained as the private property of inspired minds. The whole question of the artist's uneasy relationship to society will be found again and again in Hoffmann's writings. It was important for the romanticists that the artist should appear unsociable or egregious – in the etymological sense of that word, as someone 'outside the flock.' This psychological distance was necessary not only so that he could observe society with greater objectivity, but also in order that he could rise out of it. To retain its purity, music must resist social contamination. Only the initiated are permitted to discuss it.

Night, mystery, dreams, madness – and it is music that binds these concepts together. What is the mysterious 'euphony' that Gluck senses in the air, the euphony which affects him so profoundly? This euphony is surely more than the simple combination of agreeable sounds.[5] Jean Paul's usage of the same word provides a clue: 'The euphony of the spheres, of starry nature, played above me.'[6] This euphony is the music of the spheres, the sound of harmonious nature, the cosmic music sensed only by the visionary. The images of Gluck's dream – the sun, the knights in shining armour, the great eye, and the chords which shower down as stars – press through the dark areas of the mind and raise the spirit to a presentiment of this cosmic state.

For the romanticist the night was feminine. Now music too, was feminized. Night was feminine because it had been charmed by the nocturne of love. Music, like night, became coincidental with the beloved.

In a story entitled 'Das Majorat' this association is accomplished. The scene is the castle of R-sitten, situated on a desolate promontory high above the icy scream of the Baltic Sea. Theodore is a guest at the castle with his uncle, a lawyer attending to the estate of Baron Roderick. The nights at the castle are cold; the wind whines through the crumbling build-ing and ghosts make their appearance threatening imminent doom. The one relief in this picture of desolation is the beautiful young Baroness Sera-phina, a lover of music.

> She was scarcely nineteen years old, and her features, which were as delicate as her figure, bore an expression of angelic goodness. In the glance of her dark eyes dwelt an indescribable fascination, a melancholy desire like the dewy moonlight; and her smile was a heaven of rapture and delight.

On the night in question the guests are attempting to be gay; there is to be a ball ...

FIVE

Baroness Seraphina

All was quiet in the castle. Gentlemen and ladies busied themselves in their rooms dressing for the evening. The musicians with the scraping fiddles, the untuned basses, and the bleating oboes, of whom Lady Adelheid had spoken, had now arrived, for nothing less than a ball in the very best style was to be given. My old uncle, preferring a quiet sleep to such foolish pastimes, remained in his chamber. I had just finished dressing for the ball when there came a light tap at the door and Franz entered. Smiling in his self-satisfied manner, he informed me that the harpsichord had just arrived from the land steward's wife in a sledge and had been carried to the Baroness's apartment. Lady Adelheid wished to invite me to come over at once.

One could guess how my pulse beat, and with what deep and joyous exaltation I opened the door to the room in which *she* was to be found. Lady Adelheid approached me in a joyful manner. The Baroness, already in full dress for the ball, was sitting meditatively before the mysterious chest in which slumbered the music which I was now called upon to waken. She rose, and her beauty shone with such splendour that I stood staring at her, unable to utter a single word.

'Come, Theodore – for, according to the pleasant custom of the North, which is found also in the extreme South, she addressed everyone by his or her Christian name – 'Come, Theodore,' she said pleasantly, 'the instrument has arrived. Heaven grant that it be not altogether unworthy of your skill!'

As I opened the lid, however, I was greeted by the rattling of a score of broken strings; and when I tried to strike a chord it sounded terrible, for even the strings that remained were hideously out of tune. 'No doubt the organist has been putting his delicate hands on it again,' cried Lady Adelheid merrily; but the Baroness was distinctly annoyed and said, 'Oh, what miserable fortune! I shall never have a moment's pleasure in this place!'

I searched the case of the instrument and fortunately found some coils of strings, but no tuning key anywhere. More lamenting! I explained that any key would do if its wards would fit the pegs, and both the Baroness and Lady Adelheid ran back and forth in gay spirits so that before long a whole magazine of shining keys lay before me on the sounding board. I set to work diligently. Lady Adelheid and the Baroness herself continued to assist me in trying first one and then another peg. At length one of the tiresome keys fitted. 'It fits! It fits!' they both cried joyfully.

But when I brought the first creaking string up to the proper pitch, it suddenly snapped and they both recoiled in alarm. The Baroness, handling the brittle wires with her delicate little fingers, gave me the numbers as I called for them, and carefully held the coil as I unrolled it. Suddenly one of them coiled itself up again with a whir, drawing an impatient 'Oh!' from the Baroness. Lady Adelheid laughed heartily, and I pursued the tangled coil to the corner of the room. We all sought to extract a perfectly straight string from it, and having strung it, we were mortified when it snapped again. But at last – at last – we found some good coils; the strings began to hold, and gradually the discordant jangling gave place to pure, sonorous chords.

'Oh it will play! It will play! The instrument is getting into tune!' cried the Baroness, looking at me with her lovely smile. How quickly this common interest banished all the strangeness, all the shyness imposed by the artificial manners of society. A confidential familiarity had arisen between us which burned through me like an electric current, melting the timidity which had lain like ice in my heart. That strange mood of pathos which is engendered in such love as mine had left me completely. Thus it happened that when the harpsichord was brought tolerably into tune, I did not interpret my deeper feelings in improvisation as I had intended, but turned to those sweet and charming *canzonettas* which have reached us from the South.

During this 'Senza di te' or that 'Sentimi idol mio,' or 'Almen se non poss'io' and numberless 'Morir me sentos' and 'Addios' and 'O dios!' a brighter and brighter glow shone in Seraphina's eyes. She had seated herself close beside me at the instrument. I felt her breath fanning my cheek; and as she placed her arm behind me on the chair back, a white ribbon disengaged itself from her lovely dress and fell across my shoulder where it was kept in continual flutter to and fro by my singing and Seraphina's soft sighs, like a true messenger of love. It is a wonder that I managed to keep my head!

As I was running my fingers aimlessly over the keys, thinking of a new song, Lady Adelheid, who had been sitting in the corner of the room, came over to us and kneeling before the Baroness begged her, clasping both her hands to her bosom, 'Oh dearest Baroness! Darling Seraphina! Now you must sing too!'

To this the Baroness replied, 'Whatever are you thinking, Adelheid! How could I dream of letting our virtuoso hear such a miserable voice as mine!' She looked inexpressibly lovely, casting down her eyes and blushing like a modest child, her shyness contending with her natural desire to sing.

As can easily be imagined, I added my entreaties and did not desist until, after mentioning some little Courland *Volkslieder*, she stretched out her left hand towards the instrument and tried a few notes by way of introduction. I rose to make way for her at the instrument, but she would not permit me to do so, contending that she could not play a single chord, and for this reason her singing would, without accompaniment, be poor and uncertain.

She began in a sweet voice, pure as a bell, that came straight from her heart, and sang a song whose simple melody bore all the characteristics of those *Volkslieder* which proceed from the breast with such purity that we are induced to see in the bright light they create around us our own higher poetic nature. A hidden charm lies in the simple words of the text, forming a hieroglyph of the ineffable truth that fills our hearts. One has only to think of that Spanish *canzonetta* whose words say simply: 'With my love I sailed out to sea. It grew stormy and my love was flung about mercilessly. No! I shall never again sail the seas with my love!' Thus the Baroness's little song said simply: 'Lately I was dancing with my sweetheart at a wedding; a flower fell out of my hair. He picked it up and returning it to me said: "When, my darling, shall we go to a wedding again?"' With the second verse I accompanied her with arpeggiated chords, and as I, in the inspiration which took hold of me, stole the melodies of the following songs from the Baroness's own lips, I must have appeared in her eyes and those of Lady Adelheid to be one of the greatest masters of the art of music; for they overwhelmed me with enthusiastic praise.

The lights from the ballroom, which was situated in one of the other wings of the castle, now shone across the Baroness's chamber and a discordant bleating of trumpets and horns announced that it was time to gather for the ball. 'Oh, now I must go,' said the Baroness. I rose from the instrument. 'You have afforded me a delightful hour; these have been the most pleasant moments I have ever spent here in R-sitten.' With these words the Baroness offered me her hand; and as in the extreme intoxication of delight I pressed it to my lips, I felt her fingers close upon my hand with a sudden convulsive tremor!

··◁‖══════════‖▷··

SIX

Inspiritrice

··◁‖══════════‖▷··

A few pages later, again after she has made music with him, Baroness Sera-phina allows herself to be kissed by young Theodore – an explicit sign, if one were needed, for the fusion of music and love in Hoffmann's mind. For the poet Wackenroder, music was the gateway to all love and divine rapture. The very presence of music in so many love scenes in romantic literature illustrates the attractiveness of this idea.

> Each recognized the other at the same instant. Franz trembled, he could find no words ... meanwhile a horn could be heard sounding through the garden. And now Franz ... sank to his knees before the beautiful creature ... in tears he kissed her hands ... her lovely face was bent forward towards him, the horn improvised with the most thrilling tones ... both were lost in enchanted ecstasy. Franz could not say whether he was dreaming, or whether everything was in his imagination. The horn fell silent, and he collected himself again. (Ludwig Tieck)[1]

When music passes, the spell is broken. Here is Hoffmann again, speaking of a youthful romance:

> ... everything was so lovely. Her form seemed to hover in the particles that the sunbeams made visible, and leaning towards her I felt her soft breath on my glowing cheek. I was happy and wanted to tell her so. The word died on my lips as it struck six o'clock, and the flute music of the clock played Mozart's 'Forget Me Not' in solemn tones. Her long eyelashes drooped, and I sank back in my chair ... Finally the notes became silent. 'It's past,' I said. 'Yes,' she replied in muffled tones.[2]

In his novel *Kater Murr*, Hoffmann has his composer hero, Johannes Kreis-ler, describe how the artist's spirit stretches out a thousand feelers in ardent longing and surrounds the one whom it has seen yet never possessed, for the longing continues to exist as an endless thirst. And she, *she* herself is the glorious one who, like a dream figure, takes on living form and shines forth from the artist as song – picture – poem![3]

Much has been written of the artist's muse, about the effectiveness of the 'ideal' woman and Platonic love. And it is said that the most effective of all muses is she who remains inaccessible. Dante's Beatrice was inaccessible in death; Petrarch's Laura was inaccessible in marital faithfulness; Wagner's Mathilde was protected by marital convention, while Goethe developed the art of running away from his muses who were protected in no way.

The one shattering emotional experience of Hoffmann's life was his relationship with and eventual separation from Julia Marc. Hoffmann's Julia was indeed inaccessible and accordingly he apotheosized her. Julia became a seraph. Thus endowed with the powers and charms of a goddess, she hypnotized him throughout his life. The only way Hoffmann ever made love to Julia was in song. The whole dynamics of his love affair were pressed into envelopes of melody.

When words ceased it was music, not actions, that took over. In Hölderlin's *Hyperion*, Diotima expresses herself best in song and shuns conversation. Hyperion recalls their first meeting: 'We spoke very little together. We were ashamed of speech ... We longed to become fused in the music of a divine song.'[4]

It is precisely in vocal music that the romanticist's love is most impulsive, for a song presupposes the physical presence of the beloved as vocalist. In this way we can account for the extreme popularity during Hoffmann's day of romantic songs by composers now considered marginal: Hasse, Traetta, Graun, and so forth. Baroness Seraphina sings one of those 'divine *canzonettas* of Abbé Steffani.' Elsewhere, Antonia, the heroine of Hoffmann's story 'Rat Krespel,' sings 'an impassioned song by the old Leonardo Leo' and one by Padre Martini, which causes tears to come to her father's eyes. In the novel *Kater Murr* Hoffmann introduces one of his own Italian-styled arias as a favourite of Kreisler: 'Mi lagnerò tachendo.'

Of all the characteristics of music, melody seems to Hoffmann the most important: 'The first and foremost characteristic of music is melody, which enchants the human soul with a wonderful, magic spell.'[5] We may suppose that melody is considered the most important because it is the easiest to anthropomorphize. Just as we may see the graceful undulations of the feminine physique in a Louis XV chair or an Art Nouveau pattern (the contours of which are said to have influenced Debussy in the composition of his arabesques), just as these things reveal the feminine, so in the serpentine lines of the Italian aria with its affluence of embellishment we find a sensuousness that can be tasted with both the ear and the eye – for even the appearance of the notes on the page describes in voluptuous turns and passionate thrusts a true geography of eros. In Mozart's *Don Giovanni*, for instance, Donna Anna's arias are noticeably more embellished than those of the other singers, for Mozart has given her the most ardent personality.

tu   ben sa – i   quant'io t'a - ma – i   tu co - no – sci la – mia

fè,   tu   —   co   –   no – sci la   mia fè.

(Act II, Scene III)

For the romanticist, music is the quintessence of femininity. In languages with more than one gender the word itself is always feminine, a matter which caused the poet Kleist to rejoice.

Throughout Hoffmann's writings we may trace the development of a concept binding eros and music. At first the beloved is merely called on to sing. Although her songs are romantic, it is possible that she may contribute in no other way to the fire of romance, for as an effective muse, she must remain unobtainable. Then somehow she appears to invade the song, fashioning it into a symbol of love so strong that it would continue to exist as an erotic experience independent of her singing it. In other words, the song becomes the beloved.

This same transference is also the heart of the Orpheus legend, so beloved in the early days of opera. Orpheus attempts to bring back his beloved from the land of the dead – with music. He fails; the music alone remains. But in the song of Orpheus, Eurydice lives on forever – for she has become that song. The courtly love of the twelfth century also illustrates this thinking. In the unreciprocated love of the troubadour, the beloved becomes a song about herself. Julia Marc, in the many shapes and disguises she assumes in Hoffmann's work, is a striking example of the reappearance of this European myth in the conscience of a later author. Ultimately, by association, any or all music may come to symbolize the beloved, and the crystallization of the concept will be complete: 'In the long crescendo of the nightingale's song, the beams of light condensed into the figure of a beautiful woman – and this figure was divine, magnificent music!'[6]

A sixth concept may now be added to the five concepts of romanticism mentioned earlier: music is the beloved.

In the last chapter this transformation was merely suggested. Baroness Seraphina sang some romantic songs, thereby becoming identified with the theme of love. The following translation, 'Ombra adorata,' carries this symbolism through to a point where music has become a total substitute for the beloved, an erotic experience itself. Throughout 'Ombra adorata' the voice of the singer remains unidentified and unattached to any human form. She is pure quintessence, the 'adored shadow' alone, which leans down towards the artist and raises him up in mighty flight. It is Hoffmann's most sustained piece of lyrical writing.

SEVEN

Ombra adorata

*Who does not know Crescentini's wonderful aria 'Ombra adorata,'
which he composed for the opera* Romeo and Juliet *and sang with
such exceptional style?*

How wonderful is music, and how little are we able to fathom its deepest
secrets. But does it not dwell in the human breast, filling the soul completely with its enchantment, so that one's whole disposition turns towards a new, transfigured life, free from this world and its depressing
torments? Truly, a divine power passes through us, and by surrendering
ourselves to whatever the power provokes with an innocent, childlike
spirit, we are able to speak the tongue of the unknown, of the romantic
realm of spirits, assimilating it unconsciously as the apprentice who has
read aloud from the master's book of magic. Wonderful visions dance on
the stage of life, filling all who are able to see them with an infinite yet
inexpressible desire.

How constrained was my heart when I entered the concert hall. How
depressed I was by all the wretched minutiae which plague us in this life,
and the artist in particular, like a horde of stinging vermin. Even the violent shock of death would be preferable to this continual torment.

You, my faithful friend, understood the melancholy glance I threw you.
May you be a hundred times blessed for taking my place at the piano, while
I try to hide myself in the extreme corner of the hall. How did you manage to get a short, unimportant overture by an immature composer performed in place of Beethoven's great symphony in C minor? What pretext
did you use? For this too, I thank you with all my heart. What would become of me, crushed by the relentless outpourings of worldly misery, if
Beethoven's massive spirit had stepped up and embraced me with brazen
arms, forcing me with it into that realm of the titanic and immeasurable
which its thundering tones reveal?

When the overture had exhausted its childish jubilations of trumpets and drums, there was a quiet pause, as if something important were to come. I enjoyed that. I closed my eyes and, searching my soul for more pleasant visions than those which surrounded me, I forgot the concert and with it the whole room (which I knew well since I was supposed to play the piano).

The pause may have lasted some time when finally the ritornello of an aria began. It was tenderly performed, suggesting in simple but heartfelt tones the desire of the pious soul to raise itself towards heaven and rediscover there all that is dearly beloved, yet lost on this earth. Like a celestial light the bell-like voice of a girl rose above the orchestra:

Tranquillo io sono, fra poco teco sarò mia vità!

How can I describe the feelings that gripped me? My pain was transformed into melancholy desire. A divine balm healed my wounds. All was forgotten as I listened raptly to those tones descending as if from another world to embrace me.

Just as simple as the recitative is the theme of the following aria, 'Ombra adorata.' But equally direct is its appeal to the soul, overcoming earthly pain in the blessed hope of fulfilling the promise of a higher world. The entire composition is arranged naturally and without artifice; the phrases shift from tonic to dominant alone. There are no harsh modulations, no unnecessary embellishments. The song flows like a silver-bright stream among brilliant flowers. But is this not precisely the mysterious magic that stands at the bid of the master, that he is able to empower such an unpretentious melody with an indiscernible yet irresistible spell over every receptive soul? And the soul rejoices in its transfiguration, transported on the crystal-clear melismas and borne up through the brilliant sky.

Like all compositions conceived by a master, the work demands to be received with the whole soul – I might say, with the precise knowledge of the transcendental implied by its melodies. That there would be certain embellishments in both the recitative and the aria was clearly understood, for the genius of Italian song demands them. But is it not wonderful that a tradition has been established concerning the precise embellishments of the song, based on the interpretation of Crescentini himself, the composer and supreme performer, so that today no one would dare introduce a foreign embellishment without censure? How tastefully Crescentini has worked these embellishments into the contour of the song. They are the shimmering jewels which beautify the countenance of the beloved, brightening the sparkle of her eyes and her wine-dark lips and cheeks.

But what am I to say about you, you magnificent singer? With the glowing enthusiasm of the Italians I call you heaven-blessed! For it is indeed the blessing of heaven which enables your warm and pious soul to give expression with such magnificent tones to that which you feel deep in your heart. Like tender spirits your tones have embraced me, and every tone said: 'Raise your head, depressed one, come with us to the far-off land where pain is unknown and where the breast is filled with indestructible desire and enchantment.'

I shall never hear you again. But when vulgarity and pettiness strike me, thinking to draw me down with them; or when the despicable scorn of the mob tries to wound me with its venomous sting, then your tones and consoling spirit will whisper to me:

Tranquillo io sono, fra poco teco sarò mia vità!

And I will raise myself above all insults in a mighty flight of enthusiasm, never-before experienced. All the benumbed feelings of my wounded breast will scintillate like a salamander and I will grasp them and twirl them together into a fiery sheaf of flaming visions with which to transfigure and perpetuate your song and yourself.

EIGHT

A Romanticist's Don Giovanni

The song and the singer have become one, and will remain sustained together, so that even though the singer may depart, the song will continue
to exist as the form and the presence of the beloved. Hoffmann first entered the words 'Ombra adorata' in his diary on 25 August 1812 at the
height of his infatuation for Julia Marc, and the sketch is clearly intended
as a means of perpetuating her memory, for it was evident that she was to
be taken from him.

While numerous other Hoffmann works strive towards the same condition, few attain the purity of tone of 'Ombra adorata.' But there is at least
one other example of the total unification of music with the beautiful
woman. 'Rat Krespel' is one of Hoffmann's most frequently translated
tales and it need be mentioned only briefly here.[1] In it Antonia, the daughter of Krespel, is possessed at once with a beautiful voice and a strange
affliction that will cause her death if she dares to use her voice in song.
Antonia's father owns a rare Cremona violin, and in some way the girl
seems to be identified with this instrument so that when it is played it
seems possessed with the eloquence of her singing voice. Antonia lives a
subdued existence, resisting all impulse to sing, until one night Krespel has
a dream in which he hears his daughter's voice in song. Rushing to her bed-
side, he finds her dead. She has yielded to an ultimate impulse and it has
caused her death. Krespel's dream of Antonia on the fatal night is curiously synaesthetic; he hears her in song and at the same moment he sees
her being rapturously embraced by a lover. The question posed by the
story is this: shall life be surrendered for one brief ecstatic moment of true
art? The answer is yes; for the true artist there can be no choice.

In the story to follow, an ultimate sacrifice is again made in the name
of art. We have seen examples illustrating how the beloved could be projected into music, becoming one with it. To complete the cycle, Hoffmann

at times has presented us with pure music which is transformed back into a spectre of the beloved. In the story 'Don Juan' a young opera singer, playing the role of Donna Anna in Mozart's *Don Giovanni*, is identified so strongly with the role she is creating that she appears literally to inhabit the melodies of her arias. When she steps mysteriously out of the music to pay a nocturnal visit to 'the travelling enthusiast' who narrates the story, it is as if the music itself were revealing its most intimate message through the words she speaks. Recognizing the narrator as a composer, she says: 'I have sung *you*, for *I* am your melodies.'

Hoffmann's extreme enthusiasm for Mozart has already been mentioned. The opera *Don Giovanni* had been familiar to him since 1793 when he had heard it as a student in Königsberg. In the spring of 1795 the aspiring young composer wrote to his friend Hippel: 'Ah, my friend, to compose such a unique opera could be the joy of my life.' He never wrote such an opera, but he did write a story about it, a story which makes it impossible for anyone to view Mozart's opera in the same way after reading it. In 'Don Juan' some original Mozartian values undergo an important reinterpretation in the course of a five-page letter-essay which comes in the middle of the tale. Hoffmann makes his case so forcefully that the literary critic Leo Weinstein has claimed: 'It may be said that in its broad outlines the history of the Don Juan legend can be divided into two main parts, and the dividing line is Hoffmann's five-page letter.'[2]

To appreciate the effect of Hoffmann's examination, some knowledge of Mozart's opera is desirable. Hoffmann himself gives a fairly complete description of a performance of *Don Giovanni* in his story, and it will be necessary here merely to furnish some background information.

It has been estimated that as many as 2,500 operas of all sorts were written during the last half of the eighteenth century. When Mozart wrote *Don Giovanni*, a flux of operatic ideas and operatic styles pervaded Europe. *Opera buffa* had succeeded in gaining popularity at the expense of *opera seria*. Neapolitan opera, with Piccini and Cimarosa as its exponents, was on the wane, its artificiality challenged by Gluck's restoration of drama to opera. At the same time the German *Singspiel*, or operetta, with spoken dialogue and folk-like songs was gaining a firm footing. Mozart profited from these cross-currents and assimilated what he needed from all available sources.

Da Ponte's libretto for *Don Giovanni* was inspired by the Don Juan legend which, although it went back to medieval times, was first put into concrete form in Tirso de Molina's *El Burlador de Sevilla* of 1630. With Tirso, Don Juan is sheer spontaneity of instinct, the insolent avidity of youth, the body and mind aflutter with rough-edged masculinity. 'All

Seville calls me "the Burlador" and my greatest pleasure is to deceive a woman and leave her dishonoured,' Tirso has his hero say.[3] The play is elemental and entertaining. El Burlador is the career philanderer. For him there is nothing more to life than deceiving women, and he spends all his time calculating how to seduce his next victim.

This is substantially the same Don that Da Ponte took over and presented to Mozart. In fact, he thought nothing of borrowing from such an unsophisticated form of entertainment as the *commedia dell'arte* for the imbroglios of the second act. In a series of luminous rococo tableaux Mozart delineates for us the jocular situations of Juan's adventurous life and his final downfall when the Commendatore, whom he had murdered, comes to life again and drags him off to Hell. Mozart called his opera a *dramma giocoso* and it was appreciated as such by its first audiences.

Now little of this fits in with the intense and humourless world of the romanticist. The problem facing Hoffmann, therefore, was to discover how the psychology of the Don Juan legend could be adapted to suit the romantic conscience; for no one, least of all Hoffmann, wanted to be deprived of Mozart's magnificent music merely because his psychology was becoming unfashionable. He begins, therefore, by asking himself the question: How did Don Juan become what he is? Originally, says Hoffmann, Don Juan was equipped by nature with the highest physical and intellectual capabilities. Thus endowed, he naturally has the highest aspirations; he must always seek perfection, 'the ideal.' His soul is victim to an unending longing for the infinite. He engages in a passionate career to find the ideal woman. Disillusioned in his quest, he turns angrily against God and falls into the hands of the devil. Donna Anna is very possibly that ideal woman the Don is seeking, but he has met her too late. Contrary to previous tradition, Hoffmann assumes that Donna Anna has been seduced by the Don before either appears on stage and that her demonstrative hatred for him is in reality ill-disguised love; for she has been captivated by the one man who made her feel truly like a woman. Thus, in the confusion of her feelings she pleads with her frigid fiancé Ottavio to postpone their marriage for one year, knowing that she will die of sorrow and remorse before that year is up.

Thus Hoffmann makes Anna the heroine of the opera in what might appear to be a quite arbitrary fashion; for certainly she has a less important role on stage than Donna Elvira, and her arias are in reality much more concert arias than the powerfully dramatic arias of Elvira. But a careful study of Mozart's work reveals that there are no heroines at all. The Don alone is the animating force from which all the other characters take their existence. He is the exclusive protagonist of the work. Although he has fewer arias to sing than any of the other leading personalities, he rules the scene at all times, and all the other personalities live an existence derived from him.

With Mozart, the Don had been a carefree individualist, an embodiment of sensuality. He preyed on women in order to satisfy his physical appetites and his vanity. With Hoffmann, on the other hand, Don Juan is a victim of thwarted idealism. He becomes a Faustian man, a Sisyphus; and he is ruled by devilish and divine powers. He seeks – in vain; and as a result turns against God and man in absolute contempt.

Equally important is Hoffmann's new conception of Donna Anna. For Mozart she had been merely an item in an extended catalogue of victims of the Don's sexual prowess. For Hoffmann she becomes the 'ideal woman,' feminity incarnate, the spirit of music.

Numerous commentators have pointed out that Mozart's opera does not possess the qualities Hoffmann read into it. In his introduction to his edition of the opera, Alfred Einstein claims he has tried to rid the score of 'all the romantic and unromantic obscurities of the nineteenth century which began with E.T.A. Hoffmann.'[4]

Certainly one may search in vain for traces of the inner conflict and ambivalent love in Donna Anna's character, or the noble idealism of the Don himself. On the contrary, Da Ponte's text repeatedly emphasizes Donna Anna's affection for Don Ottavio. Could we really believe that her sense of shame and inner conflict results in continuous lying to and hypocrisy with her bridegroom? All Mozart intended her to do was to grieve like a dutiful daughter for the assassination of her father, the Commendatore, and to lead the crescendo of loathing and hatred for the Don which accumulates throughout the opera.

But sensuality is certainly present in Mozart's music as the philosopher Kierkegaard has so strongly insisted in his discussion of the opera.[5] Hoffmann's interpretation too is sensual to the extreme; and it provides the occasion for a deep expression of wish fulfilment; for Donna Anna does not pay her mysterious nocturnal visit to Don Juan, as might be expected, but to the side of 'the travelling enthusiast' himself, the composer Hoffmann ...

NINE

Don Juan:
A Fabulous Incident which Befell
a Travelling Enthusiast

A piercing bell and the shrill cry 'The show's on!' woke me from the soft sleep into which I had sunk. The double basses rumbled in confusion, a timpani stroke, trumpet calls. A long clear A sounded by the oboe and the violins tuned up. I rubbed my eyes. Could it be that Satan, ever-mischievous, had caught me intoxicated? No, I am still in the room of the hotel where I put up last night, half dead with fatigue. Just above my head hangs the elegant tassel of the bell rope. I pull it firmly; the valet appears.

'In the name of heaven, what's the meaning of this confused music next door. Is there a concert in the hotel?'

'Your Excellency,' – I had ordered champagne at the table d'hôte dinner – 'Your Excellency is perhaps unaware that the hotel is connected to the theatre. Behind the tapestry there is a concealed door which opens on a short passageway, and that leads directly to loge number 23, the visitors' box.'

'What? – Theatre? – Visitors' box?'

'Yes, the small visitors' box for two or at most three people – gentlemen of quality only. It's near the stage, all upholstered in green with a lattice to ensure privacy. If it please Your Excellency, today they are performing *Don Juan* by the famous Herr Mozart from Vienna. The entrance fee of a thaler and eight groschen can be added to your bill.'

He was already pushing open the loge door as he spoke these last words, for on first hearing the words *Don Juan* I had stepped past the concealed door into the passageway. For a moderate-sized town the house was spacious, tastefully decorated, and brightly illuminated. Loges and stalls were filled to capacity. The opening chords of the overture convinced me that, even if the singers were merely adequate, an excellent orchestra would afford me the most glorious enjoyment of the masterpiece. During the *andante* I was seized by a horror of the dreadful infernal region of lamentation; a shuddering presentiment of something terrible filled my mind. The jubilant fanfare of the seventh bar[1] of the *allegro* seemed like the voice of exulting crime itself. Out of the deep night I saw demons stretch their fiery claws towards the carefree mortals dancing on the thin edge of the bottomless pit. I saw clearly in my imagination the conflict between human nature and those unknown, monstrous powers which surround man, plotting to destroy him. At last the storm subsided and the curtain went up.

Leporello, freezing and ill-humoured, wrapped in his cloak, walks back and forth in front of the pavillion. The night is starless.

Notte e giorno faticar ...

In Italian then? Italian, here in this German town? *A che piacere*! I shall hear all the recitatives, everything just as the great master conceived and felt it!

Don Juan bursts on stage, followed by Donna Anna who clutches the cloak of the offender. What a sight! She could be taller, slimmer, and more majestic in her walk; but what a face! Eyes from which flash love, anger, despair; inextinguishable sparks, hurled from one focus and burning everything in their path like Greek fire. Loose tresses of dark hair flow down her neck and shoulders. The white nightdress treacherously displays her provocative charms. Her heart, gripped by the horrible deed, beats violently. And now – what a voice!

Non sperar se non m'uccidi ...

Through the tumult of the orchestra her notes, cast of ethereal metal, shine like glowing flashes of lightning. In vain Don Juan tries to free himself. Does he really want to? Then why doesn't he beat off the woman with his fists? Has the evil deed rendered him powerless, or is it the inner conflict between love and hate that robs him of courage and strength? The old father has paid with his life for the folly of attacking his powerful adversary in the dark. In spoken conversation, Don Juan and Leporello advance further onto the proscenium. Don Juan unwraps his cloak and now stands splendidly in a crimson suit of slashed velvet with silver embroidery. A powerful, commanding figure; a handsome face with an aquiline nose, keen eyes, sensual lips; the peculiar play of the muscles above his brow imparts something Mephistophelean to his expression at times and, without spoiling the beauty of his face, causes involuntary dread. It is as if he were able to practise the magic art of the serpent, as if women, once he has looked on them, could no longer do without him, so that, driven by a sinister power, they rush towards their own destruction.

Around him bustles Leporello, tall and thin in his red-and-white striped waistcoat, his short red jacket, and white hat with its red plume. His features are a curious mixture of good nature, roguery, lasciviousness, and ironical impudence; his black eyebrows contrast strangely with the greyish hair on his head and in his beard. The old rascal obviously merits his position as servant and accomplice to Don Juan. They have successfully escaped over the wall.

Torches. Donna Anna and Don Ottavio appear; he is a delicate, foppish little man of twenty-one at the most. Anna's fiancé, he probably lives in the house, for he has arrived so quickly. He could have rushed to the scene to save the old man at the initial alarm, but he had to spruce up first. In any case, he was always cautious about stepping out at night.

> Mà qual mai s'offre, o dei, spettacolo funesto agli occhi miei!

There is more than despair over Don Juan's shocking crime in the awful, heart-breaking tones of this recitative and duet. The murder of Donna Anna's father is only incidental to the doom which the Don must bring on himself, and those notes which wring terror from the heart describe, more than the consequences of the bloody act, the torment of a man who cannot break away from his own evil destiny.

Donna Elvira, tall and slender, with features that still bear traces of faded beauty, has also entered to complain of the traitor Don Juan:

> Tu nido d'inganni ...

The compassionate Leporello had just remarked quite cleverly

> Parla come un libra stampato

when I thought I sensed someone near or behind me. Someone could have easily opened the loge door behind me and slipped in. The thought distressed me thoroughly. I was so happy to be alone in the loge, to embrace this superb performance of the masterpiece with every nervous fibre of my being as though through tentacles, and to draw it into my innermost self. A single word, which might easily have been a silly one, could have broken the spell of this poetic and musical enchantment. I resolved to take no notice whatever of my neighbour but, wholly engrossed in the performance, to avoid any exchange of word or glance. With my head resting on my hand, my back turned to my neighbour, I kept my eyes fixed on the stage.

The remainder of the performance bore out the excellent beginning. The wanton, infatuated little Zerlina consoled the clumsy good-natured Masetto in her lovely tones and airs. In the wild aria 'Fin ch'han dal vino' Don Juan frankly revealed his innermost lacerated feelings, his contempt for the insignificant people who surrounded him, whose only purpose was to serve his pleasure, whose dull lives he destroyed remorselessly. The play of his eyebrows was more Mephistophelean than ever.

The masks appear. Their *terzetto* is a prayer that rises to heaven in shafts of pure light. Now the central curtain rises quickly to reveal a scene of gaiety. Glasses clink, masqueraders and peasants dance together in abandon under the encouraging eye of their host, Don Juan. Now appear the three plotters who have sworn vengeance. All grows more and more solemn until the dance begins. Zerlina is rescued and to the thundering accompaniment of the finale Don Juan bravely defies, with a drawn sword, the enemies ranged around him. He strikes the bridegroom's fancy-dress sword from his hand and, like mighty Roland scattering the army of the tyrant Cymork, opens himself a path to freedom while the rabble draw back in confusion, stumbling and falling over themselves.

Several times I thought I had felt a gentle, warm breath behind me and heard the rustle of a silken garment. This led me to suspect the presence of a woman in the box; but, wholly engrossed in the poetic world of the opera, I paid no attention. Now, after the curtain had fallen, I looked at my neighbour. No words can express my astonishment! Donna Anna, in the very same costume she had worn on stage, stood behind me, staring intently at me with her soulful eyes! I stared at her utterly speechless. Her lips formed a gentle, ironical smile in which I saw my own uneasy appearance reflected – or so it seemed to me. I felt compelled to address her and yet my tongue was paralyzed by astonishment – yes, I might even say by terror.

Finally, finally, almost involuntarily I managed to speak. 'How is it possible to see you here?' To this she replied in the purest Tuscan that if I did not understand and speak Italian she would have to forgo the pleasure of conversing with me for she spoke no other tongue.

These sweet words were like music. As she spoke, the expression in her dark blue eyes was heightened and the lightning flashing from them sent a stream of fire through my veins that pounded in my pulse and vibrated in my every fibre. It was Donna Anna, without a doubt. It did not occur to me to wonder how she could possibly be on stage and in my loge at the same time. Just as in a happy dream the strangest things seem natural, and just as a pious faith understands the supernatural, fitting it in with the so-called natural events of daily life, so too I fell into a kind of somnambulism in the presence of this amazing woman. I realized, too, that there were secret bonds linking her so closely to me that she could not be parted from me even by her appearance on stage.

How I should like, my dear Theodore, to impart to you the remarkable conversation that now began between the Signora and myself. But when I try to set down in German what she said in Tuscan with lightness and grace, every word seems stiff and pale, every sentence clumsy.

When she spoke of *Don Juan* and of her role, it seemed that the depths of the masterpiece revealed themselves to me for the first time; I could now begin to witness and understand the fantastic phenomena of a strange world. She said that music was her only reality and that she felt she could grasp through singing many otherwise hidden secrets of the self that no words could express. 'Yes, it becomes clear to me when I sing,' she continued with burning eyes and agitated voice, 'but everything about me is dead and cold, and when I am applauded for a difficult roulade or a successful effect, it is as if icy hands clutch at my glowing heart! But you, you understand me, for I know that you too are at home in the wonderful romantic realm where tones are infused with sublime magic.'

'But, miraculous creature, how can you know anything about me?'

'I know the frenzy and yearning love that were in your heart when you wrote the part of — in your most recent opera. I understand you; your soul revealed itself to me in song. Yes' – here she called me by my first name – 'I have sung *you*, for *I* am your melodies.'

The intermission bell rang. A sudden pallor drained the colour from Donna Anna's unrouged face. She put her hand to her heart as if in sudden pain, but saying quietly, 'Unhappy Anna, your darkest moment is upon you,' she vanished from the box.

The first act had delighted me, but after my remarkable experience, the music now affected me in new and extraordinary ways. It was as if the long-promised fulfilment of the most unearthly dreams was now being granted in real life; as if the ecstatic intimations of the enchanted soul were now embodied in sounds, moulding themselves into rare disclosures. In Donna Anna's scene I felt myself enveloped by a soft warm breath; its intoxicating spirit passed over me and I trembled with bliss. My eyes closed involuntarily and a burning kiss seemed to be imprinted on my lips. But the kiss was a long-held note of eternal passionate longing.

The finale began in outrageous merriment:

Già la mensa è preparata.

Don Juan sat philandering between two girls, drawing one cork after another, releasing the fermenting spirits which had been hermetically imprisoned to allow them full reign. It was a short room with a large Gothic window in the background, through which the night could be seen. Even while Elvira reminded the faithless lover of his vows, one saw frequent flashes of lightning and heard the muffled rumbling of the approaching storm. At last a mighty crash.

Elvira and the girls flee. The marble colossus, accompanied by the terrible chords of the netherworld, enters to tower over the pygmy form of Don Juan. The ground shakes under the thundering strides of the giant. Through the storm, through the thunder, through the howling of the demons, Don Juan shouts his terrifying 'No!' The hour of damnation has come. The statue vanishes. The room is filled with thick smoke, out of which hideous spectres emerge. Don Juan writhes in the torments of hell; from time to time one catches sight of him among the demons. Suddenly an explosion, as if a thousand thunder bolts were striking. Don Juan and the demons have vanished, one knows not how! Leporello lies in a corner of the room.

What a relief now to see the other characters return, still vainly seeking Don Juan, who has been snatched from earthly vengeance by the infernal powers. It is as if only now the fearful circle of evil has been broken. Donna Anna looks quite altered; a deathlike pallor covers her face, her eyes are dim, her voice trembles and is uneven. Yet for this very reason the short duet she sings with her sweet little bridegroom is heart-rending. He is now eager to get married at once, for Heaven has conveniently delivered him of the perilous duty of revenge.

The fugal chorus rounded out the work to a splendid whole, and I hurried back to my room in the most exalted state of mind I had ever experienced. The waiter called me to the table d'hôte and I followed him mechanically.

There were distinguished people in town as a result of the fair and the conversation turned, naturally, to today's performance of *Don Juan*. There was general praise for the Italians and their gripping performance, but little remarks, dropped rather facetiously here and there, showed that probably no one had the slightest idea of the deeper significance of this opera of all operas.

Don Ottavio had been well liked. Donna Anna had been too passionate for one gentleman. He felt that in the theatre one should observe a moderation and avoid all excess of emotion. The description of the attack upon her father had upset him terribly. At this point he took a pinch of snuff and turned his indescribably stupid, sly eyes on his neighbour. The neighbour maintained that the Italian woman, although certainly quite beautiful, was too little concerned about her dress and jewelry; in the scene just mentioned one of her curls had come loose and had cast a shadow on the semi-profile of her face! Now another man began to intone very softly

Fin ch'han dal vino,

at which a lady remarked that Don Juan had seemed to her the least satisfactory of the whole cast. The Italian had been much too sinister, too intent, and had failed to play the character with enough levity and frivolity. The effect of the final explosion was universally praised. Tired of this rubbish I hurried back to my room.

IN VISITORS' BOX NO. 23

I felt so constricted, so oppressed in the musty room. At midnight I thought I heard your voice, dear Theodore; you clearly spoke my name and there was a rustling at the concealed door. What is there to prevent me from revisiting the scene of my wonderful adventure? Perhaps I will see you there, and the woman who fills my whole being! How easy it is to carry in the little table, two candles, and writing materials. The waiter brings the punch I have ordered, finds the room empty, the tapestry swung back. He follows me into the box and regards me with suspicion. At my nod he sets the drink on the table and retires, glancing back with a question on his tongue as he goes.

Turning my back on him, I lean over the railing of the box and look into the deserted auditorium. Illuminated magically by my two candles, the architecture quivers and glimmers weirdly. The curtain sways in the draft. Suppose it were to billow up and reveal Donna Anna frightened by gruesome monsters? 'Donna Anna!' I cry involuntarily. My cry is lost in the empty house, but it has aroused the spirits of the instruments in the orchestra pit – a mysterious tone issues from them and seems to repeat the beloved name. I cannot help shuddering, but it is a thrill of pleasure that tingles through my nerves.

I recover my self-possession and feel inclined, my dear Theodore, at least to indicate to you that for the first time I really grasp the inner meaning of the divine master's work. Only a poet understands a poet; only a romantic soul can pass through the portals of romanticism; only the exalted spirit of an artist undergoing initiation within the temple of art itself can comprehend what the initiated utters in his exaltation.

If one considers the libretto of *Don Juan* alone, without ascribing to it any deeper significance, but appreciating it only as a story, it is scarcely understandable how Mozart could conceive and compose such music as he did. A *bon vivant* who loves wine and girls to excess, who arrogantly invites the stone statue to his rowdy table, the statue of the old father whom he stabbed to death in defence of his own life – really there is not much poetry in this; and to tell the truth, such a man is really not worth being singled out by the powers of hell as a unique specimen for their collection. Nor does he deserve that the stone statue, animated by a transfigured spirit, should take the trouble to descend from his horse and urge the sinner to repent before his last hour on earth; nor, finally, that the devil should send out his best henchmen to escort him to the netherworld.

Believe me, Theodore, nature fashioned Juan as the dearest of her children, with everything that raises man towards divinity, everything that elevates him above the commonplace, above the factory products which are ciphers for lack of individuality. This destined him to conquer and command: a powerful, handsome physique, a personality radiating the spark which kindles the most sublime feelings in the soul, a profound sensibility, and a quick, instinctive intellect.

But the terrible consequence of the fall of man is that the devil retains the power to seduce man and prepare wicked pitfalls for him, just when he is striving for that perfection which most expresses his divine nature. This conflict between the divine and the demonic forces is the essence of earthly life just as the hard-won victory gives us the concept of supernal life. The demands upon life exacted by his physical and mental qualities exalted Don Juan but, insatiable in his desires and fired by a longing which sent the blood boiling through his veins, he was driven to the greedy, restless pursuit of experiencing all phenomena of this earthly world, hoping in vain to find satisfaction in them.

Here on earth nothing so much elevates the inner nature of man as love. It is this which, by its mysterious yet powerful agency, destroys or improves the elements of our being. What wonder, then, that Don Juan had hoped love might calm the yearnings of his heart. It was here that the devil slipped the noose around his neck. Through the cunning of man's hereditary enemy, the thought was planted in Don Juan's soul that love, the pleasure of the flesh, could actually achieve here on earth that which exists in our hearts as a heavenly promise only, that longing for infinity which weds us to heaven. Fleeing restlessly from one beautiful woman to another, enjoying their charms with the most burning ardour to the point of drunken and exhausted satiety, believing himself always deceived in his choice, always hoping to find the ideal of ultimate satisfaction, Juan was finally doomed to find all earthly life insipid and shallow. Moreover, since he despised humanity anyhow, he revolted against the delusion which, seeming to be the best life could offer, had ensnared him so bitterly.

Every enjoyment of woman was now no longer a gratification to his sensuality, but became a cynical mockery of Nature and the Creator.

He was driven on by a deep contempt for the common features of life, to which he felt himself superior. He felt bitter scorn for a humanity which hoped to find in love, and the homely union it produces, some slight fulfilment of the higher aspirations which nature has treacherously planted in our hearts. He was forced to rebel against the thought of any such relationship and to wreck it whenever he found it. Thus, he was at war with that unknown Being which guides our destiny, a Being which seemed to him to be a malicious monster playing a cruel game with the wretched creatures it created. Every seduction of a beloved bride, every blow delivered to happy lovers causing irremediable grief, represented a fresh triumph over that hostile monster and raised the seducer forever above our narrow life, above Nature, above the Creator. He really wants more and more to leave life, but only to plunge deeper into hell. The seduction of Anna with its attendant circumstances is the very summit of his achievement.

Donna Anna is in all natural endowments the counterpart to Don Juan. Just as Don Juan was originally a wonderfully strong and handsome man, so she is a divine woman over whose pure soul the devil has no power. All the arts of hell could destroy her only physically. As soon as the devil has accomplished this ruin, according to the decree of heaven, the execution of the revenge may no longer be delayed by the powers of hell.

Don Juan mockingly invites the statue of the murdered old man to his bawdy feast, and the transfigured spirit, seeing Don Juan for the first time as the Fallen Man and grieving for him, does not disdain to visit him in an awesome disguise and exhort him to repent. But so corrupt is his soul that not even heavenly salvation can throw a ray of hope into his heart and light his way to a better life.

You have undoubtedly noticed, my dear Theodore, that I have spoken of Anna as seduced, and I shall tell you in a few words to the best of my ability at this late hour, when thoughts and ideas come from the depths of my mind, how the music alone, quite apart from the text, seems to me to reflect the whole conflict between these two opposing natures, Don Juan and Donna Anna.

I have already mentioned that Anna is the counterpart of Juan. Suppose Donna Anna had been destined by heaven to let Don Juan recognize, in the love that ruined him through the arts of Satan, the divine nature that dwelled within him, and to tear him away from his desperate efforts at self-destruction? No! It was too late. When he first saw her he was already at the height of his crimes and could feel only the demonic desire to destroy her. She herself could not be saved. When he fled the deed was done. The fire of a superhuman sensuality, a fire from hell, surged through her being and she was powerless to resist. Only he, only Don Juan, could arouse in her the erotic madness with which she embraced him, he who sinned with the superhuman frenzy of the hellish spirits within him.

The deed once done, he wanted to escape. But for Donna Anna the thought of her sin was like a terrible, poisonous, death-spewing monster. Her father's death at Don Juan's hand, her betrothal to the frigid, effeminate, and prosaic Don Ottavio, whom she once thought she loved; even the love that in a moment of ecstasy had flooded her being and now burns as annihilating hatred – all these things are tearing her heart to pieces. She feels that only Don Juan's destruction can bring peace to her mortally tortured soul; but this peace demands her own earthly destruction. Thus she incessantly spurs her indifferent bridegroom to revenge. She pursues her betrayer herself, and relents only after the powers of the underworld have dragged him down into the pit.

But she cannot yield to her eager bridegroom:

> Lascia, o caro, un anno ancora allo sfogo del mio cor!

She will not survive that year. Don Ottavio will never embrace the woman whose devotion has saved her from becoming Satan's chosen bride!

How vividly I felt all this in the devastating chords of the recitative and narration of the duel by night! Even Donna Anna's scene in the second act – 'Crudele' – which superficially refers only to Don Ottavio, really speaks in subtle overtones of that state in which the soul is bereft of all earthly happiness. What other meaning is there in those strange words which the poet added, perhaps unconsciously: 'Forse un giorno il cielo ancora sentirà pietà di me!'?

The clock strikes two. A warm, electrifying breath glides over me. I recognize the faint fragrance of the Italian perfume that yesterday informed me of my fair neighbour's presence. I am seized by a blissful feeling that I could only express in music. The air stirs more violently through the house; the strings of the grand piano in the orchestra vibrate. Heavens! From a great distance, born by the floating tones of an ethereal orchestra, I think I hear Anna's voice:

> Non mi dir bell'idol mio!

Open out, oh distant, unknown realm of spirits! Open out, you land of genies! Open out, realm of glory, in which an inexpressible heavenly pain, akin to the most ineffable joy, brings fulfilment beyond all earthly promises to the enraptured soul! Let me enter the circle of your lovely apparitions! From thy dreams, which may terrify or serve as benign messengers to earthly men, choose me one which will carry my spirit to the ethereal fields as my body lies imprisoned in the leaden bonds of sleep!

MIDDAY CONVERSATION AT THE MAIN TABLE
(As an Epilogue)

CLEVER MAN (*taking out his snuffbox and tapping emphatically on the lid*): It's really unfortunate that we shall hear no more good opera for some time. But that's what comes of overdoing things.

MULATTO-FACE: Yes, yes. I warned her often enough. The role of Donna Anna always affected her oddly. Yesterday she carried on like a woman possessed. They say she lay unconscious in her dressing room throughout the intermission. In the scene in the second act she had nervous fits.

INSIGNIFICANT PERSON: You don't say!

MULATTO-FACE: Absolutely! Nervous fits, and they couldn't get her out of the theatre.

MYSELF: Good Lord! I hope the fits weren't serious. We shall hear the Signora again soon, I hope?

CLEVER MAN (*taking a pinch of snuff from the box*): Hardly! The Signora died this morning at exactly two o'clock.

TEN

Composers

The heroine makes the ultimate sacrifice for the sake of art and her death is announced like the snipping of scissors. Hoffmann is careful, as usual, to draw a clean line between the true artists – Donna Anna and the narrator – and the unmusical *bourgeoisie*, who now begin to emerge as the aggressive enemies of art.

A possessive psychic relationship is established between 'the travelling enthusiast' and Donna Anna. He knows 'that there were secret bonds linking her so closely to me that she could not be parted from me even by her appearance on stage.' Their exclusive and telepathic exchange of ideas is at once erotic and deathful. When Donna Anna offers the narrator her love in the form of an intoxicating breath of perfume and a burning kiss sent on the wing of song, she is identifying him clearly with none other than Don Juan himself, that arch-human of fatal splendour by whom women want and need to be possessed. From other evidence in the story we know that the narrator is no ordinary man; he is, in fact, a composer. Thus, to close the circle of Hoffmann's private mythology, it is the composer himself who symbolically becomes the seeker of ideals, the *homme revolté*, deceived and betrayed by the world as he seeks the ultimate inspiration in the divine and fiendish regions of the imagination. And Donna Anna is that inspiration – that quintessence of music which he hears and sees and breathes and touches. Anna surrenders herself completely to the creative artist and in death she elevates and ennobles him. These same themes were again picked up by Wagner for his *Tristan*; and at least one Wagnerian critic has suggested that with him also they conspired as a eulogy, not so much to the triumph of love over death as to the spirit of music itself.[1]

Fatality was fashionable in art and artistic life during the romantic era. Had not Goethe's *Sorrows of Young Werther* precipitated a whole wave of suicidal thoughts and actions? As the age grew elderly and more grim, both physical and intellectual suicide grew so common that society eventually gave artists a special licence to indulge in such activities without being outraged; but in 1813, the year 'Don Juan' appeared, the coupling of an opera commonly considered convivial and *amusant* with a morbid love-death motif must have appeared puzzling, even outrageous. The purpose of music was to embellish life; it was not a matter to be taken so seriously.

The eighteenth century had considered the composer in no way a unique member of society. In fact, the whole concept of the composer in the present-day sense of the word did not begin to be formulated until around 1800. Previously there had been simply musicians, versatile portmanteau men, some of whom also composed. A musician was valued by his employer for his dexterity, not for his creative abilities. Bach, who wrote music while performing a multiplicity of other duties, would have been unemployed had he made the claim for special privileges that society was later willing to condone in creative artists. To understand this helps us, too, to realize why many musicians whose creative talents were demonstrably inferior to Beethoven's – Friedrich Kuhlau, for instance, or Muzio Clementi – could have been considered his peers by contemporary audiences and critics. The change in status can be observed by comparing the lives of Haydn, Mozart (after he gave up his career as a pianist), and finally Beethoven. Here we see the gradual emergence of a kind of human being distinguishing himself from the other practitioners of the craft and demanding from society an acknowledgment of this distinction. The romanticists fashioned the concept of the composer in our sense of the word and flung him upward, a luminary, above other kinds of men and musicians.

Attention has already been drawn to Hoffmann's curious grouping of Haydn, Mozart, and Beethoven as the first true 'romantic' composers. I shall let Hoffmann himself describe precisely what he values in their music to qualify them for this distinction. It remains to be said that the division between 'classicist' and 'romanticist' in music was by no means conspicuous for those living at the time this alleged distinction was taking shape. It is a critical hindsight, and suggests an antagonism between schools of thought that was unpronounced at the time. There was never any desire in either romantic literary or musical circles to break completely with the past. The Schlegel brothers' Jena group, the nest of literary romanticism in Germany, maintained exceptionally good relations with Goethe's Weimar group, the fortress of classicism, at least until well on into the century. The romanticists were fond of emphasizing their historical bonds with many traditions – with the Middle Ages, for example, or with Shakespeare. As for music, the inclusion of Haydn's name in a romantic manifesto would have been unquestioned, at least until much later when Schumann eventually expelled him in 1841 by writing that he was 'like an old friend of the family who is always received with pleasure and respect,' though 'he is no longer highly interesting for the present day.'[2]

Hoffmann's characterization of Haydn as a popular composer, comprehensible to the multitude, may contain a touch of disdain when studied together with his remarks on Mozart and Beethoven. Haydn did not escape criticisms of this kind from other contemporaries as well, as is suggested in this brief conversation from Dittersdorf's autobiography:

> KAISER: What do you think of his chamber music?
> I: It is making a sensation in the world, and rightly so.
> KAISER: But isn't he often too playful?
> I: He has the gift for playfulness without debasing art.
> KAISER: Yes, you are right.[3]

Hoffmann also confessed to a certain irritation with Haydn's light-heartedness when he wrote in his diary in October 1803: 'Haydn would be a truly great composer of instrumental music if he would only take himself more seriously.'[4]

Criticisms aside, Schumann was still able to comment with approval on Haydn's joyful and sanguine temperament as late as 1836:

> ... heavenly harmony resides in these sounds, so free from traces of boredom, so productive of nothing but gaiety, zest for living, childlike joy in everything, and – what a service he has thereby rendered, especially to the present age, this valetudinarian period in music when men are so seldom *inwardly* satisfied.[5]

In the early stages of romanticism aspects of a complete figure that did not fit in with the evolution of the new philosophy were simply ignored, or else underwent adaptation, as is the case with Mozart in the Don Juan story. Thus 'ennobled' with demonic powers, *Don Giovanni* became the favourite Mozart composition for the romanticists, to the exclusion of many of his other masterpieces. For the romanticist, Mozart is the composer of *Don Giovanni* and not, for instance, of *Così fan Tutti*, for the irridescent merriment of this opera seemed beyond all philosophical salvation. One observes this with Ludwig Tieck, for example, who, while he came under the influence of Mozart's confirmed enemy Reichardt, was later able (in *Phantasus*) to write enthusiastically about a single Mozart work, *Don Giovanni*, undoubtedly influenced in this enthusiasm by Hoffmann's story. Similarly Kierkegaard shows himself to be a romanticist in his consideration of Mozart in *Either/Or* when he writes:

In Mozart's case it also happens that there is one work, and only one, which makes him a classical composer, and absolutely immortal. That work is *Don Juan*. The other things which Mozart has produced may give us pleasure and delight, awaken our admiration, enrich the soul, satisfy the ear, delight the heart; but it does him and his immortal fame no service to lump them all together, and make them all equally great. *Don Juan* is his reception piece.[6]

In the chapter which follows, Hoffmann leads us through Haydn and Mozart to – more correctly *up* to – Beethoven. For Hoffmann, Beethoven exists on the highest plane. Today we may view with envy a situation in which the most recent achievements are prized as the finest, in which the public is encouraged to believe that art slants up from the past, not down to the present. Hoffmann realized that any age which prizes the inheritance of the past more than its own achievements is tacitly admitting its own spinelessness. Although the romantic musician by no means dismissed the past, he observed no obsequiousness in respect to its omnipotence or immortality. The romanticist had a healthy respect for the past, but boundless confidence in the present and the future.

For Hoffmann, Beethoven is the greatest composer of all time. Beethoven is Hoffmann's almost exact contemporary. As the first 'composer' in the nascent romantic sense of the word, Beethoven was unique, and Hoffmann was one of the first to declare this special distinction for him. The 'genius' was now to replace the prince, who had dominated the scene during the baroque and rococo eras. To personify this bold concept of the creative musician, Beethoven's music had to be vigorous, vibrant, mighty, unfathomable in depth, immeasurable in surface. But Beethoven was not always or immediately popular, the most frequent complaints being that his compositions were too long and too chaotic. It was also alleged that he reasoned in music instead of feeling it. Another criticism, though perhaps less clearly formulated, seems to have been that Beethoven's music was not intimately enough associated with nature – that it lacked the pastoral caress. In romantic philosophy, nature, art, and the soul were harmonized and received their finest expression in sound, in the bell-like tones of the glass harmonica, the voice of the beloved, the soft sighing of the aeolian harp. Music was subjected to a kind of aesthetic eudemonism, just as the *Aufklärung* had in its last phases fallen to a position of ethical eudemonism. In rococo times, music had been a tonic, a prescription for pleasure. Beethoven's music was hard-driving and, as Goethe complained, 'utterly untamed.' It seemed perhaps that Beethoven had fought with nature and that his music bore the scars of this fight. Goethe's musical correspondent, Carl Friedrich Zelter, accused Beethoven of 'borrowing the club of Hercules' for his music; and it seemed to Zelter presumptuous that a mortal should dare to take such a weapon to beat out the soft and subdued sounds of God's harmonious earth. This, too, is the essence of the poet Grillparzer's heated attacks against Beethoven, that he had created an interest in the strong rather than the beautiful, and that he had upset the delicate natural balance established by Mozart.[7]

It is true that, just prior to Beethoven's appearance, Rousseau had called for a return to the pastoral life, but the call had been interrupted by the cry of the industrial revolution which exhorted man not to surrender to but to command the natural elements, and this cry was beginning to be heard even in Germany and Austria, where the magnetic pull of urban as opposed to rural life was increasing.

This transformation can be sensed as it takes hold of the life of a single man. For instance, writing in 1774 the composer J.F. Reichardt observes:

> The author has here the honour to assure his readers that henceforth he will never again be charmed by any great city, no matter how beautiful it may be. Having seen many great cities and finding in all of them much unhappiness and incurable disorder, he has come to agree with his friend Rousseau that all the splendor and all the amusements of the great cities are as nothing in comparison with a green meadow and a merry harvest dance and that all the art of a thousand artists is nothing in comparison with the charm of laughing nature.[8]

But thirty-six years later in 1810, Reichardt had converted to urban life:

> For anyone, surely, who can enjoy the good things of life, especially for the artist, perhaps quite especially for the musical artist, Vienna is the richest, happiest, most agreeable residence in Europe ... Thus I had the good fortune to spend in Vienna a whole winter, richer in amusements and pleasures of every kind than any winter I have ever before experienced for all my good fortune in my earlier travels.[9]

This change from rural to urban life style is everywhere present throughout the eighteenth and nineteenth centuries, nor is it absent among artists. Beethoven spent most of his life in cities or on their outskirts. Could one call him the first truly urban composer? Is there, in the heart and pulse of his music, something of the noise and excitement, the dissonance and drama of city life? This is not to imply in any sense that Beethoven's music possesses the motor impulses of an 'industrial' composer, but rather that by reflecting cosmopolitan life and its objectives he is engaged in an audacious experiment to conquer nature and bend it to man's will. 'Brazen,' was the word Hoffmann used in 'Ombra adorata' to describe Beethoven's music. Man wrestles with wild forces and seeks to civilize them. Beethoven's music reflects this struggle between the natural elements and the human will, this new-found desire to aspire to a position of control previously held by the Creator alone. Like Don Juan, his ideals are the highest and if he is defeated he plunges into depths of despair hitherto unimaginable. Beethoven's music, Hoffmann will say, 'opens to us the realm of the colossal and the immeasurable.' It 'moves the levers of fear, of horror, of terror, of pain.' But behind it there is always the infinite longing, the infinite desire to rise upward, to overcome and command these forces. For those who had been accustomed to the well-behaved repertoire of the eighteenth century it was difficult to understand that music could be produced out of these kinds of conflict. Beethoven presented them with problems when all they wanted were cameos of pleasure.

We have left the world of the glass harmonica and the aeolian harp, vibrating sympathetically with nature, and even all consideration of music as a sensuous reincarnation of the beloved; for we are entering a fateful realm where man and the elements compete for supremacy. Hoffmann now seeks complete detachment from the impurities of vocal music so that his own fantasy can roam freely throughout this realm. It is instrumental music that now assumes the dominant position, for it is the purest form of expression and disdains involvement with all other arts. Haydn and Mozart are romantic because it was through them that music was liberated from its dependence on the art of poetry so that Beethoven could force open the door and grapple with these new forces of expression.

In an 1809 review of a symphony by Friedrich Witt, Hoffmann wrote:

> Everyone knows that instrumental music has now reached heights which could
> in no way have been conceived even a few years ago; further, that the symphony,
> especially through the impetus given it by Haydn and Mozart, has become the
> highest form of instrumental music – has become the opera of the instruments.
> It was a difficult task to explore all the characteristic qualities of each instru-
> ment in the orchestra and to unify them in drama, so that each individual instru-
> ment was responsible to the whole and not as is the case in the stiff and tedious
> *concerto grosso*. But this task was beautifully accomplished by the giants of
> music and their inspired works in this genre have rightly become the norm from
> which later composers will develop their symphonies.[10]

The essay that follows, 'Beethoven's Instrumental Music,' is a compilation Hoffmann made of different reviews he had written for the *Allgemeine Musikalische Zeitung*. Beethoven's Fifth Symphony forms the basis of the essay. Hoffmann's remarks on this work, which are among the most eloquent and powerful he ever penned, need to be prefaced by some contemporary remarks on the same work, for only by comparison can the profundity of Hoffmann's perceptions be measured.

Johann Friedrich Reichardt, who may have been won over to cosmopolitan life but whose music never detached itself from the pastoral eighteenth century, found Beethoven's Fifth Symphony 'very elaborate and too long. A cavalier sitting near us reported having observed at the rehearsal that the violoncello part, busily copied, amounted alone to thirty-four sheets.'[11] And here is another contemporary review of the symphony from the *Allgemeine Musikalische Zeitung*:

> The first movement in C minor is a fiery *allegro*, a little obscure, noble in feeling and in working out, firmly and evenly developed. It is a worthy piece, which will afford real pleasure even to those who are attached to the older way of composing large symphonies. The *andante* is most original and attractive, composed as it is of the most heterogeneous ideas – gentle reverie and warlike fierceness. Its handling from beginning to end is *sui generis*. Under its appearance of arbitrariness it is possible to find in this remarkable piece much thought, a firm grasp of the whole, and a very careful elaboration. As for the following *scherzando* (which is hardly playable by a large orchestra), we must confess ourselves unable to enjoy it, owing to its far too insistent whims. But humour in art – if I may be permitted the comparison – is not just like fine cooking, however elaborate it may be one must try and try again in order to ascertain what might prove pleasing. The finale is a tempestuous explosion, born of a powerful fancy, and such as one would hardly find in any other symphony.[12]

ELEVEN

Beethoven's Instrumental Music

When we speak of the independence of music, are we not really referring to instrumental music, which, scorning every aid, every admixture of another art (poetry), expresses the pure essence of this particular art alone? This is the most romantic of all the arts – one might say, the only purely romantic art – for its sole subject is the infinite. The lyre of Orpheus opened the portals of Orcus. Music discloses an unknown realm to man, a world that has nothing in common with the outer material world in which he lives, and for which he abandons all concrete feelings to surrender himself to an inexpressible longing.

Have you ever even sensed this true nature, you miserable composers of instrumental music, as you toil assiduously to depict concrete emotions, even concrete events?[1] How could it ever have occurred to you to treat the very art which stands in opposition to the plastic arts in a plastic manner? Your sunrises, your storms, your *Batailles des trois Empereurs*, and so on, were certainly ridiculous aberrations and have been deservedly punished by total oblivion.

In song, definite emotions are suggested by means of words, and the magic power of music acts as the wonderful elixir of the wise, a few drops of which may render the drink more priceless, more glorious. Every passion the opera gives to us – love, hate, anger, despair, etc. – is clothed by music with the purple lustre of the romantic, and those very things experienced in life lead us out of life to the realm of the infinite.

So strong is the magic of music, that, growing ever stronger, it had to break every chain that bound it to another art.

The gifted composer of instrumental music has been able to raise himself to his present height not only by means of the greater technical facility of this art (improvement of instruments, greater virtuosity of performers), but rather as a result of a deeper insight into the truly characteristic spirit of music itself.

Mozart and Haydn, the creators of today's instrumental music, were the first to show us the art in its full glory; the man who then looked on it with all his love and penetrated its innermost being is – Beethoven! The instrumental compositions of these three masters breathe the same romantic spirit, displaying a similar intimate understanding of the specific nature of the art; but their compositions show marked differences in character.

The expression of a serene and childlike disposition prevails in Haydn's compositions. His symphonies lead us into vast green woodlands, into a gaily coloured throng of happy men. Youths and maidens dance in a row, swaying back and forth; laughing children peer out from behind trees and rose bushes and tease one another by throwing flowers. A life of love, of bliss, as before the Fall, of eternal youth, without sorrows, without pain, only a sweet melancholy yearning for the object of love which sways in the glimmer of the setting sun, without coming nearer, without disappearing, and so long as it is there night will not come, for it is the sunset itself, glowing above the mountain and forest.

Mozart leads us into the heart of the spirit realm. Fear grips us, but without tormenting us, so that it is more a presentiment of the infinite. Love and melancholy resound with beautiful spirit voices; night descends with bright purple lustre and we are drawn with indescribable longing towards the shapes that beckon us to fly through the clouds to their ranks and join the eternal dance of the spheres (Mozart's symphony in E-flat major, known as the 'Swan Song').[2]

Now Beethoven's instrumental music opens to us the realm of the colossal and the immeasurable. Glowing beams of light shoot through the deep night of this realm and we perceive giant shadows surging back and forth, closer and closer around us, destroying everything in us except the pain of that endless longing in which each joy that had risen in jubilant tones sinks back and perishes; and it is in this pain which consumes love, hope, and happiness without destroying them, in this pain which seeks to break our breast with the chords of all the passions that we live on and become enchanted visionaries!

Romantic taste is rare; rarer still is romantic talent. Thus there are only a few who are able to touch the lyre whose sound discloses the wonderful realm of the romantic.

Haydn conceived the human element of this life romantically; he is more commensurable, more comprehensible for the majority. Mozart is concerned with the superhuman, the miraculous element that inhabits the inmost soul.

Beethoven's music moves the lever of fear, of horror, of terror, of pain, and awakens just that infinite longing which is the essence of romanticism.

Thus he is a purely romantic composer; and is this not perhaps the reason why he has been less successful in his vocal music, which excludes the character of indefinite longing and merely represents emotions defined by words?

The musical rabble is oppressed by Beethoven's mighty genius; it would rebel in vain against it. But the wise critics look about themselves with a superior air and assure us as men of great intellect and deep insight that, while the good Beethoven by no means lacks a very rich and lively fantasy, he does not know how to curb it. Thus, they claim, he doesn't bother to select or to shape his ideas, but, following the so-called demonic method, he dashes everything down the moment it is prompted to him by the fire of his fertile imagination. But how is it that the deep inner continuity of every Beethoven composition eludes your casual glance? Could it be *your* fault that you do not understand the master's language as the initiated understand it, so that the portals of the inmost sanctuary remain closed to you? The truth is that, as regards self-possession, Beethoven stands quite on a par with Haydn and Mozart and that, separating his ego from the inner realm of harmony, he rules over it as an absolute monarch. Aestheticians have often complained about Shakespeare's complete lack of the unities and inner continuity, although for those who inspect more closely, a beautiful tree springs from a seed and puts forth leaves, blooms, and fruit. In the same way, Beethoven's supreme self-possession – inseparable from true genius and nourished by dedication to the art – is revealed only after a thorough investigation of his instrumental music.

Can there be any work by Beethoven that confirms all this to a higher degree than his incomparably magnificent and profound symphony in c minor? How this wonderful composition leads the listener imperturbably forward in a climax that climbs up and up into the spirit world of the infinite. Nothing could be simpler than the two-bar principal subject of the first *allegro*. Heard at the beginning in unison, it nevertheless leaves the tonality undecided. The nervous, unsettled passion of this movement serves to set up the melodious second subject even more decisively. It is as if these cutting tones represent the breast, oppressed and alarmed by premonitions of the monstrous and by the threat of annihilation, breaking free from itself; but soon a shining friendly spirit draws near, lighting the depths of the horrible night (the lovely theme in G major, first heard by the horn in E-flat major). How simple – to say it once again – is the theme that the master conceived as a foundation for the whole, and how wonderfully all the secondary and bridge sections follow on as a result of their rhythmic relationship, to extend the character of the principal subject little by little over the entire *allegro*. All phrases are short, almost all are

composed of two or three bars; moreover, they are constantly divided
between altering winds and strings. One might think that only something
broken and incomprehensible could come from such elements; but instead
it is precisely this arrangement of the whole, together with the constant
repetition of sections and single chords, that stimulates the feeling of indescribable longing to the highest degree. Aside from the fact that the contrapuntal treatment testifies to a deep study of the art, it is the bridge
sections with their constant allusions to the principal theme which prove
how the great master comprehended and mentally refined all the details
of the whole passionate movement.

Does not the lovely theme of the *andante con moto* in A-flat major
affect us like a gracious spirit, filling our breast with consolation and hope?
The frightful spirit that ruled the first *allegro* with terror has disappeared
in storm clouds, but even here he glowers down, and at his lightning the
friendly spirits which surrounded us vanish. What should I say about the
minuet? Listen yourselves to the original modulations, the close on the
dominant major chord, which the bass then takes up as the tonic of the
following theme; listen to the theme constantly expanding itself by a few
bars. Do you not sense once again the turbulent, inexpressible longing and
see the wonderful spirit realm which the master rules? How like a dazzling
sunbeam is the splendid theme of the last movement with the rejoicing
exultation of the whole orchestra! What an amazing contrapuntal intricacy
binds the whole together once again. For many, everything rushes by like
an ingenious rhapsody, but the soul of each thoughtful listener is stirred
deeply and intimately by just that ominous feeling of longing, and right
up to the final chord – indeed even in the moments that follow it – he will
be powerless to step out of that wondrous spirit world where pain and
pleasure embrace him in the form of sound. The internal structure of the
movements, their execution, their instrumentation, the order in which they
are arranged, everything moves to a single end; but above all it is the intimate relationship of the themes that engenders that unity which alone
has the power to hold the listener firmly in a single mood. This relationship is frequently clear to the listener when he overhears it in the connection of two movements or discovers it in the fundamental bass they have
in common, but a deeper relationship which does not reveal itself in this
way speaks only from mind to mind, and it is precisely this relationship
that prevails between sections of the two allegros and the minuet and
which imperiously proclaims the self-possession of the master's genius.

How deeply have thy magnificent compositions for the piano impressed
themselves upon my soul, thou sublime master; how shallow and insignificant everything seems to me that does not belong to thee, to the gifted

Mozart, or to that mighty genius Sebastian Bach. With what joy I received thy opus 70, the two splendid trios, for I knew well that after a little practice I should be able to hear them in truly glorious style. And, in fact, this evening things have gone so well with me that even now, like a man who wanders deeper and deeper into the mazes of a fantastic park filled with all sorts of exotic trees, plants, and wonderful flowers, I am powerless to find my way out of the marvellous turns and windings of thy trios. The lovely siren voices of their resplendent and varied movements lure me in further and further. The gifted lady who indeed honoured me, Kapellmeister Kreisler, by playing today the first trio in such splendid style, and before whose piano I still sit and write, has made me realize quite clearly that only that which the mind produces calls for respect and that everything else is worthless.

Just now I have repeated at the piano from memory certain striking transitions from the two trios. It is certainly true that the piano remains more useful as an instrument for harmony than for melody. The finest expression that can be given melody on this instrument cannot create for it the versatile life with thousands upon thousands of nuances that the string player's bow or the wind player's breath can fashion. The performer struggles in vain against the insuperable difficulties of a mechanism in which tone is produced by striking the string and allowing it to vibrate. Against that, however, there is not a single instrument that spans the realm of harmony so fully as the piano, allowing the expert to explore its treasures in the most wonderful forms and shapes. (The great limitations of the harp keep it from being considered.)[3] If the master's fantasy is stirred by a whole canvas of sounds in rich clusters from bright lights to dark shadows, then he can bring the whole to life on the piano and it will come forth from the inner world in shining colours. The many-voiced full score, the magic recipe of music, which holds in its secret signs all the wonders of music, the clandestine chorus of the most diversified instruments, this score will come to life under the hands of the master at the piano. An orchestral piece, well rendered with all the parts in this manner, might be compared with a skilful etching copied from a great painting. The piano is primarily intended for improvising, for playing from the full score, for individual sonatas, chords, and so forth; also for trios, quartets, quintets etc., where the customary stringed instruments join in, actually submitting to the conventions of the piano composition. For are not such works, composed for four or five voices, dependent on a harmonic development which prohibits individual instruments from stepping out in brilliant solo passages?

I have a real antipathy for all true piano concertos. (Mozart's and Beethoven's are not so much concertos as symphonies with *obbligato* piano.)

Here the virtuosity of the individual performer is supposed to shine forth in passages and in the expressiveness of melodies; but the best performer on the most elegant instrument would struggle in vain to create the kind of effects that, for example, a violinist could achieve almost effortlessly. After the full tutti of the wind and strings every solo sounds lifeless and dull; one is impressed by the dexterity of the fingers but little is said to the soul.

How well the master has understood the specific character of the instrument and fostered it in its most characteristic manner! A simple but fruitful theme, susceptible to the most varied contrapuntal protractions, abbreviations, and so forth, forms the basis of each movement; all remaining secondary themes and figures are related to the main idea in such a way that the details all interweave and arrange themselves among the instruments in highest unity. Such is the structure of the whole; yet in this artful structure the most marvellous pictures are seen in which joy and pain, melancholy and ecstasy alternate in restless flight, emerging beside and around one another. Strange figures begin a merry dance, now floating off to a point of light, now splitting apart, flashing and sparkling, evading and pursuing one another in numberless constellations; and at the centre of the spirit realm the intoxicated soul hearkens to the unfamiliar language and understands all the secret premonitions that have touched it.

Only the composer who knows how to use harmony to work on the human soul has truly mastered its secrets. Numerical proportions, which for the talentless grammarian remain dull and lifeless problems in arithmetic, become for him magical compounds from which to conjure up a magic world.

Aside from the good nature that prevails, especially in the first trio, and despite the melancholy largo, Beethoven's genius is in the last analysis serious and solemn. It is as though the master thought that, in speaking of deep mysterious things – even when the spirit, intimately familiar with them, feels itself joyously uplifted – one may not use an ordinary language but rather a sublime and glorious one. The dance of the priests of Isis will always be an exultant hymn.

If instrumental music is to produce its effect simply through itself as music and is not to serve a definite dramatic purpose, it must avoid all trivial facetiousness, all frivolous *lazzi*. A deep soul seeks for the intimations of that joy which is more glorious and beautiful than the joy of our constricted life, a joy imported from an unknown land to enkindle an inner life of bliss within our breasts, a higher expression than can be put into mere words – for words can express mere earthly pleasures. This seriousness in all Beethoven's instrumental and piano compositions is the best possible antidote for those breakneck passages with both hands rushing up and down, those queer leaps, those farcical *capriccios*, those notes towering high above the staff on their five- and six-line scaffolds, which fill the compositions of our day. On the side of mere digital dexterity, Beethoven's compositions for the piano really present no special difficulty, for every practised performer will have at his fingers the few runs, triplet figures, and whatever else is called for; nevertheless their performance is still quite difficult. Many a so-called virtuoso condemns the master's piano compositions, claiming that they are not only 'very difficult' but also 'very unrewarding.'

Now, as regards difficulty, the correct and proper performance of a work by Beethoven demands nothing more than that one should understand him, that one should enter deep into his being, that, aware of one's own consecrated nature, one should dare to step into the circle of the magical phenomena evoked by his powerful spell. Anyone unaware of this consecration, anyone who regards sacred music as a mere game and a means of whiling away an empty hour, as a momentary titillation for dull ears, or as a means of self-ostentation, let him leave Beethoven's music alone. Only to such a person does the objection 'very unrewarding' apply. The true artist lives only in that work which he has comprehended and now performs as the master intended it to be performed. He is above putting his own personality forward in any way, and all his endeavours are directed towards a single end, to call to life all the enchanting pictures and shapes the composer has sealed into his work with magic power, that they may surround mankind in luminous sparkling circles, and, enkindling our imagination and innermost soul, may carry us off in rapid flight to the faraway spirit realm of sound.

TWELVE

The Critic

Sir:

I am taking the opportunity afforded me by Herr Neberich of making myself known to such a gifted person as you are – Moreover you have written about my humble self. And our *weak Herr Starke* showed me in his album some lines of yours about me. So I am bound to think that you must take some interest in me. Allow me to tell you that this interest on the part of a man like you who is endowed with such excellent qualities is very gratifying to me. I send you my best wishes and remain, Sir, with kindest regards, your most devoted

Beethoven[1]

Beethoven appears to have taken a lively interest in Hoffmann following the appearance of his reviews in the *Allgemeine Musikalische Zeitung*, and he wrote a short composition on his name.[2] Certainly his letter to Hoffmann is one of the few in his entire output displaying untempered respect and warmth of expression, especially for a man he was never to meet.

As for Hoffmann, his Beethoven reviews occupy a special place in his critical output, for in them the author, seized by the pure excitement of present-tense music, has focused his imagination on the music itself and abandoned all desire to frame his comments, as in the preceding translations, within the context of a story.

Although Hoffmann regarded his musical stories as genuine music criticism and published many of them as such, it is only when we come to the Beethoven reviews that we begin to approach the condition of contemporary critical literature. Yet some may still object to the subjective impulsiveness of the reviews and the manner in which many observations are left unsupported by theoretical analysis. Our notion of music appreciation today has come to depend heavily on grammatical analysis and less on subjective vagaries. In Hoffmann's day it was the duty of the critic to describe first the ecstasy of his vision and only after he had, in Schumann's words, created 'an impression identical with the one called forth by the thing criticized' could he proceed, now assuming the sympathy of his readers, to touch on the constructional features of the work that had produced these effects. Many of the most enthusiastic commentators on music, such as Wackenroder, never carried through to this second stage at all, yet their reading public appears not to have been disturbed by this omission. On the contrary, we may suppose they delighted in it, for there was a strong feeling among the romanticists, as evidenced by 'Ritter Gluck,' that the secrets of music should not and could not be explained.

The exact extent of Hoffmann's music criticisms is only now becoming known with certainty. Hitzig, Hoffmann's friend and first biographer, testified to the authenticity of several that appeared in the *Allgemeine Musikalische Zeitung.* Others we know for certain are by him because he rewrote them or parts of them for inclusion in collections of his work such as the *Fantasiestücke* or the *Serapionsbrüder.* Between 1894 and 1912 Georg Ellinger, Hans von Müller, Edgar Istel, and Erwin Kroll found many more and exposed some others as unauthentic. The latest and most scrupulous scholar of the criticism is Friedrich Schnapp, who has come up with something like a definite list of fifty-eight reviews, based on exhaustive linguistic and stylistic analyses.[3]

As a trained musician, Hoffmann was perfectly capable of analysing a piece of music technically and was by no means opposed to doing this when writing for trade publications. His best reviews fall naturally into two sections. For those pieces which impressed him as worthy of romanticism he always attempts at the outset to secure the sympathy of his readers by confessing the depth of his own inner response to the music; and only after this cathartic burst of lyricism does he go on to make his technical assessment of the work. The form the review of Beethoven's Fifth Symphony took in its original printing is exemplary. First he dismisses all forms of music except instrumental music and pleads that its purity places it on the highest plane, the most romantic plane; then he directs us towards Beethoven's music by comparing it with that of Haydn and Mozart. We are moving by stages from the past to the present and from the general to the particular. The spiritual ecstasy produced by Beethoven's music is evoked, and we are taken by means of visionary utterances on a metaphorical tour of a Beethoven composition. Only then is the reader prepared to be drawn through the rational analysis of an actual work.

For the revised printing of the Fifth Symphony review Hoffmann chose to extrapolate his analysis of the work for the less technically minded reading public of his *Fantasiestücke.* The original review included twenty-one musical illustrations and a thorough analysis of the composition in which Hoffmann discovered for the first time the now famous thematic and rhythmic relationships between the movements.[4] I have hesitated to reproduce that version, partly because it lacks the overall richness of the later study, and partly because its contents are no longer new to students of music, having been duplicated in every textbook analysis. However, in order to compare that anonymous review in the *Allgemeine Musikalische Zeitung*, which dismissed the third movement of Beethoven's symphony as a failure, with Hoffmann's study, published in the same magazine, the third-movement section of Hoffmann's review might be included here. It indicates the breadth of Hoffmann's conception, both his grasp of the movement's dominant spirit and his perception of its harmonic and thematic detail.

The minuet[5] which follows the *andante* is again so original that the spirit of the listener is gripped by the piquant and ingenious manner in which the master, in following the Haydn formula, has turned it into the most original movement of the whole composition. Above all, it is the original modulations, the cadences on the dominant major chord which the bass then takes up as the tonic of the following theme, and the constantly expanding principal theme itself that achieve the character of Beethoven's music as I have described it above. All the unrest, all the presentiment of the wonderful realm of spirits that the opening *allegro* had provoked in the mind of the listener is now excited anew.

The C minor theme, introduced by the lower strings, moves to G minor in the third bar; the horns hold the G and a bar later the violins, violas, and bassoons, now joined by the clarinets, reply with a four-bar phrase which concludes in G major. The bass theme is repeated, but after the third bar the G minor cadence moves to D minor, then to C minor as the preceding violin phrase is repeated.

The horns now introduce a phrase leading to E-flat major, accompanied by the strings which punctuate the first beat of each bar with chords. The orchestra then leads this phrase further to E-flat minor, closing on the dominant, B-flat major; but in the same bar the bass begins a restatement of the principal C minor theme, this time in B-flat minor. The violins etc., repeat their phrase and a point of repose is reached in F major.

The bass repeats its theme again, extending it through F minor, C minor, G minor, and back to C minor, at which the tutti that had first been heard in E-flat minor now leads the phrase through F minor to C major; but just as the bass had turned B-flat major into B-flat minor the last time, it now seizes the fundamental C as the tonic of a C minor statement of the theme. The flutes and oboes reply with the phrase that had first been taken by the strings, while the strings repeat one bar of the tutti subject.

The horns hold the G and the cellos begin a new theme, against which the violins repeat their opening phrase, then extend this with a new eighth-note figure, heard for the first time. The new theme of the cellos itself contains references to the original theme and is in this way, as well as through an identical rhythm, intimately related to it. After a short repetition of the tutti section this part of the minuet closes in C minor *fortissimo* with trumpets and timpani.

The lower strings open the second section, the trio, with a subject in C minor which the violas imitate in fugal fashion leading to the dominant, followed by abbreviated imitations in the second and the first violins. The first half of this section closes in G major. In the second part the lower strings start the theme twice over but each time are restrained, only to carry it forward the third time. While some may find this comical, for the reviewer it is a sinister effect. After several imitations of this, the subject is picked up by the flutes, supported by the oboes, clarinets, and bassoons and the tonic G held throughout by the horns. Finally the trio dies away in isolated notes, first from the clarinet and bassoon, then from the lower strings.

Now follows a repetition of the principal theme of the first section in abbreviated note values on the lower strings. Again the repose of a cadence. Then the extended version of the same theme is heard. This time instead of half notes, quarter notes are employed followed by quarter-note rests. Most of the other phrases of the first section are also repeated in this abbreviated fashion. The restless longing which the material expressed originally is now intensified to a fear which breaks in on the breast. Only a few abrupt sounds escape this feeling. The chord of G major seems to lead to a conclusion; but the bass now holds A flat *pianissimo* for fifteen measures while the violins and violas hold C, the major third above, and the timpani plays first the rhythm of the frequently quoted tutti, then four bars with one stroke per bar, then four with two strokes, and finally beats in quarter notes. The first violin at last sounds the first theme and leads us twenty-eight bars further along, constantly alluding to this theme, until the dominant seventh of the original key is reached. The second violins and violas have meanwhile sustained the C throughout while the timpani beats in quarter notes together with the bass which has moved from A-flat to F-sharp, back to A-flat and finally to G. Now the bassoons enter, and one bar later the oboes, then three bars later the horns, flutes, and trumpets, while the timpani continues to beat C in eighth notes and the movement leads directly into the C major with which the final *allegro* begins.

Why did the master allow the timpani to remain throughout on C in dissonance with the dominant chord? It is in accord with the character he sought to give the whole work. These dull, dissonant beats excite the terror of the extraordinary, the fear of the supernatural, like a fearful and unknown voice. The reviewer has already mentioned above the progressive nature of the principal

theme which expands itself in order to render each effect more conspicuous.
Here are these extensions grouped together:

With the repetition of the first section, the phrase appears like this:

Although so simple, how strong is the impression made by the reappearance of
the first movement motive in the subsequent movements of the work. It is the
same thought as the opening theme of the tutti section in the minuet.

It seems to me that something of the greatness of Hoffmann's music
criticism lies in his ability to join both the imaginative and the analytical
forms of description without treating them as contradictory or exclusive
ways of responding to music. How many critics are too self-conscious to
indulge in the first or too unprofessional to manage the second? There is
something inherently natural about Hoffmann's division of the musical experience into two phases, for is not any new work first accepted as a sensuous expression and only afterwards grasped intellectually?

It is true that with less inspiring compositions, Hoffmann dismissed all
prefatory discussion and engaged immediately on a perfunctory analysis

of the music. These decapitated reviews show only that such works drew no initial response from him, cast no fire into his soul. As a professional music critic, Hoffmann was not at liberty to choose the music he was to review, and thus his collected criticisms include extensive articles on works by such insignificant composers as Friedrich Witt, C.A.P. Braun, Joseph Elsner, and others, along with the occasional Beethoven or Mozart or Gluck review. Hoffmann's editor, Georg Ellinger, has noticed a certain stylistic stiffness in the regular music criticisms, which is scarcely surprising. Shortly after he took up his duties as critic for the *Allgemeine Musikalische Zeitung* he wrote in his diary, 'It went better than I thought' – a remark which indicates he did not find reviewing simple. As we shall see, in Hoffmann's aesthetic cosmology the world of words ranks below that of tones, so that for an aspiring composer to have to make a living at emulating other people's music with his prose must at times have seemed to him to be doubly frustrating.

Nevertheless, Hoffmann is an epoch-making critic, one of the greatest in the history of music. He is this because he was able to distinguish truly great musical achievements from mere trivialities; because he placed music above the other arts, thereby establishing the aesthetic order for the future; because he attempted to understand the new music of his own time and proclaimed its merits with vigour and eloquence; and because despite an inadequate knowledge of the past he sensed that which was great there and that which deserved revival. On the whole, he was a generous music critic, though not so generous as Schumann, who discovered a genius in every second paragraph. But Schumann was much less trustworthy in his discoveries than was Hoffmann. From the constellation of composers living and dead, Hoffmann points directly at Palestrina, Bach, Gluck, Haydn, Mozart, and Beethoven. Other composers may have their talents, but these are the great ones; these are the models to be followed.

On the other hand, his enthusiasm was not blind. There were reservations in his respect for Haydn. Beethoven, too, was not beyond the occasional reproach. In his criticism of Beethoven's *Coriolanus* overture, for instance, he suggests that the work is too muscle-bound to serve as an introduction to Collin's reflective drama, and commends Beethoven to more 'romantic' authors such as Shakespeare or Calderón. In his review of Louis Spohr's first symphony he says 'this work ... must draw the attention of the music-loving public,' though he refrains from committing his own enthusiasm to it, for he was highly suspicious of Spohr's peculiar brand of romanticism. On the other hand, a work such as Étienne Méhul's overture *La Chasse*, which to a modern audience would seem like a pale imitation of the hunt music from Weber's *Freischütz*, was for Hoffmann an exciting model of descriptive music. (*Der Freischütz*, of course, had not yet been written.) Without knowing precisely what the composer had in mind, Hoffmann invents a program for the work:

> Out of the thicket springs the royal stag, pursued by the ferocious hounds; on panting horses the hunters storm after. The animal escapes. The dogs have lost the scent; they slink about sniffing. The hunters are still. Then the dogs start off again. Over stone and bush leaps the stag, the horns peel out, the hunters hasten after, and the hunt is on.[6]

We note parenthetically that the description suggested by Méhul's music, as by that of Haydn, is purely terrestrial compared with the supernatural imagery of the Beethoven landscape.

A revealing comparison could also be drawn between Hoffmann's analyses of Beethoven themes and those in less significant works. In Friedrich Witt's fifth symphony the *allegro* theme

is found to be 'pleasant' (*angenehm*), the *andante* theme

is 'charming' (*lieblich*). But these four notes alone

have the power to carry the listener 'imperturbably forward in a climax that climbs up and up into the spirit world of the infinite.' There is no mistaking the terrestrial for the transcendent experience.

The impulse to be propelled upwards, so common in romantic aesthetics, has its roots in Christianity, where paradise exists above earth and the good Christian aspires upwards towards its attainment. This parallel was sensed by the romanticists themselves. The writer Wackenroder had developed it in his story of Joseph Berglinger, a fictional musician for whom music had become a mystical experience, related to all that is serene and divine. Berglinger listens to music in church:

> Full of expectation he awaited the first sound of the instruments; and as this now broke forth from the muffled silence, as a mighty and attenuated sigh of wind from heaven, and as the full force of the sound swept over his head, it seemed to him as though his soul had suddenly unfurled great wings and he was being raised above the barren earth; the curtain of clouds before the mortal eye diffused and he soared up into radiant heaven. Then he held his body still and motionless, fixing his gaze steadfastly on the floor. The present sank away before him; his being was cleansed of all earthly trifles, which are mere dust to the lustre of the soul. The music set his nerves tingling with a gentle thrill and with its transformations conjured up a variety of images.[7]

For Berglinger music is a great purifying force, a 'spiritual wine.' Berglinger's creator had studied music with Johann Nikolaus Forkel, the biographer of Bach. Forkel had himself dreamed of reuniting music with religion as Bach had achieved it, and he had no use for the contemporary music of Haydn and Mozart, which he considered secular and trifling. To Forkel, Bach's works 'carry us away with them.'[8] The same upward sweep is encountered here as in the writings of Wackenroder and Hoffmann.

In extending Wackenroder's story and preparing it for publication, Ludwig Tieck inserted the description of a conversion to Catholicism, produced by the effect of religious music.[9] Hoffmann too, who had heard in Poland a great deal of music associated with the Catholic church, indicates strongly in his unfinished novel *Kater Murr* that he was preparing his composer hero, Johannes Kreisler, for conversion in order that he might ultimately devote himself exclusively to religious music.

The close identification of music with religion can be sensed everywhere in German romanticism. The poet Kleist entrusted to music a seraphic charm which could, nevertheless, have a terrifying power if debased. In his short story 'Saint Cecilia, or the Power of Music' he tells of four iconoclasts who would destroy a nunnery while the sisters were performing the music of 'an ancient Italian mass.' Their punishment takes the form of a conversion to an incurable religious mania in which, with frighteningly inhuman voices, they sing a perpetual *Gloria in excelsis* to the Creator.[10]

In his essay 'Ancient and Modern Church Music,' a translation of which may be found in the next chapter, Hoffmann asserts that music is a purely Christian art as distinct from the plastic arts, whose spiritual essence belongs to pre-Christian times. In this assertion he anticipates the fully formulated arguments of Kierkegaard (in *Either/Or*) and Spengler (in *The Decline of the West*). This leads him directly into the question of whether *all* music can be qualified as religious or whether some kinds are more suited to this end than others. Goethe had maintained there were basically two kinds of music: that which inspires us to pray and that which impels us to dance. The question, then, is how to distinguish between the sacred and the secular, and indeed how to separate out inferior forms of sacred music from the best expressions.

The romanticists felt the Middle Ages held the secret to many things and they longed to duplicate the purity and nobility of medieval philosophy and art. Characteristically, Hoffmann looks back nostalgically into the depths of the past to find his solution, not to the Middle Ages (for medieval music was unknown or misunderstood in his time), but to the nearest musical equivalent he can find, that is, to the Italian composers of the renaissance and early baroque.

Hoffmann criticizes the secular influences and the emotionalism of the religious music of his own time and compares it unfavourably with that of the sixteenth century – or what little of it he knew. He does not realize that the music he is idealizing and reducing to a serene ghost of unearthliness had in its day a strength and a worldliness of its own, and that the influences of opera and instrumental music were every bit as conspicuous in early baroque music as they were in the religious music of his own time. Elsewhere Hoffmann had criticized a statement by the opera composer Sacchini in which the latter claimed that one could modulate at liberty in religious music but that in stage works a simplicity is prescribed which makes rapid and numerous changes of tonality hazardous. To Hoffmann precisely the opposite seemed true. He would eliminate from religious music all sensation of passion, of excitement, of drama. Certainly when this concept of religious music is applied to the works discussed in 'Ancient and Modern Church Music' a mythical species of music results which had, in fact, never existed.

Nevertheless, an attempt is made here towards correct stylistic restoration and evaluation. The problems lie in the lack of materials and the method of study. The talent for looking at music objectively and carefully, which we call musicology, did not come into existence properly until almost the middle of the nineteenth century. In fact, Alfred Einstein has noted that the birth of musicology, while ostensibly undertaken in the spirit of objectivity, was at the same time an expression of the romanticist's subjective longing to recover an irrecoverable past.

I shall have occasion later to show how Hoffmann's enthusiasm for Bach – and there is no denying that he was among the first to call for his

revival – was also an expression of his necessity to champion socially unpopular causes. Hoffmann prides himself on appreciating Bach while others
misunderstood him. There is a snobbery here; and one may assume that it
attached itself to some of the other 'obscure' figures mentioned in the
essay to follow.

In 1805 Breitkopf und Härtel issued a Mass for Double Choir under the
name of Bach, which Rochlitz unctuously introduced as 'an obelisk disin-
terred from the ruins of a grey, prehistoric age.' The work was not by
Bach. When Hoffmann planned his 'Ancient and Modern Church Music'
and attempted to secure something by this composer he was sent this mass.
Thus he drew his conclusions about the nature of Bach's religious music
from a single spurious composition. He knew none of the Passions, none
of the cantatas, nor the *Magnificat*, nor the B minor Mass. One may wonder altogether how much religious music of the past was known to him.
A mass by Johann Gottlieb Naumann that he heard once in Dresden became, in one of Hoffmann's reviews, *the* mass by Naumann. Which mass he
was describing out of Naumann's twenty-seven manuscript masses known
to have existed at that time in Dresden is not stated, indeed does not concern him. Hoffmann's telescoped view of history may also be observed
with some alarm. From Guido d'Arezzo we are directed immediately to
Palestrina; and from Palestrina the masters of the baroque such as Alessandro Scarlatti seem to spring forth as disciples, without stylistic cleavage. I
have pointed out other inconsistencies or errors of fact in the footnotes
to the translation.

More important than its minor historical difficulties is the philosophical
ambivalence of the essay. The very fact that it falls so easily into conversation form in which conflicting ideas are put forward illustrates Hoffmann's
uneasy approach to his subject. Although he favours the religious music of
the past, he cannot disguise the fact that he prefers the *music* of the present. Music originated in religion, Hoffmann argues, but soon it longed to
pour 'its unending treasures over mankind so that even the secular, even
the petty mundane affairs of life, may adorn themselves joyfully in the
splendour of its rays.' This glorification of the secular could not come
about until recent times, for ancient music was uncertain of itself and
needed the church as its guardian. Although the liturgical music of the past
achieved great purity, it is only the music of Hoffmann's own time that
'arouses the feeling of the unknown and the mysterious' so that 'the spirit
surrenders itself to dreams in which it perceives the supernatural and the
infinite.' In the present essay he develops the idea that all music is in some
way religious and impels us upwards to some higher reality; but it becomes
obvious that the heaven to which contemporary music with its secular and

instrumental impurities beckons us is by no means the heaven of Christianity. 'Unknown' and 'mysterious,' it lacks completely the felicitous detail of a paradise improvised by centuries of Christian writers. Hoffmann appears here to be labouring towards the realization which came to him so effortlessly elsewhere, that the higher realm suggested by music is not merely a place where one is caressed by an indulgent diety, but rather a place where one challenges the dynamic and buffeting waves of destiny. There is a secret disappointment tucked into the essay that Beethoven did not face this destiny squarely in his Mass in C; but this would have been impossible, for Beethoven's triumph was in achieving the altitude of the divine in his instrumental music, independently of the church.

The essay takes the form of a conversation between members of the Serapion's brotherhood (*Serapionsbrüder*), each character representing a different aspect of the personality of the author himself. This technique was also copied by Schumann in his *Davidsbündler*, where Eusebius, Florestan, and Meister Raro exchange points of view. In the following account the characters are more subordinate to the arguments put forward than in Schumann's work, where they have a life of their own. We come upon the *Serapionsbrüder* in the middle of one of their regular meetings ...

THIRTEEN

Ancient and Modern Church Music

'Don't forget that next to our invigorating meetings I, who live in the country, miss another pleasure which permeates my whole being and raises it up. I am thinking particularly of the great variety of musical productions and the performances of the finest choral music. Just today I comprehended, in the highest sense of the word, Beethoven's Mass in C, which as you know was performed in the Catholic church.'

'And that,' Cyprian said morosely, 'is not astonishing to me because it is precisely as a result of having deprived yourself of such things, Sylvester, that you see them in a better light. For the hungry, simple food is tasty. To put it more directly, while Beethoven may have given us some pleasant, even great music in his mass, he has by no means given us a mass. What has happened to the austere church music?'

'I know already,' Theodore interrupted, 'that you, Cyprian, champion only the old masters, and since you are afraid to see black notes in liturgical music, you are unjustifiably severe on all recent composition.'

'Nevertheless,' Lothar said, 'as far as I am concerned, Beethoven's mass sounds too jubilant and too earthly in its rejoicing. I would certainly like to know in just what way the various parts of the liturgy differ to allow the composer such complete liberty of contrasts in setting them.'

'Exactly!' cried Sylvester. 'That has never been clear to me either. One might think, for example, that the words *Benedictus qui venit in nomine domini* could only be set one way, in a pious, quiet manner; but I know that they have been set quite differently by different masters. Moreover, although I have been affected differently by each composition, I have never been able to reject any setting by a great composer as wrong. Theodore should explain this to us.'

'I would do so gladly,' said Theodore, 'and to the best of my ability; but to do so I would have to read you a little essay which would transform into earnestness the light-hearted mood with which our meeting today began.'

'But isn't it one of the Serapion principles,' replied Ottmar, 'that earnest-
ness and light-heartedness should alternate? Have no fear of opposition,
Theodore, for all of us are interested – with the possible exception of
Vinzenz, who understands nothing about music. But I would bid our new
Serapion's brother, Vinzenz, to swallow the scurrilous remark that is on
his lips and not to interrupt the speaker.'

'O Serapion!' sighed Vinzenz with his eyes turned skyward. But Theodore began immediately in the following manner.

'Prayer and worship undoubtedly affect the mind according to its pre-
dominant or even momentary disposition, resulting from its physical or
mental well-being or suffering. At one time worship is inward contrition,
even to the point of self-accusation and shame, grovelling in the dust before
the lightning of the Lord of all worlds, who is angry with the sinner; at another time it is vigorous elevation towards the infinite, at another, childlike
trust in divine grace, and at another, anticipation of the promised bliss. The
words of the mass present only the motive, or at best the clue for devotion,
and for every mood they will awaken the appropriate response in the soul.

'In the *Kyrie*, God's mercy is implored; the *Gloria* praises His omnipotence and majesty; the *Credo* gives expression to the faith on which the
pious soul firmly builds; and after the holiness of God has been exalted
in the *Sanctus* and blessings are promised to those who approach Him in
confident faith in the *Benedictus*, a prayer is offered to the Mediator in
the *Agnus* and the *Dona* that He may send down His peace and gladness to
the faithful soul. This general character of the text in no way encroaches
on the personal interpretation of the inner meaning which each of us feels
according to his individual disposition. Rather it is precisely this general
character which lends itself to the most infinite variety of musical settings.
This is why there are so many *Kyries*, *Glorias*, and so forth, so completely
different in character. For example, compare the two *Kyries* from Haydn's
masses in C major and D minor; also the two *Benedictuses*.[1] From this it follows – and this ought always to be the case – that the composer who sets
out to write a mass inspired with true devotion will let the individual religious disposition of his own mind govern. The words will adapt themselves
to that. But he should never allow himself in the *Miserere*, the *Gloria*, the
Qui tollis and so forth, to express the heart-rending sorrow of the contrite
heart with jubilant clangour. Works of this kind, and there have been a
great number, lately thrown together in the most frivolous manner, are
abortions engendered by impure minds. I reject them just as eagerly as
Cyprian does.

'But I deeply admire the glorious church music of Michael and Joseph
Haydn, Hasse, Naumann, and others, not forgetting the old works of the

pious Italian masters, Leo, Durante, Benevoli, Perti, and others; since the lofty and noble simplicity of their art, which without ostentatious display touches the soul with its simple modulations, seems to have been completely lost in recent times. I do not cling to the original pure church music exclusively because holy things ought to shun all mundane displays and artful sophistry; but also because simple music is most effective in the church. It can't be denied that the faster the notes follow one another the more they are lost in the lofty vaults, so that the whole effect becomes confused and unintelligible. Hence, to a good degree, the immense effectiveness of chorales in church.

'I certainly agree with you, Cyprian, that the sublime church music of ancient times is superior to that of recent times, for it was always faithful to its holy style. At the same time I think that the richness which music has gained in more recent times, chiefly through the employment of instruments, should be utilized in churches, not to produce mere idle display, but in a noble and worthy manner. The bold simile that the ancient church music of the Italians holds a similar relationship to that of the more recent Germans as does St Peter's at Rome to the Strasbourg Minster, may not be inapt. The grandiose proportions of St Peter's elevate the mind because it finds them commensurable; but the viewer gazes with a strange inward disquiet at the Strasbourg Minster as it soars aloft in the most daring curves, and with its strange interlacings of fantastic figures and ornamentation.[2] This disquiet arouses the feeling of the unknown and the mysterious; and the spirit surrenders itself to dreams in which it perceives the supernatural and the infinite. Now this is exactly the effect of that purely romantic element which pervades the compositions of Mozart and Haydn.

'It's easy to explain why it would be difficult these days to write a church composition in the lofty, simple style of the ancient Italians. Aside from the fact that the pious faith which gave those masters the power to proclaim holiness in noble and earnest strains probably seldom dwells in the hearts of artists these days, it is enough to mention the incapacity arising from the lack of true genius, and also the lack of self-renunciation. Does true genius not achieve its greatest moments in absolute simplicity? But who does not take delight in letting his treasure glitter before the eyes of all? Who is content with the approval of individual connoisseurs? Few indeed are those for whom the genuine and unadorned is the best, or even the *only* work. Everywhere people have begun to adopt the same form of expression. We have almost reached a point where there is no longer any such thing as a style. In comic opera we often hear solemn, striding passages, and in serious opera we hear playful little tunes. In the church, masses and oratorios are performed that are directly inspired by operas.

'It takes a rare degree of genius and depth of spirit to employ vocal embellishments and all the resources of instrumentation humbly and respectfully – in short, religiously. Mozart, who is a bit gallant in his two masses in C major,[3] has solved this problem beautifully in his *Requiem*; for here he has created from the depth of his soul a truly romantic and sacred music. I don't need to mention how excellently Haydn has achieved sublimity and holiness in his masses, although here and there one justifiably detects trifling.

'As soon as I learned that Beethoven had written a mass, and before I had seen or heard a note of it, I felt certain that the master would take old Joseph Haydn as his model for style and character. Yet I found I was wrong; for he felt the words of the liturgy quite differently. Beethoven's genius is usually prone to devices of awe and terror. I thought the vision of the transcendental would fill his soul with awe and his music would reflect this. On the contrary, the whole mass expresses a mind filled with bright, childlike clarity, which in its purity and faith confides in the grace of God, and prays to Him as to a father who cares for his children and hears their petitions. The general character of the composition, together with its inner structure and intelligent instrumentation, is quite worthy of the master's genius, when considered as a composition intended for the service of the church.'

'But, in my opinion,' Cyprian urged, 'this is quite false and can only lead to a wicked desecration of the holy. Let me explain my views on church music and you will see that I am at least clear on the subject in my own mind. I believe that no art proceeds so directly from man's spiritualizing ability as does music. It demands a pure and spiritual means of expression. Music is thus the expression of this highest and holiest spiritual power which kindles all nature. Through song it becomes an experience of the highest fulfilment of existence, a hymn of praise to the Creator. In its deepest, most characteristic sense, music is therefore a religious cult and its sole origin is to be found in religion. From there it is passed on into life. Ever richer and mightier, it pours its unending treasures over mankind so that even the secular, even the petty mundane affairs of life, may adorn themselves joyfully in the splendour of its rays. Thus adorned, even the secular, it seemed, longed after the heavenly realm and sought to gain entrance to it. But precisely because of this special peculiarity of its nature, music could not become the property of the ancient world where everything proceeded from sensuous corporealization; rather it had to be reserved for more modern times.

'The two opposite artistic poles of heathenism and Christianity are sculpture and music. Christianity destroyed the former and created the latter, along with painting, which stands in the nearest relation to it. In painting, the ancients knew neither perspective nor colouring; in music neither melody nor harmony. I use the word melody here in its higher sense, as the expression of an inner emotion undominated by words and their rhythmic relationships. But beyond this particular defect, which may perhaps indicate only the narrower footing on which music and painting stood at the time, the germs of those two arts could not develop in that unfruitful soil. Not until the advent of Christianity could they grow gloriously, and bring forth flowers and fruit in luxurious profusion. Both music and painting maintained their place only *in appearance* in the antique world; they were kept down by the power of sculpture, or rather they could assume no adequate form amid the mighty masses of sculpture. Those arts were not in the least what we now call "music" and "painting." In the same way, sculpture disappeared as a result of the Christian tendency to expression. But even though the holy mystery of music was discovered only in Christian times, a germ existed in ancient times which contributed to life in its most characteristic manner, namely as religious cult. For this is what dramas were from the earliest times, a depiction of the joys and sorrows of the gods. The declamation of those dramas was accompanied by instrumentalists. And this proves that the music of the ancients was purely rhythmic, even if it is not otherwise demonstrable; for as I have already said, melody and harmony, the two pillars on which modern music rests, were unknown in ancient times. Therefore, although Ambrose and later Gregory – about the year 591 – based Christian hymns on ancient hymns, and although we see traces of purely rhythmic music in the so-called *cantus firmus* and in antiphonies, these are only inheritances of germ ideas handed down from the past.

'Certainly a deeper study of ancient music can interest only the antiquarian. As for the practical composer, the divine profundity of the purely Christian art of music was recognized only when Christianity was shining in its brightest splendour in Italy, and great masters proclaimed in consecrated tones the holiest mysteries of religion, never before heard.

'It is noteworthy that not long afterwards, when Guido d'Arezzo had penetrated deeper into the mysteries of music, it began to be misunderstood and was thought to be a subject for mathematical speculation.[4] Thus, its true essence was misunderstood just as it was beginning to reveal itself. The wonderful tones of this language of the spirit were awakened and went sounding forth over the world. Man soon succeeded in capturing the hieroglyphs of intertwining melody and harmony. I mean the method of writing music down in notes. But soon the writing itself passed for the thing written; for the masters sank themselves in harmonic subtleties. Music would have become pure speculative science and no longer music if these tendencies had been carried to their extreme. Religion was desecrated by the contrived art which was passed off in the name of music, though for the pure heart the spirit of music remained truly religious.

'The contest was brief and ended with a glorious victory for eternal truth over falsity. Pope Marcellus II was on the point of expelling all music from the church, and thus was about to deprive divine worship of its most glorious adornment.[5] But the great master Palestrina revealed to him the sacred mystery in the pure essence of music. From that time on music became the most characteristic feature of the Catholic form of worship. And from that time a true comprehension of the spirit of music dawned in the pious hearts of composers, and holy inspiration filled their immortal and inimitable compositions. You, Theodore, know well that the mass for six voices which Palestrina composed at that time – was it in 1555? – in order that the angry pontiff might hear real music, became known by the title *Missa Papae Marcelli*.[6]

'With Palestrina began the most glorious era of religious music, and thus of all music. This lasted for nearly two hundred years, prospering in this state of pious dignity and strength, though it cannot be denied that even in the first century after Palestrina this lofty, inimitable simplicity and dignity was lost in a certain "elegance" in which composers began to indulge. What a master is Palestrina! Without any ornamentation, without anything approaching melodic sweep, his works consist mainly of strings of consonant chords which grip the mind by their strength and boldness and raise it on high. Love, the harmony of all spiritual things in nature – as is promised to the Christian – is expressed in these chords; for it was through Christianity that it was given life. Thus the chord and harmony are the images and expression of the spiritual communion and union with the eternal and the ideal which reigns above and around us.[7]

'The purest, holiest, and most religious music must be that which flows from the soul as an expression of love, uncontaminated by all that is worldly. And such are Palestrina's simple and majestic compositions. Conceived in the highest fervour of piety and love, they proclaim the divine with might and glory. To his music really belongs the phrase used by the Italians to describe the shallow and miserable works of others: it is truly music of another world – *musica del'altro mondo*. Successions of perfect triads are strange to us today and it is our weakness to see in them nothing but technical ineptitude. But considered only from the point of view of effectiveness, it is clear, as you have already remarked, Theodore, that in a large resonant building such as a church the blending effect of passing notes weakens the power of the music. In Palestrina's music each chord strikes the listener with all its force; the most elaborate modulations could never affect the mind as these bold, weighty chords which burst upon the mind like dazzling beams of light.

'Palestrina is simple, true, childlike in piety, strong, and mighty. He is as truly Christian in his works as the painters Pietro of Cortona and Albrecht Dürer. For him, composition was an act of worship. But I must not forget the great masters Caldara, Bernabei, Scarlatti, Marcello, Lotti, Porpora, Bernardi, Leo, Valotti, and the others now forgotten who always remained simple, dignified, and forceful. I have a vivid memory still of Alessandro Scarlatti's mass for seven voices *alla Capella*[8] which you, Theodore, once performed with a number of your pupils. That mass was a model of the true and powerful ecclesiastical style, in spite of the melodic "swing" which music had acquired by this time (1705).'

'And the mighty Handel,' said Theodore, 'the inimitable Hasse, the profound and thoughtful Sebastian Bach – don't forget them!'

'By no means,' replied Cyprian. 'They are also members of the sacred fraternity whose hearts were strengthened by the power of faith and love. It was just this power which kindled the inspiration and led them to communion with the Almighty so that they created works which served not worldly ends, but were written in praise and honour of religion and the highest things. These works bear the true mark of integrity. They do not strive after effects. Nothing in them detracts from the divine.

'One finds here none of the so-called "striking" modulations, nor the clever embellishments which weaken the melody, nor any of those powerless, confusing rushes of instrumentation intended to deafen the listener so that he does not notice their emptiness. Hence it is that only with the masters just mentioned – and a few in more recent times who, like them, have remained faithful servants to the true church which exists no longer on this earth – only with these masters do we have works which elevate and edify the pious soul. Let me mention here the glorious master Fasch, who belongs to the old pious times, and whose profound works have been so little understood by the frivolous crowd since his death that his mass for sixteen voices could not be published for want of support.[9]

'You do me a great injustice, Theodore, if you believe that my mind is closed to more modern music. Haydn, Mozart, and Beethoven have in truth unfolded a new art, the germ of which began to show itself in the middle of the eighteenth century. It is scarcely the fault of these three masters if through frivolity and misunderstanding the legacy of the past was valued so lightly, or if counterfeiters tried to pass off their products as the real thing. It's true that to the extent that instrumental music gained in popularity, vocal music declined. With this development there were the ecclesiastical reforms (dissolution of the monasteries and so forth) and true choral music disappeared.

'Clearly it is impossible to go back to Palestrina's simplicity and grandeur. A more important question is: to what extent can the new resources be brought without ostentation into the churches? The force which rules this world drives onward unceasingly, and although the spirit of the past can never return in its original form, truth is everlasting. A wonderful spiritual communion gently binds a mysterious band around the past, the present, and the future. The sublime old masters are still alive – in spirit. Their music still sounds, though with the roaring and tumultuous strife which has broken in on us, it is difficult to hear it. May time bring early fulfilment to our hopes! May piety, peace, and joy return! And may music, free and strong once more, fly on seraph's wings to the life beyond, to her home from whence comfort and salvation beam down on the restless hearts of mankind!'

Cyprian spoke these words with a conviction which showed they came from his heart. The friends, deeply moved by them, kept silent for some time ...

FOURTEEN

The Absolute Musician: Johannes Kreisler

As the shapes of the Hoffmannesque cosmology of music emerge, we are made aware increasingly that if music is to accomplish the noble destiny intended for it, all the fetters tying it down in collaborative enterprises must be broken.

The music of the church may indeed have achieved noble heights in the past, but this was due to the humility of the composers entrusted with important liturgical texts. There is no way of resolving Hoffmann's argument as to whether contemporary religious music could achieve the same high distinction; but one thing is certain: Haydn, Mozart, and above all Beethoven, achieved their best moments of musical expression independently of religious texts.

The whole argument of 'Beethoven's Instrumental Music' is for the superiority of music unfettered by poetry. This same argument is repeated with some compromise in another celebrated Hoffmann essay entitled 'The Poet and the Composer,' of which a good translation is available in English.[1] The basic position is again incontrovertibly clear: music must be true to itself alone and everything outside music must be subservient to it in collaboration. 'The Poet and the Composer' is a closely argued dialogue between the two principal operatic collaborators. Hoffmann goes to considerable pains to instruct the librettist in how to fashion a text that will not fetter the composer. Music will dominate the situation. The libretto must shape itself to the musical demands, for 'even plot and action take on musical shape.' Words are specific and concrete, and are therefore tied to reality. Whenever words and music are brought together, as in opera, an inclined line joins the world of reality with the world of the spirit. The words are intensified, exalted, transfigured; but music by its implication loses some of its original altitude. 'But now music must enter wholly into our lives, it must take its visions, and clothing them in words and deeds, must speak to us of particular passions and events.' How can the noble art of music be made to express commonplace things? 'Can music do anything but inform us of the wonder of that place from which it originated to descend to us?' Rather it is the poet who must 'prepare himself for a bold flight into the land of the romantic,' where the language spoken is 'the language of music.'

In a similar imaginary dialogue between a poet and a composer, Wagner later had his poet say: 'Expand your melody boldly, so that it pours forth like a ceaseless stream. In it say what I refrain from saying because only you can say it ...'[2] It is no exaggeration to say that Hoffmann's essay laid the philosophical foundation for all romantic opera, and particularly for Wagner's later works, written after he had revised his thoughts concerning the practicality of the *Gesamtkunstwerk*.

'The Poet and the Composer' was written in Dresden in 1813, the very year Wagner was born. In his preface to the first edition of Hoffmann's *Fantasiestücke* Jean Paul had suggested that Hoffmann might himself be the one to effect a perfect wedding of words and music in opera;[3] but for whatever reasons, Hoffmann was never able to follow his own argument through in practice. He merely opened out the problem and suggested the lines along which a solution must move.

This consideration of music as the apogee of spiritual attainment was accompanied by an attitude towards the composer in which he is elevated to the status of a very special human being, soaring to dizzy heights above and beyond all other men. The age was just beginning to adjust to this new concept of the creative musician when, about 1810, Hoffmann introduced a character into fiction who was destined to become, over the course of the next decade, as he was elaborated by the author, and for generations after he was created, an extreme personification of the composer in the modern sense; a figure who, perhaps more than any real composer, defined this new role in society and at the same time exposed the tragic consequences of a compulsive and overindulgent philosophy of music.

I have already discussed the distinction between the composer and the practitioner, the artist and the artisan, which was developing at the beginning of the nineteenth century. For the first time in history the composer was allowed to feel the full height of his stature and to be fully conscious of his role for posterity. Only then was music permitted to have at least theoretical existence above and beyond its specific utilitarian function. Haydn, who was forced to conduct Prince Esterházy's orchestra dressed in his lackey's uniform, wrote works for specific occasions and could only conjecture privately about how they would be viewed by the public of the future. Mozart, who threw over his steady patron, was nevertheless dependent on Viennese society, and seldom wrote works that were not assured of performance. Beethoven was the first composer to transfer his energies to the works *he* wanted to compose, regardless of whether they were appreciated by those around him. His last quartets are, like a diary, evidence of solitude.

It was as if in reply to some epochal demand for a vivid and firmly outlined musician *par excellence* that Hoffmann created his Kapellmeister, Johannes Kreisler. To complete Hoffmann's musical philosophy we must turn now to this fascinating and enigmatic figure, registering how he thought, dreamed, and behaved, and how society reacted towards him.

Hoffmann introduced his hero first as a flicker of shadow passing across the lives of his readers. Who was Johannes Kreisler? The first fragment of the cycle of writings about and by him entitled *Kreisleriana*, gives the reader a brief but memorable contact.

Where did he come from? No one knows. Who were his parents? Also unknown. Whose pupil is he? Certainly the disciple of a good master, for he plays splendidly, and since he possesses both intellect and culture one tolerates him, and even permits him to teach music. Truly he has been a Kapellmeister; so testify the diplomatic people to whom he once, while in a good mood, showed a document certified by the management of the Court Theatre in ——. In it one learned that Kapellmeister Johannes Kreisler had been dismissed for adamantly refusing to set to music the libretto of an opera composed by the court poet; also that he had talked in a derogatory manner in public of the *primo huomo* and had been persistent in his preference for a young girl, to whom he taught singing, over the *prima donna*, expressing his opinion publicly in no uncertain terms. It was also stated that he could have retained the title of Regal Kapellmeister on condition that he mend his ways and abandon certain foolish prejudices – for example, that the true Italian music had disappeared, and so forth – and provided that he would humbly acknowledge the excellence of the court poet who was generally taken to be a second Metastasio.

His friends maintained that nature had tried out a new recipe in creating him, but that it failed owing to too little phlegm in his constitution as a counterforce to his hypersensitivity and the almost destructive flame of his fantasy. Thus the balance that is so necessary in order for an artist to live and create was broken. Be that as it may, Johannes was drawn constantly to and fro by his inner visions and dreams as if floating on an eternally undulating sea, searching in vain for the haven which would grant him the peace and serenity needed for his work.

Thus it was that even his friends couldn't bring him to finish a composition or to prevent him from destroying what he had written. Occasionally he composed at night in extreme excitation, waking his friend whose room was nearby

to play him the compositions he had written with incredible speed in this inspired state of mind. He would shed tears of joy over his success, holding himself
to be the luckiest of men. But the next day the splendid composition would lie
in the fire.

Singing was almost fatal for him, for his fantasy became overexcited and his
spirit moved into a realm where no one could follow without peril. On the other
hand, he frequently found hour-long pleasure in playing the oddest themes on
the piano in artful and quaintly contrapuntal arrangements. When he was successful he passed several days in the best of spirits and a roguish irony spiced his
conversation, which was the joy of his small but intimate circle of friends.

Then one day, no one knew how or why, he disappeared. Many believed they
had seen traces of madness in him, and actually he had been seen wearing two
hats stacked one upon the other and sporting two pens arranged as daggers in his
belt, singing lustily as he frisked out of the gate. But his friends had taken little
notice of this, for such bizarre outbursts were caused by some inner grief over
which there was no control.

All investigations as to his whereabouts having proved in vain, his friends
busied themselves with his few remaining belongings, musical and otherwise.
Then Miss von B— appeared and explained that she alone should be entrusted
with the belongings of her dear teacher and friend who she believed would certainly return. The friends gladly turned everything over to her. On inspecting the
musical manuscripts they found some short, largely humorous essays jotted down
on the reverse sides. The faithful student permitted a friend of the unfortunate
Johannes to make copies of these and to distribute them to others as an unpretentious testament of inspired moments.[4]

The *Kreisleriana* consist of two groups of papers on music, originally published in the *Fantasiestücke* of 1814-15.[5] The titles of the individual sections are as follows:

PART ONE

1 / 'Johannes Kreislers, des Kapellmeisters musikalische Leiden' (Of Kapellmeister Johannes Kreisler's Musical Sorrows)
2 / 'Ombra adorata'
3 / 'Gedanken über den hohen Wert der Musik' (Reflections on the High Value
   of Music)
4 / 'Beethovens Instrumental-Musik' (Beethoven's Instrumental Music)
5 / 'Höchst zerstreute Gedanken' (Highly Scattered Thoughts)
6 / 'Der vollkommene Maschinist' (The Consummate Craftsman)

PART TWO

1 / 'Brief des Barons Wallborn an den Kapellmeister Kreisler' (Baron Wallborn's Letter to Kapellmeister Kreisler)

2 / 'Brief des Kapellmeisters Kreisler an den Baron Wallborn' (Kapellmeister Kreisler's Letter to Baron Wallborn)

3 / 'Kreislers musikalisch-poetischer Klub' (Kreisler's Musical-Poetical Club)

4 / 'Nachricht von einem gebildeten jungen Mann' (Account from an Educated Young Man)

5 / 'Der Musikfeind' (The Music Hater)

6 / 'Über einem Ausspruch Sacchinis und über der sogenannten Effekt in der Musik' (Concerning a Statement by Sacchini and the Alleged Power of Music)

7 / 'Johannes Kreislers Lehrbrief' (Johannes Kreisler's Letter of Achievement)

The letter from Baron Wallborn was actually written by de la Motte Fouqué. Many of the papers had appeared in the *Allgemeine Musikalische Zeitung* and other periodicals from 1810 onwards, prior to their collection in the *Fantasiestücke*. But whoever wishes to know Kreisler thoroughly must piece together information from a number of other sources. The tale 'Nachricht von den neuesten Schicksalen des Hundes Berganza' (An Account of the Latest Fortunes of the Dog Berganza) provides some details concerning one of Kreisler's early love affairs. Another fragment, 'Der Freund' (The Friend), presents a terrifying picture of an insane musician with the initials 'J.K.' There is also the early sketch for an unwritten novel, 'Lichte Stunden eines wahnsinnigen Musikers' (Lucid Hours of a Mad Musician), only a few lines long but most informative in its evocations. Here are a few of the notes:

> The love of the artist
> The mysticism of the instruments
> Musical twilight
> Modulations
> Intimation of the music of the kingdom of heaven
> The secret of the fugue – question and answer – two words, or the inn in the woods
> Piano – forte – crescendo – fortissimo – decrescendo – ritardando – dolce a tempo – smorzando ...[6]

Finally, there is the elaborate exposition of Kreisler in the novel Hoffmann eventually did write about him. Here we learn much about Kreisler as a character in a social setting. The full title of the novel suggests something of its unusual form: *Lebensansichten des Katers Murr nebst fragmentarischer Biographie des Kapellmeisters Johannes Kreisler in zufälligen Makulaturblättern* (Tom-cat Murr's Opinions on Life, together with a Fragmentary Biography of Kapellmeister Johannes Kreisler in Chance Wastepaper Scraps). Murr is the cat of Kreisler's friend and biographer, Meister Abraham. From a habit of sitting on his master's desk, littered with papers, he has succeeded in teaching himself to read. He soon learns to write as well, and though a little diffidently at first, he eventually comes to write his autobiography, now confidently signing himself *étudiant en belles lettres.* As he writes, Murr has been using as blotting paper the pages of another notebook that lies at hand, stuffing them between his own pages as necessary. As it happens, the second manuscript is a biography by his master of Johannes Kreisler. By a publisher's oversight the two works are published together.

There can scarcely be a more bizarre novel in romantic literature than Hoffmann's *Kater Murr* with its truncations and *non sequiturs*, for fragments of each story are interpolated between one another, breaking the narration in mid-sentence. Murr's autobiography, though broken, is chronological in its development, but Kreisler's is haphazard and incomplete, for Murr has been tearing pages out of the book quite at random.

The two volumes of *Kater Murr* appeared in 1819 and 1821, and a translation has finally recently appeared in English.[7] A third volume was apparently projected, but never undertaken. Thus the narrative is left suspended and the final fate of Kreisler is not known. A number of suggestions throughout the book and elsewhere would seem to indicate that Hoffmann had intended that his hero would either go mad or pass his final days in a monastery, but there is no conclusive proof of this.

The scene of *Kater Murr* is a small annexed principality in Germany. Kreisler mysteriously appears on the scene and is retained at court. The narrative of the novel is ambitious and complex. Kreisler is drawn into a net of intrigue and social complications involving the principal characters, who include the entertaining but ineffectual reigning Prince Irenäus and his half-witted son; the old organ builder and magician, Meister Abraham, who has been responsible for persuading the prince to allow Kreisler to remain at the lilliputian court; Rätin Benzon, a scheming and social-climbing woman of influence (having been a former mistress of the prince); and two girls, Julia Benzon, daughter of the Rätin, and Princess Hedwiga, daughter of the prince.

Kreisler's position at court is precarious. The prince will tolerate him only if he abjures some irritating habits, such as failing to lower his eyes when spoken to by the prince and giving the impression that what the prince says is unimportant. In this way Hoffmann suggests that Kreisler feels much the same as Beethoven felt on the day he took his celebrated walk with Goethe and refused to move off the path for the aristocrats. But Kreisler's musical abilities, his witty conversation, and his moody states of elation and depression fascinate the court, and interest is constantly centred on him.

The former Kapellmeister teaches singing to the two young girls, Princess Hedwiga and Julia Benzon, who is one of the many reincarnations of Hoffmann's own Julia Marc. Each of the girls possesses an outstanding singing voice. Hoffmann does not miss the chance here to develop at greater length the themes outlined earlier which exist between music and the beautiful woman. His very first encounter with Julia Benzon reveals to him a voice which causes his heart to 'soar up to bright celestial spaces in a thousand shimmering colours.' Each of the young girls comes to love Kreisler, though neither loves him with anything approaching a physical passion. Julia's love is religious almost, a reverence of worship for a man whose power she senses instinctively. Hedwiga's love is more effervescent, but for that no less heartfelt. Each seems to love Kreisler for a mysterious protective power he possesses, and when Julia dreams of falling on his breast, it is simply in order that he might save her from premonitions she has of sinister events. It is entirely different when Prince Hector, a visitor to the court, after hearing Julia sing, and on the pretence of having been deeply moved, rushes forward and attempts to kiss the girl. This event symbolizes the complete debasement of art by sensuality. It must be considered beside the 'Ombra adorata' fragment where passion was sublimated in the contemplation of the disembodied singing voice, the lyrical strains of which ennobled and enraptured the narrator.

In *Kater Murr* we see Kreisler in an unideal social setting. There is a stinging contrast between the musician and the unmusical society in which he is forced to live. The negative insight of irony is frequent with Kreisler. He tells us in a catalogue of humiliations how he has learned to smile pleasantly when a Lord Chamberlain tells him Haydn's *Seasons* is boring, and how he has learned to sit patiently while a member of the court informs him that Rossini and Pucitta are greater composers than Mozart and Beethoven. He is speaking to Rätin Benzon here and concludes by telling her what music means for him:

> Often I find surging up within me a wild, frantic desire for something which I seek outside myself with an ever-unsatisfied eagerness, because in reality that something is in my own heart, an obscure mystery, a confused and enigmatic

dream of a paradise of utter peace, which the dream itself can foreshadow but never name; and that foreshadowing inflicts on me the agonizing tortures of Tantalus. Ever since childhood this feeling has come over me, sometimes so abruptly that in the midst of the liveliest game I would flee to the forest or to a hill and there I would throw myself down weeping, quite inconsolable; yet in the game I had been the most reckless and exuberant of any. Later I learned to control myself better, but I cannot describe the martyrdom I went through at times. It would happen when I was surrounded by the best and most charming friends, even at the moment of some aesthetic pleasure or when for some reason or other my vanity came into play. Suddenly everything round me would seem disconsolate, colourless, lifeless, and I would be transported into a hopeless solitude. Only one bright angel has power over this evil demon – it is the spirit of music which often rises up victoriously within me, silencing with its mighty voice all earthly pains and miseries.[8]

Kreisler is kept alive by music. The Rätin's comment after the above confession is that he takes music too seriously. In the letter to Baron Wallborn in the *Kreisleriana* cycle, he speaks again of his relationship to music:

You must know what people say about me – that the music which dwells in my innermost being has broken out with excessive violence, holding me imprisoned in its tentacles, so that I can no longer escape, and must turn everything in my life into music. Perhaps they are right.[9]

Kreisler is the personification of the romantic soul in its struggle to bring to the surface the deepest of its personal feelings, often at the risk of madness or death. Plunging into the unconscious the true romanticist fights with equivocal and unpredictable forces and returns to give them form in the abrupt and contradictory moods and tempos of his art:

Never imbibe what is foreign to you, but go down into the depth of your nature to discover its own profound inclinations. Then bring to light what you have discovered however small it may be.[10]

So wrote Karl Philipp Moritz in 1797 on the very breast of the movement. To go down into the depth of one's nature – that is true originality. It is also true romanticism. In a world without form, a sudden tiny light is seen deep beneath the clouds of darkness. Kreisler is that light. He is that tiny flame of sincerity in a society decadent and counterfeit, wholly lacking the courage to burn.

The age was spellbound by Kreisler's audacity. As the most influential fictional hero of his time, he informed the world of the artist's torments, dreams, and hopes; and his desperate denunciations of the prostitution of music by the insensitive were soon heard throughout Europe. More than any other figure, real or fictional, Kreisler became symbolic of the spirit of music itself. Schumann wrote his *Kreisleriana* in celebration of the passionate musician. The young Brahms often spoke of himself as Johannes Kreisler, Junior, and wrote down all his favourite sayings about music in a little volume he called *Des jungen Kreislers Schatzkästlein* (Young Kreisler's Little Treasure Box). Of Kreisler, as the ideal towards which an entire age aspired, Oswald Spengler has written:

> There used to be, especially in eighteenth-century Germany, a real musical culture which pervaded all life; and it was typified by Kapellmeister Johannes Kreisler ... Today it is scarcely more than a memory.[11]

To Spengler, Kreisler was in a category with Faust and Don Juan as figures who characterized whole epochs of thought. Certainly music pervaded the society of which Spengler speaks to a degree perhaps never experienced before or since, but, as we shall see, Kreisler does not really typify this society. Rather he is the archetype of a new social order in which musicians are distinguished from dilettantes and true musicians are disinherited by society. Kreisler does not harmonize with society – he clashes with it; and it is precisely this collision of forces which gives the whole Kreisler situation its special temperament. Caught in the vicissitudes between his own idealistic spirit and the stupid and dull society in which he must live, Kreisler at times becomes hubristic and insolent. At other times his distemper is twisted into cynicism. For him the world was an 'eternal inexplicable misunderstanding.' But if his outward behaviour is ugly, this ugliness does not come from within, for his heart is pure.

When music and musicians are debased at court, Kreisler responds with defiance. But it is little better with the bourgeois, for it was among the bourgeois that he had suffered earlier throughout the *Kreisleriana* cycle. Here again it is music alone – his own kind of music – which saves him from ignominious defeat. One of the most brutal sketches in the *Kreisleriana* is an account of how the composer suffers as a lackey-pianist through that chattering paradigm of all social triviality, the tea party ...

FIFTEEN

Of Kapellmeister Johannes Kreisler's Musical Sorrows

They have all gone. I was informed of their departure by a variety of whisperings, shufflings, and grumblings. Truly, they were like a swarm of bees leaving its hive. Gottlieb has now lighted new candles and put a bottle of Burgundy on the piano. I can play no longer, for I am quite exhausted. To blame is my dear old friend here on the music stand who carried me once again so high through the air – like Faust on the cape of Mephistopheles – that I didn't notice the people far below me, despite the rude noises they may have made.

A senselessly wasted evening. But I am now at ease and relaxed. Even while playing I took out my pencil and below the last stave on page 63 I jotted down a couple of good modulations in numbers with my right hand while my left carried on with the flow of notes. On the blank page at the back I continue to write. I'll leave numbers and tones and with the true pleasure of the convalescent patient, who can't refrain from telling what he has suffered, I'll recount here in detail the abominable torture of the tea today. But not for myself alone; rather for everyone who has enjoyed and been edified by my performance of Johann Sebastian Bach's piano variations (as published by Nägeli of Zurich); so that, reading the Latin word *verte* at the end of the thirtieth variation – I'll write it in as soon as I have concluded this lamentation – they will turn the page and read. They will guess the real connection at once.

You know that Privy Councillor Röderlein has a charming house here and that he has two daughters who are the darlings of society. They dance like goddesses, converse in French like angels, and sing and draw like the muses. Privy Councillor Röderlein is a rich man; he produces the best wines at his quarterly dinners, the best dishes – everything is arranged to please the most discriminating gourmet. Whoever cannot amuse himself divinely at his teas lacks tone, spirit, and above all, taste for art. They are arranged precisely for this reason; for with the tea, punch, wine, ice cream, and so forth, some music is always presented, and this, together with the other things mentioned, helps to make the fashionable company feel more sociable. The matter is arranged like this: after each guest has had time to consume enough cups of tea to his liking, and after the punch and ice cream have been passed around twice, the servants draw up the gaming tables for the older, more solvent members of the company who prefer cards to music – an activity which, by the way, creates only a slight disturbance, for little money falls.

This is the signal for the younger members of the company to join the Röderlein daughters. A tumult ensues; one can distinguish what is being said: 'Gracious Fräulein, please do not deny us the pleasure of your divine talent! Oh sing something, my dear one! – impossible? – a cold? – at the last ball? – out of practice? Oh please, please, we implore you!' and so on.

Meanwhile Gottlieb has opened the piano and burdened down the music stand with the well-known volumes of music. From the gaming table dear Mamma calls over: 'Chantez donc mes enfants!' That's my cue. I seat myself at the piano, and in triumph the Röderleins are escorted to the instrument. Now another dispute arises; neither will sing first. 'You know, dear Nanette, how terribly hoarse I am.' 'Am I less so, dear Marie?' 'I sing so badly.' 'Oh dearest, just begin.' And so on. A sudden inspiration from me (I have it every time): they should both begin by singing a duet. The suggestion is strongly applauded; the book is opened, the well-thumbed page is located, and they're off: 'Dolce dell'anima,' etc.

Actually the Röderlein daughters are quite without talent. I have been here now for five years, and have been their teacher for four-and-a-half years. During this time Fräulein Nanette has reached a point where, after hearing a melody only ten times in the theatre and after playing it over no more than ten times on the piano, she can sing it so that one can immediately recognize what it is supposed to be. Fräulein Marie knew it after the eighth time, and although she often sang it a quarter of a tone flatter than the piano, she had such a pretty little face and such nice rosy lips that in the end one could put up with it. After the duet, a general chorus of acclamation. Now ariettas and duettinos alternate and I hammer out the accompaniments brightly for the thousandth time.

During the singing the wife of Finance Minister Eberstein, by means of clearing her throat and gently humming along, gave us to understand that she sang too. 'But dear Frau Eberstein, now you must also let us hear your divine voice!' Fräulein Nanette cries. A new tumult arises. She has a cold. She doesn't know anything from memory. Gottlieb drags in a couple armfuls of music; they are thoroughly thumbed through. At last she will sing

'The Diabolical Revenge' etc., then 'Rise up and See,' etc., then 'Ah, How I Loved,' etc. Panic-stricken I suggest 'Violet in the Meadow.' But she is for the big stuff; she wants to display herself. She decides to do Constanza's aria.

O cry, squeak, miaow, gargle, groan, moan, tremulate, stridulate, strangle it to death! I strike the *fortissimo* blow and strum myself numb. O Satan, Satan, which of your diabolical spirits has entered this throat? Four strings have snapped already; one hammer is broken. My ears tingle, my head roars, my nerves tremble. Are all the obscene sounds of the market-criers' trumpets built into this small throat?

I'm exhausted. I drink a glass of Burgundy. The applause is excessive, and someone remarks that the finance minister's wife and Mozart have fired me up. I smile with downcast eyes and look quite silly. But now all the musical talents, previously withdrawn, bloom forth in profusion. We are bombarded with musical excesses; ensembles, finales, choruses, all have to be performed. It is well known that Canon Kratzer sings a divine bass, as is observed by someone with a Titus haircut, who at the same time modestly asserts that although he is a mere second tenor himself, he is nevertheless a member of several choirs. Quickly everyone is organized to perform the first chorus from *Titus.* It was quite splendid. The canon, standing close behind me, thundered the bass over my head as if he were entering a cathedral with *obbligato* trumpets and drums. He carried the notes quite well, though he had an individual notion about the *tempo.* But at least he was consistent about it and dragged exactly half a bar behind throughout the entire piece. The others displayed a decisive proclivity for ancient Greek music which, as is well known, knew no harmony and was performed in unison. They all sang the upper voice with slight accidental sharpenings and flattenings of roughly a quarter-tone. This rather noisy production provoked an unfortunate social discord, namely the strong displeasure of the card players who, for the moment, were prevented from making their melodramatic contribution to the production with declamatory punctuations. For instance: 'Ah how I loved' – 'forty-eight' – 'was so happy' – 'I pass' – 'I know not' – 'whist' – 'the pain of love' – 'in the same suit.' The whole affair was quite jolly. (I fill up my glass.)

'That was the high point of today's musical exhibition; now it's over.' At least that's what I thought as I closed the book and stood up. Then the baron, my antique tenor, approached me and said: 'My dear Kapellmeister, won't you improvise for us, just a little? I implore you!' I break out in a cold sweat. The improvisatory gift has left me completely today. And while we are speaking thus, the devil in the guise of a double-vested dandy in the next room discovers the Bach variations lying under my hat. He thinks they are like the little variations on 'Nel cor mi non più sento' or 'Ah vous dirai-je, maman,' and wants me to hurry up and get at them. I object and they all fall on me. 'Well then,' I think to myself, 'listen to them and die of boredom!' and I begin to play.

At the third variation several ladies moved away followed by several members of Titus's army. Since it was their teacher playing, the Röder-leins remained, though not without effort, until the twelfth variation. At the fifteenth the double-vested dandy fled. Out of exaggerated respect the baron himself remained until the thirtieth, though he almost emptied the glass of punch which Gottlieb had placed on the piano for me. I would gladly have ended, but the theme of this thirtieth variation drew me imperturbably onward. The pages suddenly expanded to giant size and leapt about me, revealing a thousand imitations and variations of the theme, all of which I was forced to play. The notes were alive; they glittered and spun about me. An electric shock travelled through my fingertips to the keys; the spirit which caused it overcame all my thoughts. The whole room was filled with a fragrant vapour in which the candles burned mournfully. Occasionally a nose appeared, or two eyes, but they disappeared again at once.

So it happened that I was left alone with my Sebastian Bach and was served by Gottlieb as by a *spiritus familiaris*. (I drink.) Should people be allowed to torture honest musicians as I have been tortured today and will be tortured again? Surely no art is so frequently and humiliatingly abused as the heavenly art of music, whose gentle airs can be so easily profaned. If you possess true talent, true discrimination for art, learn music and honour the worthy art to the limits of your ability. If you just want to fool with it, have the goodness to keep it to yourself and stop torturing Kapellmeister Kreisler and others like him.

I could go home now and finish my new piano sonata; but it's not yet eleven o'clock and it's a beautiful summer night. I'll bet the daughters of my neighbour, the game keeper, are standing at the open window shrieking out the first stanza of 'When Your Eyes Are Beaming' for the twentieth time. Across the street someone will be torturing the flute while his neighbour conducts acoustic experiments on the horn. The numerous dogs of the neighbourhood are unruly and my landlord's tom-cat, aroused by the sweet duet, will come to my window (you know that my musical-poetical laboratory is a garret on the roof) to howl up and down the chromatic scale – sweet nothings for the neighbour's cat, with whom he has been in love since March. After eleven it grows quieter. I have remained sitting that long for there is still some white paper and Burgundy at hand and I am enjoying them.

There is, I am told, an ancient law which prohibits noisy labourers from living next to educated gentlemen. Why couldn't poor oppressed composers, who have to sell their inspirations for a price in order to make ends meet, turn this law on themselves and banish themselves from the neighbourhood of windbags and bores? What would the painter do if he was offered a collection of apish masks as a subject for a painting of the 'ideal?' He would close his eyes; at least then he could create an undisturbed image in his imagination. Cotton in the ears won't help; one still hears the murderous assembly. Just to think about them! – now they're singing, now the horn, etc.! It is the devil who fishes up such sublime ideas!

The page is completely full. Just enough room in the margins around the title to note why I have resolved a hundred times never to allow myself to be tortured at the councillor's and why I have always broken my resolution. It is the Röderleins' wonderful niece who ties me to this house where art is patronized. Anyone who has been lucky enough to hear Fräulein Amalia sing the final scene of Gluck's *Armida* or Donna Anna's big scene in *Don Giovanni* will understand that an hour with her at the piano is like a balm from heaven flowing into the wounds and discords of the music master's tortured day. Röderlein, who believes neither in the immortality of the soul nor in keeping time, maintains that it is totally irrelevant for the success of the tea party that she refuses to sing and that she sings gladly only for quite common people such as musicians. The long, swelling tones she produces – tones which draw me to heaven – she has learned from the nightingale. But Röderlein contends that the nightingale is an unintelligent creature living only in forests and ought not to be imitated by sensible, thinking human beings. At times she is so indiscreet as to accompany Gottlieb's violin at the piano in sonatas by Beethoven and Mozart, though not a single tea drinker or whist player is ever aware of it.

That was the last glass of Burgundy. Gottlieb snuffs the candles for me and seems to be wondering what I am writing so diligently. One is quite right to prize this Gottlieb, even though he is only sixteen years old. He has a wonderful profound talent. Why did his father, the toll collector, have to die so young? And did his guardian have to place the youth in the servants' profession? When Rode was here Gottlieb listened to him from the foyer, his ear pressed against the door, and then went and played all night. During the following days he went about reflectively, dreamily. The scar on his left cheek, left there by the jewel on Röderlein's finger, is testimony that the hand can be used for other purposes than to induce dreaminess with caresses. Among other things I have given him Corelli's sonatas. He charged into them on the old Oesterlein piano in the attic among the mice until, with Röderlein's permission, he moved the piano to his own little room.

Cast off that wretched servant's uniform, Gottlieb, and in a few years let me embrace you as the valiant artist you could become, for you have a splendid talent and a deep understanding for art!

Gottlieb stood behind me and wiped the tears from his eyes as I spoke these words. I pressed his hand silently and we went up to play the sonatas by Corelli.

SIXTEEN

Philistines

The Germans were seldom so outspoken against philistinism as the French. But there were signs about the turn of the century that philistinism in Germany was inspiring more hearty denunciation. Clemens Brentano catalogued many charges against the philistines in his writings, and in 1802 Fichte wrote his crusty *Naturgeschichte des Philisters.*

We have already had occasion to observe how clean is the line which Hoffmann always drew between true artists and philistines. Kreisler divides society into two quite distinct groups: 'good people,' who live righteously but are poor musicians, and 'true musicians,' for whom a secret knowledge of the mysteries of music compensates for all other deficiencies in living.

Hoffmann's intense and continuing opposition to the bourgeois resulted in part from the circumstances of his own life, for he was constantly at war with the bourgeois within himself. Abandoning the security and respectability of a career in law to enter on the notoriously uncertain career of a professional musician, he was eventually driven back to the *Staatskrippe*, as he termed it, having failed to overcome the vicissitudes of artistic life.

There is much self-portraiture in Hoffmann's Kreisler, though perhaps not so much as some biographers have been tempted to see. Kreisler is more a projection of the man Hoffmann would have liked to be, had he possessed the talent and courage. Perhaps as a result of his own moral defeat in having abandoned music, Hoffmann does not seek to infuse Kreisler with outgoing missionary zeal. Kreisler does not exhort society to wake up out of its vegetable bondage and acquaint itself with 'truth.' The truth which Kreisler represents is a secret reserved for the initiated. He is no mediator standing among crowds, but a shadowy and strangely uncommunicative figure. He haunts society; he does not convert it. If there is little respect for the nobility of a life dedicated exclusively to music, then this very fact gives a special asperity to his creed, for society acts as an abrasive to the perilous path he treads. As Ronald Taylor has put it, 'the Scylla of artistic unbalance' is steadied by 'the Charybdis of bourgeois unconcern.'[1] How dramatic is the contrast between the garrulous *Liebhaber der Musik* with their uncharming talk and performances and Kreisler's inspired interpretation of Bach's *Goldberg* Variations!

It is obviously important for the impact of the preceding chapter that the unpopular spectre of Bach should have been invoked. I have mentioned before that Hoffmann's motivation to champion the music of J.S. Bach may not have been entirely pure. When Bach died in 1750 one of his successors at St Thomas drew up a list of composers in order of greatness and appeal. Bach ran fifth, after Telemann, Stoelzel, Fasch, and Pfeiffer.[2] During the following decades he fell into even greater neglect, although he continued to inspire isolated musicians of vision. When Mozart visited Leipzig in 1789 he enthusiastically reconstructed some of the motets for himself from the parts, and was observed in this occupation by a quite bewildered Friedrich Rochlitz, editor of Germany's leading music magazine.[3] Gerber's *Lexikon der Tonkünstler* of 1790 shows that at that time only nine of Bach's works had been published.[4] In 1802 J.N. Forkel's spirited biography of Bach had appeared, but his revival did not really begin until 1829 with Mendelssohn's famous *St Matthew Passion* performance.

In 1810 then, the year Kreisler was performing the *Goldberg* Variations at tea parties, Bach was still largely a mystery. Although many of Bach's keyboard works were available, no one could more than roughly sense Bach's greatness. It is indeed a credit to Hoffmann that he did roughly sense it. It is apparent, however, that although he was excited enough by Bach's music to write about it frequently, he did not 'understand' it in any true sense of the word. Elsewhere in the *Kreisleriana* he has written:

> There are moments, especially when I study the works of the great Sebastian Bach, in which the mystical rules of counterpoint and the relationships of the notes fill me with terror. Music – with mysterious horror, yes, even profound terror – I call thee – Thee! – the Sanscrit of nature expressed in tone![5]

It is precisely the unintelligible Sanscrit quality of Bach's music that Hoffmann finds so attractive. It suits his plan. Bach is an enigma. Hoffmann does nothing to clarify him for us. He supports Bach blindly: 'the uncomprehending fight over you childishly; the apelike blasphemers sink in their own scorn!'[6] but this is not an explanation. It is important for Hoffmann to have someone he can hold slightly out of focus so as to confuse the myopic philistine, for this strengthens by association the egregious social position of Kreisler as well. Bach and Kreisler were the 'true musicians' opposed by the 'good people' of society.

German society in the eighteenth and nineteenth centuries still laboured under a multiplicity of class distinctions. They were more pronounced there than in France or England, due to the fragmentation of the country into a chequerboard of independent principalities, each with its own tiny hierarchy. Below the numerous strata of the nobility came the numerous strata of the bourgeoisie, with the church and the army forming further and separate hierarchies. It was the privilege of the musicians (who, as Hoffmann says, 'arise from the poorer classes') to be permitted to cut across all these barriers and mix with all classes by virtue of their abilities to entertain. Some artists found this agreeable and rewarding enough. One has the impression, for example, in reading Dittersdorf's autobiography that the life of a successful musician was an endless stream of balls, parties, intrigues with the nobility and their mistresses, and frequent payments in gold watches and snuff boxes, or more infrequently in grants and stipends. Nevertheless, the freedom granted the musician to mix with all levels of society was a privilege and in no way raised him to a level of social equality. For the upper classes, musicians were figures on the periphery of their lives to whom they threw trinkets whenever they were made favourably aware of their existence. Artists were merely the cultural upholsterers of society. In description after description of social gatherings we see that musicians occupied the anteroom of society.

> The company assembles in four fine long rooms that form a suite and are lighted by some hundreds of wax candles. Of these eighty people, thirty or forty will play cards. Of the rest some sit and work at their 'entoilage' or 'réseau' while others of us entertain them with our conversation, or they walk hand in hand and arm in arm from sofa to sofa and room to room. At the end of this suite of rooms there is an anteroom where musicians are usually playing. Both ladies and gentlemen are attired in all their finery, the ladies in satin dresses, deeply décolleté and richly trimmed with 'blondes' and lace, and with shawls of Flemish lace over their shoulders. They all wear diamond hair ornaments, earrings and necklaces, their coiffure is in the latest Parisian fashion, their gowns are imitations of the latest models from Paris. Not a word of any language but French is spoken. You flirt and rally and kiss all à la Française.[7]

In one of Hoffmann's most cynical stories, an educated ape becomes a great virtuoso because he can span two octaves with each hand.[8] This, together with his extraordinary agility in executing octaves and trills – a skill gained from having leapt about rapidly in trees during his youth – makes him the darling of musical society. This is Hoffmann's way of saying that musicians are animals kept to perform tricks.

In distinguishing sharply between 'true musicians' and the rest of society Hoffmann is opposing the picture society had of itself, indeed the picture of German musical life at this time kept alive in many flattering posthumous studies, such as that by Spengler quoted earlier. It is true that Germany was seething with music making during the eighteenth and nineteenth centuries. The trouble was that there existed as yet no adequate distinction between the amateur and the professional musician; or rather, the professional musician does not yet have the respect to which he is entitled from the amateur musician. Where everyone makes music, few listen to those who are making the best music. Hoffmann is trying to force society into a consciousness of the distinction between amateur and professional status.

Of course, these are our terms. Hoffmann's day recognized at least three categories of musical accomplishment. First of all there was the *Liebhaber der Musik* (the music lover); he might be a passive listener or an amateur performer. Above him there was the *Kenner* (the so-called connoisseur), who probably played an instrument reasonably well, may have moved the parts in holy procession through the odd counterpoint exercise, and may even have published these exercises. Thirdly, there was the *Meister* (master), who was that versatile musical personality mentioned before, the portmanteau musician who could write a birthday ode for a king as easily as he could fiddle for a wedding or accompany society's budding *prima donna* on the piano. Of these, only the *Meister* expected to be paid for his musical services, but this was natural, for as Hoffmann has already said, these musicians 'arise from the poorer classes.'

But let us underline once again that the occupation of 'master' musician had at this time little of the lustre it later acquired. Society did not glorify or apotheosize its master musicians. Danhauser's celebrated 1840 painting of Liszt improvising at the piano with Marie d'Agoult draped adoringly at his feet could not have been painted in 1800. The figure grouping would have been socially outrageous.

Contrast this painting with the humiliations suffered by composers less than half a century earlier at the hands of the arrogant and ubiquitous *Liebhaber* and *Kenner*. Contemporary with Kreisler's sufferings is this account by Carl Maria von Weber.

On the following morning I waited on Herr von Y— for I had heard much about the musical taste of his family and knew he had great influence in the town.

He saluted me with 'Ah, welcome! I am very happy to make your acquaintance, for I have been written to most favourably of you.' I bowed. 'You, of
course, know my newest sonatas?'

I looked embarrassed. 'I cannot say that I ...'

'But,' he interrupted, 'the quartet ...?'

'I am *particularly* sorry,' I muttered, colouring, 'but I do not recall ...'

'Well,' said my host, raising his eyes in astonishment, 'at least the caprices will
be familiar to you!'[9]

Indeed the age did embrace 'a musical culture which pervaded all life' –
but with more stultifying than stimulating consequences. In the *Kreisleriana* fragment entitled 'Der Musikfeind' (The Music Hater) Hoffmann
argues that the farcical displays of amateur musicians did nothing to develop one's taste for music, but on the contrary could lead to blind hatred
of the art. Here is his amusing description of the ritual of inculcation:

My father [Hoffmann puts these words in the mouth of Kreisler; in reality they
are autobiographical and refer to his uncle Otto] was certainly a dedicated musician. He played the piano diligently, often until late at night. When occasionally
there was a concert at our house, he played very long pieces in which the others
attempted to accompany him on violins, basses, flutes, and horns. When such
long pieces were at last over, everyone cried out 'Bravo! Bravo! What a beautiful
concert! How accomplished and well played!' and they respectfully mentioned
the name of Emanuel Bach. My father, however, always hammered so tumultu-
ously that it seemed to me he couldn't possibly be interested in music – for I had
in mind heart-warming melodies – but rather that he did it for the sport and the
others made a game out of it with him.

On such occasions I was perched on a high stool near my mother, dressed in
my Sunday best, and was forced to listen without fidgeting or moving. Time
would have been unbearably long and I wouldn't have been able to stand it if I
hadn't found the grimaces and comical movements of the performers so amusing.
Above all, I recall an old lawyer who always played the violin near my father and
was always referred to as a quite extravagant enthusiast. Music made him half
mad so that in his semi-crazed exaltation he performed Emanuel Bach or Wolf or
Benda without understanding what he was doing or keeping time. I can see him
clearly still. He wore a plum-coloured coat with gold-woven buttons, a little silver sword, and a slightly powdered wig, from which a small round bun of hair
dangled at the back. He was indescribably earnest in everything he undertook.
'Ad opus!' he used to cry when my father had distributed the parts. Then he
would raise his violin with his right hand and remove his wig with his left hand

to hang it on a nail. Now he began, bending closer and closer to the music as he played so that his red eyes popped out of his head and drops of sweat stood on his brow. Sometimes it happened that he reached the end sooner than the others, which caused him much wonderment and he would look scornfully at the remaining players.[10]

One would like to think matters stood better with the nobility, for the nobility is expected to possess more taste and sensitivity than the bourgeois. Certainly their opportunities for study were greater. It has been pointed out, however, that the German nobility contributed surprisingly little to letters and art, at least by comparison with their French and English counterparts. Certainly the number who made positive contributions is very small. Occasionally a member of the aristocracy excelled at music, such as Louis Ferdinand of Hohenzollern, some of whose compositions are still performed. But the real resource of most courtiers in their idle hours was not music but card parties. Gambling was one of the chief vices laid against the aristocracy when their superiority began to be challenged. Dittersdorf records bitterly in his autobiography: 'Cards had been substituted for music in the evenings ... They used to play commerce at two or more tables; and the Prince was brought in, in an armchair, to watch the game.'[11]

When the aristocracy did attend concerts, they were surrounded by a number of empty chairs in direct proportion to their rank. On the whole the taste of the nobility was as insipid and undistinguished as that of the lower classes, and when someone as close to the scene as Max Maria von Weber, in writing about his father, says of the nobility that 'beyond dance-hall and the "table" music of the period they were utter nonentities as regards musical taste,'[12] it may be understood that waves of discontent and disrespect among artists for their benefactors were growing.

Not long after Hoffmann arrived in Bamberg the Princess of Neufchâtel visited the city to see her mother. Hoffmann was requested to prepare a 'Prologue' for presentation at the theatre. He describes the affair in a letter to Hitzig:

I threw together some very ordinary sentimental stuff, composed equally sentimental music to it, and the whole was produced, not sparing lights, horns, echoes, mountains, rivers, bridges, trees with names carved on them, flowers, wreaths. From the mother of the Princess I received, together with gracious words, thirty Carolins for the emotional experience I had provided for her. At a certain place in the *Prologue*, 'I went, I flew, I plunged into her arms!' (an uncommonly fine climax) and mother and daughter embraced tearfully in the ducal box. The audience applauded rather ironically ...[13]

Hoffmann makes war on all shallow musical experiences. He makes war on all prologues, battle symphonies, birthday cantatas. He makes war on the minuet, the quadrille, and the waltz, that apotheosis of Biedermeier sentimentality. Hoffmann detests everything that establishes the subordination of art to entertainment. Johannes Kreisler, arch-musician, is the deliverer of art. He exists as an assertion for an order of priorities. He is an impulse pitted against his time, a martyr laying his life against a dream of artistic maturity.

In *Kater Murr* Hoffmann, poignantly and with great skill, pits Kreisler against Tom-cat Murr, his rival, the arch-philistine. Although apparently well-informed, Murr is smug, self-satisfied, and prudish. An *étudiant en belles lettres*, he has filled himself with useless knowledge and classical scholarship. He is a parody of a scholar, crammed with information but without the slightest glimmer of enlightenment. Nevertheless the local professor of aesthetics at the university fears him as a powerful threat.

Murr's whole story is told with such scintillation and humour that we might be inclined to forget what he stands for. It is only when Murr, to the chorus of applauding ladies, catches mice with amiable agility that he inadvertently betrays to the attentive reader that his discriminating sense of taste is in reality merely culinary. But his conceit is masterly. 'Can indeed anything unimportant ever happen to a great genius?' Murr asks in the process of telling us the trivial details of his own life.

One night Murr is attracted to the beautiful white cat Miesmies, whom he meets on the roof and serenades ecstatically. Miesmies, who is a singer herself, sings the aria 'Di tanti palpiti' from Rossini's opera *Tancred*. 'From the heroic strength of the recitative she stepped into the truly catlike sweetness of the *andante*. The aria seemed to be created for her ...'[14] With what clever irony is Rossini's famous aria being labelled *Katzenmusik*! Later a black cat with an excellent bass voice joins them and the three sing operatic trios until some unappreciative barbarian throws a piece of slate at them. Such episodes are ludicrous parodies of the agonizing recitals by talentless amateurs with which Kreisler and Hoffmann both were so familiar.

Hoffmann saw in the philistine a mediocrity of soul which stimulated his bitterest sarcasm. If Kreisler exists as an assertion of the divine nobility of music, Murr is his absolute enemy and represents a total betrayal of the artist. In his introduction to the *Fantasiestücke*, Jean Paul had warned Hoffmann that 'love of the artist' could easily turn into 'hatred of mankind.' But the older Jean Paul did not understand the compulsion with which it was necessary to deliver music from its abuses and return it to its true custodians.

SEVENTEEN

Reflections on
the High Value of Music

It cannot be denied that in recent times, thank heaven, the public's taste for music is improving so that it is now more or less part of a decent education for children to be allowed to study the subject. Thus one finds a piano in every house, or at least a guitar – whatever that may signify. Nevertheless, there are a few isolated scorners of this undeniably beautiful art and it is my task here to give them a sound rebuke.

The real purpose of art is to provide people with an amusement and thus to divert them from the much more important tasks of earning bread and fame. Then afterwards they may return to the real purpose of their existence with redoubled energy and dedication – that is, to be a faithful cog in the treadmill of the state and (I remain with the metaphor) to let themselves be manipulated like mechanical gadgets.

Now no art is more qualified to achieve this end than music. It would be fortunate if, in reading novels or poetry, one could find something completely free of the tasteless fantasy apparent in much of the most recent literature. Imagination, too, which is the most insidious aspect of original sin, must be crushed. One must keep clear of its influence. What I mean to say is that reading carries with it the unpleasantness that one is more or less obliged to think about what one is reading, and this is obviously contrary to the purpose of amusement. The same applies to recitations, especially the kind that fail to hold the attention, so that one drops off to sleep very easily, or rests from serious thought; for as we may observe, in the spiritual metabolism of the average businessman it is necessary to have periodic rests. The pleasure of a painting can last only a very short time, for the interest wanes completely as soon as one has guessed what it is supposed to represent.

As for music, it is only those wretched scorners of this beautiful art who deny that a successful composition is one which respects its own limitations, allowing one pleasing melody to follow after another without storming about in all sorts of contrapuntal meanderings and modulations. Thus it gives rise to a charming pleasure in which one is quite liberated from thinking, or at least is restrained from serious thoughts, and one experiences merely the pleasant and frivolous variety which consort happily without even making their presence felt!

But we may go further and ask: should one be prohibited during music from engaging in conversation with one's neighbour about politics or morals or anything else? Certainly if this were possible a double purpose could be achieved in a pleasant way. It is therefore to be heartily recommended, since music, as one will have occasion to notice in all concerts and musical circles, facilitates conversations exceedingly. During the intermissions everything is quiet, but when the music begins, a flow of conversation is immediately unleashed to mingle and swell with the tones. Many a fine lady whose conversation is normally limited to the words 'Yes, yes!' or 'No, no!' when enthused by music is induced to extend her vocabulary, which, though wicked according to the Bible, is definitely in keeping with the spirit of the concert hall; and many a husband or lover, intoxicated by this sweet and uncommon volubility, falls into the trap. The advantages of beautiful music are most unpredictable!

You, the despicable scorners of the noble art, let me lead you now into a domestic circle where father, tired after the hard work of the day, relaxes in his dressing gown and slippers smoking his pipe. Hasn't dear little Rosie practised the 'Dessau March' and 'Bloom, Sweet Violet' just for his sake, and played them so beautifully that mother has shed tears of joy on the stocking she is darning? Wouldn't the squealing of the youngest child get on his nerves if it were not for this lovely child's music?

But if your spirit is turned completely against this domestic idyll, the triumph of simple nature, then follow me into that house with the brightly illuminated windows. You enter the room. The steaming kettle is the focal point, around which the elegantly dressed men and women move. Gaming tables are set up, but the lid of the piano is also open, for here too music serves to inspire pleasant conversation and amusement. Carefully selected, it interrupts in no way, for even the card players, although involved in the more important matter of wins and losses, tolerate it willingly.

Finally, what should I say about the great public concerts which give one the splendid opportunity to speak to one's friends accompanied by music, especially for those still young in heart who desire a becoming accompaniment to frame a pretty remark to this or that lady. Such concerts are the true places of diversion for the businessman and are to be preferred to the theatre, for there performances are sometimes given in which the mind is compelled to fix itself on futile and fictional subjects, so that one runs the risk of being drawn into poetry – a thing every good bourgeois must be on his guard against!

In short, as I mentioned right at the beginning, it is a decisive sign that the true purpose of music has been recognized and that it is studied with so much industry and earnestness. How important it is that children should be kept at their music, even if they have only the slightest talent for art – for that, indeed, is not the issue here. Thus when they move out into society, even though they may be otherwise ineffectual socially, at least they will be able to contribute something pleasurable and diverting.

Another excellent advantage of music over all the other arts is that it is pure (unmixed with poetry) and is therefore completely moral and has no detrimental effect on tender youth. A police officer was quoted in a statement concerning the invention of a new musical instrument: 'It contains nothing against the state, religion, or morals.' By the same token all teachers and parents may be reassured that my new sonata contains not a single immoral thought.

Of course it is understandable that as children grow older they will stop practising, for such things are not in keeping with the activities of serious men. As for women, they can easily find better ways to keep society amused. These then enjoy the pleasures of music only passively inasmuch as they allow themselves to be played to by children or professional artists. From an accurate assessment of the purpose of art it follows naturally that artists (that is, those undoubtedly insane individuals who dedicate their whole lives simply to diverting and amusing society) are to be tolerated because they bring *miscere utile dulce* into practice. No one with good judgment and mature insight would prize the best artists as highly as a good chancery clerk, or even an artisan who stuffs the mattresses on which the councillor sits in the palace antechamber or the salesman in his office, for we are comparing here a necessity with something that is merely decorative.

Therefore, when we associate with artists in a polite, even friendly manner, it is only a consequence of our cultivation and *bonhomie* which requires us also to be kind to children and other human beings whose company is pleasant. Many of these unfortunate dreamers are apprised too late of their folly and as a result fall victims of madness, as is evidenced by their statements about art. They maintain that art intimates a higher principle to man and leads him out of the trivialities of everyday life to the temple of Isis where nature speaks to him in sacred tones never before heard, but completely intelligible. These fools cherish an eccentric belief concerning music: they call it the most romantic of all the arts because it aspires to the infinite; the mystical Sanscrit of nature, spelled out in tones which fill the human soul with infinite longing, leading man to understand the sacred hymn of the trees, flowers, animals, stones, and waters. The completely useless game of counterpoint, which does nothing to cheer up the listener and therefore deceives the true purpose of music, these people compare to the mysterious interlacing of moss, leaves, and flowers. The talent – or in the language of these fools, the genius – of music glows, they say, in the breasts of those people who practise and cherish the art, and if an inferior principle imposes itself on the spark hoping to extinguish it, it is itself consumed by indestructible flames. Those people who, as observed at the outset, have come to the right conclusion about the true value of art, and especially music – those people are called ignorant blasphemers who must forever remain locked out of the sanctuary of higher existence. In this way they confirm their madness.

Therefore, quite rightly I ask, who is better, the businessman who lives on his money, who eats and drinks well, takes walks, and is greeted by everyone with respect, or the artist who struggles along in his miserable life of fantasy? Indeed these fools maintain that their special lot enables them to raise the poetical above the common and that that great privation transforms itself into pleasure. Well, kings and kaisers in a madhouse with straw crowns on their heads are happy too!

The best proof that all this posturing is empty and only intended to cover up an inner sense of guilt for not having struggled after something more solid is the fact that almost no one becomes an artist by free choice and also that artists arise from the poorer classes. Given birth by obscure, untitled parents or by other artists, they make the distress and misery of their condition an opportunity to gain entry into higher classes of society than would otherwise be possible. This remains an eternal consolation for their imaginations.

If a titled family of high standing were ever so unlucky as to have a child who was drawn especially to art – or in the ridiculous language of those fools, a child who was consumed beyond all opposition by the divine flames – and there were a danger that he might be deluded into pursuing a career as an artist, it might be necessary for a good teacher to set him straight by readjusting his spiritual diet, i.e. through the total removal of all fantastic, exaggerated entertainment (poetry and the so-called 'violent' compositions of Mozart, Beethoven, and others), as well as by repeated inculcations of the idea that art is a subordinate activity and that artists are quite secondary individuals possessing neither titles, fortunes, nor any other distinctions. By this means it should be easy to bring the straying youth back to his senses so that in the end he will develop a healthy contempt for art and artists. This is a remedy against eccentricity that cannot fail to work.

If I may give a little advice to those poor artists who have fallen into the above-described state of insanity in the interests of helping them break free from their purposeless existence, I would tell them to learn some simple handicraft along with their art. That way they will be appreciated as useful members of society. A wise person told me that I had a talent for slipper-making, and I am not disinclined to establish a precedent in this matter by asking Herr Schnabler, the local slipper-maker if he will teach me the trade. After all he is my godfather.

Reading over what I have written I find I have described the madness of many musicians very shrewdly and with a secret horror I feel myself related to them. Satan whispers in my ear that to them many of my ingenuous remarks could be construed as dreadful irony. But I assure you once more my remarks have been directed exclusively against you, the despisers of music, who refer to the edifying singing and playing of children as useless noise and appreciate music only as a secret sublime art. With all the weapons at my disposal I have attempted to prove to you that music – that wonderful and profitable discovery of awakened Tubal-cain[1] – has as its purpose to make men happy, to divert them, and to bring joy into the household. It is, therefore, the highest duty of every cultivated person to further it in an acceptable and satisfying manner.

···◈▥══════▥◈···

EIGHTEEN

Ecstasy

···◈▥══════▥◈···

For the philistine the sole purpose of art is to bring a little *brio* into life.
Elsewhere in the *Kreisleriana* a certain Baron Wallborn (who has obviously
seen the foregoing article) writes a letter to Kreisler in which he attempts
to defend the music-making of amateurs and children by asking the composer 'Is there such a thing as absolutely bad music? ... And again, on the
other hand, is there such a thing as absolutely perfect music?'[1] Baron Wallborn is really enquiring whether the simple urge to make music is not in
itself a noble thing.

Kreisler replies that he can be deeply moved by music which may be far
from perfectly performed as long as it is heartfelt and honest. He does not
reject elementary musical experiences outright. But he does denounce
music which caters to people for whom art is a shallow and unaffecting
experience.

The great weakness in most of the nineteenth-century German aesthetic
theorizing was that it regarded a work of art in the pure state of antisepsis,
stripped bare of all sociological considerations. Considered in this way art
becomes a mere configuration of abstracted elements in space and time.
But art cannot exist independently of those who study it. The error of
Fichte's and Schelling's aesthetic speculations is the assumption that art
had one fixed exposure (that of their own time) and that this could be
taken as axiomatic for all times. They ignored the fact that the *Anschauung*
of an age could change, and when it eventually did, of course their speculations became valueless.

Hoffmann was never guilty of ignoring the social implications of art.
By comparison with the philosophers his aesthetic theories are 'impure,'
but this very impurity makes them more valid and more interesting as the
insights of an individual reacting in and against a particular society. Hoffmann was immensely interested in the way art affects people, and the

conscious and unconscious associations it produces in the mind of the beholder. Thus he associated the voice and image of his beloved Julia with Italian song literature, and consequently this music gained for him – and for those of his readers who are infected by his writings – a great beauty and charm. Similarly, socially undesirable people may like certain kinds of music (Kater Murr's love of Rossini, for instance), with the result that this music is contaminated and must be dispossessed by true artists.

But these social considerations do not prohibit us from giving an affirmative answer to Baron Wallborn's question 'Is there such a thing as absolutely perfect music?' In individual pieces we experience merely glimpses of an imagined perfection, which exists as an infinite dream and may be experienced by every composer when he undertakes a new work, just as it was described in 'Ritter Gluck.' Only the genius is permitted entry into this ecstatic realm.

Ecstasy is the opposite of that squandering and tepid imitation of musicianship practised by the 'good people.' Kreisler, who is the spirit of music, lives perpetually in this state of ecstasy. 'His spirit moved into a realm where no one could follow without peril.' Kreisler's great failure, however, is his lack of *Besonnenheit*, of presence of mind. Unlike a truly great composer he frequently, in the words from 'Ritter Gluck,' 'dreams away the dream of this dream-world.' We recall that although he often wrote with incredible speed in the middle of the night, 'the next day the splendid composition would lie in the fire.'

Although Joseph Berglinger, 'der erste Musik-Verkündiger im Wort,' certainly did achieve ecstasy, he achieved it vicariously, for he was not a composer. In fact not a single real composer is ever mentioned in Wackenroder's writings. Berglinger achieves ecstasy because he holds music as absolute, even to the point of regarding daily social intercourse as a betrayal of this noble purpose of existence:

> As long as you live, he thought, you must hold fast, unwavering, to this beautiful poetic ecstasy, and your whole life must be a piece of music. When he went to lunch with his relatives and had thoroughly enjoyed his meal in their hearty company, it displeased him that he had let himself be drawn again so soon into the prosaic life and that his rapture had vanished like a gleaming cloud.[2]

Berglinger's commitment to music, like Kreisler's, is total. When his musical reveries are interrupted by domestic quarreling he cries:

> Dear God! is this the world as it is? – and is it Thy will that I should plunge into the turmoil of the crowd and share the general misery? ... No! No! You have been born to a higher, nobler end![3]

Berglinger's lofty idealism brings tragedy into his life when he discovers the uniqueness of his artistic reverence. He discovers that even few practising artists themselves share the nobility of his feelings towards music.

Kreisler too has travelled to the apogee of the realm of absolute music, but he has not succeeded in communicating his insights to humanity. Thus in society he will be forever frustrated. Even when most enraptured and deliriously optimistic, he leaves his listeners bewildered and unable to grasp his meaning. Hoffmann is, of course, optimistic enough himself to leave us with the impression that the future will understand him. As the spirit of music, Kreisler inspires the age as an example of the heights to which human awareness can aspire. As a figure improvising at the piano he prefigures the typical romantic musician to follow him who, having lost all contact with reality, evolves completely subjective visions and values. What Marcel Brion has said of Schumann applies equally to Kreisler: 'With him and for him, all things sang.'[4] His is the absolute and ecstatic glitter of vision, the uncounterfeiting inspiration.

The penalty for this extreme vision in a blind society is expulsion. More than this, if the constitution is not rugged enough to stem the inflow of absolute music, the extreme penalty of madness is exacted. Absolute music possesses the dangerous power to turn men into maniacs. In a fragmentary story entitled 'Der Freund,' an insane musician with the initials 'J.K.' is confined to the country home of a friend. The friend attempts to cure him with music therapy. J.K. flies into a rage and loses control of himself completely. Later, when the friend leaves a guitar in his room, the musician dares to touch it. At the sound of the C major chord J.K. suddenly smashes the instrument.[5] Music, then, is the means by which the incalculable demonic forces of the universe burst in on the calculated life of man, setting up tremendous and destructive upheavals in his personality.

In our last glimpse of Kreisler, just before his disappearance or madness, we see the composer inspired. In a few powerful and suspenseful flashes he will run the full gamut of musical experience from reverence to eroticism, from tranquility to fear, from heroism to madness, seeking to embrace the absolute, while his friends and disciples with their limited range of emotional responses can understand little of these flamboyant displays and nothing of the total ecstasy ...

NINETEEN

Kreisler's Musical-Poetical Club

All clocks, even those that were late, had struck the hour of eight; the lamps had been lit, the piano stood open; the landlady's daughter, who attended to cleaning Kreisler's quarters, had already notified him twice that the tea-kettle was boiling. At last a knock at the door; the True Friend entered with the Prudent One. They were soon followed by the Dissatisfied One, the Jovial One, and the Indifferent One. The club was in session. As usual Kreisler was ready to spin his symphonic-like fantasy of tones and rhythms which would lift the club members – each of whom possessed a strong musical sensitivity – out of the dusty atmosphere in which they were forced to pass their days, and raise them a few fathoms higher into purer air.

The Prudent One looked serious, almost melancholy, and said: 'How unfortunate it was, dear Kreisler, that one of the hammers was broken during your last performance. Has it been repaired yet?'

'I hope so,' replied Kreisler.

'We'll have to see for ourselves,' the Prudent One continued and with that he deliberately lit a candelabra which was standing on the desk, and holding it over the piano, searched for the invalid hammer. But the heavy candle shears, which were attached to the candelabra, fell and with a shrill crackling sound twelve to fifteen strings snapped. The Prudent One said simply, 'Oh! Look what happened!' Kreisler's face bore the appearance of someone who has just bitten into a lemon.

'Damn! Damn!' cried the Dissatisfied One. 'I wanted to hear Kreisler improvise today above all others; never in my life have I been so desperate to hear music!'

'Actually,' the Indifferent One remarked, 'it doesn't matter much whether we begin with music or not.' The True Friend added that it was nevertheless a pity that Kreisler wouldn't be able to play; but that they should not let this destroy their mood completely.

'We'll have plenty of fun anyway,' said the Jovial One, laying a certain emphasis on his words.

'But I *will* improvise,' Kreisler declared. 'The strings in the bass are not broken; that will be enough for me.'

Then Kreisler donned his little red cap, drew on his Chinese dressing gown, and turned to the instrument. The club members took their seats on the sofa and chairs and the True Friend, at Kreisler's request, extinguished the lamps so that everything was in complete darkness. With the sustaining pedal down Kreisler now played the chord of A-flat major, *pianissimo* in the bass. As the tones died away he spoke:

'What is it that rustles so miraculously, so strangely around me? Invisible wings glide up and down. I am swimming in an ethereal fragrance. But the fragrance shines in flaming circles, mysteriously intertwining. They are tender spirits, moving their golden wings in magnificently voluminous tones and chords.'

A-flat minor chord (mezzo forte)

'Ah, they are carrying me to the land of unending desire. But as they lay hold of me they give rise to a pain which would rend my breast asunder in an effort to escape.'

E major; second inversion (ancora più forte)

'Be steadfast my heart; do not break at the touch of the burning ray that has penetrated my breast! Be refreshed my gallant spirit! Rise and move in the element which has given you birth and which is your home!'

E major; first inversion (forte)

'They have offered me a magnificent crown! But those diamonds sparkling in it are in reality the thousand tears which I have shed, and in its gold shine the flames which have consumed me. Courage and strength to him who is destined to reign in the realm of spirits!'

A minor (arpeggio dolce)

'Why are you fleeing, lovely maid? Why do you try, since invisible bonds hold you completely. You cannot tell what it is that gnaws painfully at your breast, at the same time filling you with sweetest joy. But you will understand everything when I caress you with the language of the spirits, the language I speak and which you understand so well!'

F major

'Ah, how your heart rises with desire and love when I embrace you with melodies filled with glowing enchantment. You can flee from me no longer, for those secret desires which have oppressed your soul are fulfilled. Like a consoling oracle, tones pour out of my soul and speak to you.'

B-flat major (accentuato)

'How joyful are the meadows and forests in spring! All the flutes and panflutes, which during the winter lay frozen in dusty corners, are awake and are recalling their favourite melodies which they are now trilling as happily as the birds.'

B-flat major seventh (smanioso)

'A mild west wind arises like a mournful secret in muffled grief and as it passes the fir and birch trees whisper: "Why has our friend become so sad? Do you harken to him lovely shepherdess?"'

E-flat major (forte)

'Go after him! Go after him! Green is his coat, like the dark wood. His yearning words are the sweet sounds of horns. Do you hear the rustling in the underbrush? Do you hear the sound of horns, full of gaiety and melancholy? It is he! Let us go to meet him!'

G major seventh; second inversion (piano)

'The game of life is a game of provocation. Why wish, why hope, why demand anything?'

C major (fortissimo)

'But let us dance with furious frenzy over the open graves. Let us rejoice! They cannot hear down there. Hurrah! Hurrah! Dancing and rejoicing! The devil is coming with trumpets and drums!'

Several C minor chords (fortissimo)

'Don't you know him? Don't you know him? Look, he clutches after my heart with his fiery claw. He grimaces, masquerading himself as a quack doctor, a corporation director, a concert master. He throws candle shears on the piano strings so that I cannot play. Kreisler! Kreisler! Pull yourself together! Can you see him lurking, this pale ghost with the gleaming red eyes, a claw-like bony fist stretching out of this torn coat? The crown of straw shakes on his bald skull. It's madness! Johannes, be brave! Mad! Mad! Phantom, why do you ensnare me? Let me go! I curse the singing and the music, only release me from this pain. Oh! Oh! you have tramped all over my flowers. Not a single stalk of green is left in this dreadful desert. Everything is dead, dead, dead!'

Here a tiny flame crackled; the True Friend had quickly struck a match and lit both lamps, cutting off all further fantasies from Kreisler, for he knew well that Kreisler had reached that point from which he usually tumbled into a gloomy abyss of hopeless despair. Just at that moment the landlady's daughter brought in the steaming tea. Kreisler sprang up from the piano.

'What was all that supposed to be about?' enquired the Dissatisfied One. 'I'd rather have a clever *allegro* by Haydn than all that rubbish.'

'It wasn't as bad as all that,' the Indifferent One commented.

'But too gloomy, far too gloomy,' the Jovial One added. 'Our conversation today should turn to pleasanter things.'

The club members endeavoured to follow the advice of the Jovial One, but Kreisler's ghastly chords and terrifying words sounded on in distant echo and preserved the tense atmosphere Kreisler had created. The Dissatisfied One, quite disgusted with the evening which, as he put it, had been ruined by Kreisler's mad fantasy, left with the Prudent One. The Jovial One followed them, and only the Travelling Enthusiast and the True Friend (both of whom, let it be stated explicitly, are the same person) still remained with Kreisler. He sat quietly with crossed arms on the sofa. 'I don't know,' said the True Friend, 'what to make of today's performance, Kreisler. You were so excited, without a trace of humour, not at all as usual.'

'Ah, friend,' Kreisler replied, 'the gloomy shadow of a cloud is passing over my life. Don't you think that a poor innocent melody, which does not wish any place at all on this earth, should be permitted to roam free and harmless through the wide space of the heavens? Ah, right now I'd like to fly out of that window on my Chinese dressing gown as upon a cloak of Mephistopheles.'

'As a harmless melody?' the True Friend interrupted with a smile.

'Or a *basso ostinato*, if you'd prefer it,' answered Kreisler; 'but in some way or other I must soon be off.'

And soon it happened, just as he had said.

TWENTY

Synaesthesia

Kreisler disappeared. Perhaps he returned to the element which had given him birth. Or became insane. Or stabbed himself with an augmented fifth, as Hoffmann bitterly suggested elsewhere.

Like the entire foregoing vignette, the image is synaesthetic. The nervous systems of two sense-areas have collided in metaphor. From the translations in this volume it will be clear to the reader that Hoffmann had a special ability to draw the senses together in synthesis and relate the sensations of one art to those of another. Sometimes this collision of sensations is whimsical, as when Kreisler speaks of wearing a 'garment that I had bought in a state of the highest depression over the failure of a trio, whose colour was C sharp minor, over which I wore a collar in E major, simply to pacify onlookers.'[1] At other times the synaesthetic undertaking is earnest and sustained, as in the foregoing chapter where a whole vocabulary of audio-visual correspondences is established.

Hoffmann's preoccupation with synaesthesia was by no means unique in his day. Someone with much patience has taken the trouble to read the collected words of Ludwig Tieck, Hoffmann, and Robert Schumann in search of images that are synaesthetic in character. The results were: Tieck 696; Hoffmann 652; Schumann, a prolific 824.[2] It is appropriate at this point to recall again Schlegel's advice to the young:

> We should strive to bring the arts closer together and search for bridges from one to the other. Statues will come alive to become perhaps paintings; paintings will become poems; poems will become music; and who knows, perhaps solemn religious music will rise up again as a temple in the sky.[3]

Preoccupations of this kind have a firm basis in the philosophies of the time, particularly in that of Fichte, who stressed the productive strength of what he called 'the absolute I.' For Fichte the whole world arises as a result of 'the absolute I' of the individual, so that all objectivity is inevitably lost in subjectivity. Thus it is understandable that the romanticists should cultivate the sovereignty of 'the artistic I' which broke through all boundaries of the separate senses to combine them arbitrarily in fantastic synaesthetic constellations.

It was in this spirit that writers such as Karl von Eckartshausen wrote works in which they felt quite at liberty to make idiosyncratic correspondences between the various modes of sensorial experience and offer them to the public as tested and objective disclosures. In his treatise *Disclosures of Magic from Tested Experiences of Occult Philosophic Sciences and Veiled Secrets of Nature*, von Eckartshausen tells us how he had 'long tried to determine the harmony of all sense impressions,' and had built a machine 'so that whole colour chords could be produced.'[4] His colour organ, which was a technical advance over that of Père Castel, projected candlelight through a number of coloured glasses so that as one played a keyboard 'the beauty of the colours was indescribable, surpassing that of the most splendid jewels.' Von Eckartshausen wrote a poem and accompanied it with sounds and colours to demonstrate the effectiveness of his technique:

A THEORY OF OCULAR MUSIC

WORDS: Sadly she wandered, loveliest of maidens ...
MUSIC: The notes of a flute, plaintive
COLOUR: Olive, mixed with pink and white

WORDS: ... in flowery meadows ...
MUSIC: Gay, rising tones
COLOUR: Green, mixed with violet and daisy yellow

WORDS: ... singing a song, joyful as a lark ...
MUSIC: Soft notes, rising and gently falling in quick succession
COLOUR: Dark blue streaked with scarlet and yellowish-green ...

Why a sadly wandering maiden should sing a joyful song is merely one of the more whimsical idiosyncracies of the author. Careful as one must be in assigning objective relevance to the world of synaesthetic correspondences, those of 'Kreisler's Musical-Poetical Club' do at least possess greater consistency. To begin, here is the series of chords Kreisler played.

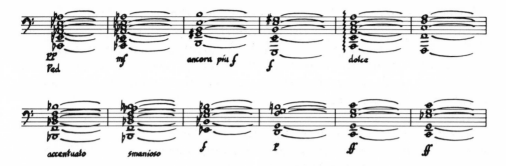

The modulations and their dynamic markings are bold and dramatic, not unlike Beethoven. Hoffmann attaches distinct qualities to each of these chords and thus implies that each tonality and modulation has a character of its own. The extent to which there was disagreement on these qualities is evident when Hoffmann's characterizations are placed in parallel with a similar attempt at key-characterization by his contemporary, the poet-musician C.F.D. Schubart.

TONALITY	HOFFMANN	SCHUBART[5]
A-flat major	Ethereal; shines in flaming circles, tender, golden, magnificently voluminous	Funereal tone, decomposition; judgment; eternity; black
A-flat minor	Unending desire, pain, effort to escape	
E major	Burning ray; crown, diamonds, tears, flames, courage, strength	Loud rejoicing; jovial happiness and great but not unsurpassable pleasure
A minor	Lovely maid; caresses, sweetest joy, but gnawing pain, uncertainty	Innocent femininity; tenderness of character
F major	Heart rises, desire and love; glowing enchantment; secret dreams fulfilled; comforting oracle	Agreeability and repose
B-flat major	Joyful, happy; spring	Serene love; clear conscience; hope, aspirations for a better world
B-flat major seventh	Mild west wind, mournful secret; sad, muffled grief	

TONALITY	HOFFMANN	SCHUBART
E-flat major	Green colour, woodlands; sound of horns, full of gaiety and melancholy	Tonality of love; devoted prayer (the three flats denote the Holy Trinity)
G major seventh	Provocation	
C major	Rejoicing; furious dance over the open graves; trumpets and drums	Innocence, naïveté; children's voices
C minor	Premonition of the devil! Fiery claws clutch after the heart; grimaces, madness; pain, desert, death	Declaration of love; lament, disappointed love, languishing, pining, sighing of the love-drunk soul

Such a table reveals the lack of concordance even between contemporary commentators, drawing on roughly the same musical experience. Even where there is relative agreement on the temperament of a given tonality, this could more likely have arisen from a shared acquaintance with specific popular pieces of music possessing a strong character over and above that suggested by their tonality. This is the case, for instance, when one thinks of the character affinities between several of Beethoven's best-known pieces in C minor.[6] At a time when the subject of synaesthesia in romantic literature was being critically investigated, one commentator provided the following statistical analysis of Hoffmann's synaesthetic imagery.[7]

	OPTIC	ACOUSTIC	OLFACTORY	GUSTATIVE	TACTILE
OPTIC		8	1	0	0
ACOUSTIC	45		2	0	0
OLFACTORY	5	7		0	1
GUSTATIVE	0	0	0		0
TACTILE	0	2	0	0	

By far the greatest number of images are in the area of acoustic-optic sense-associations. As regards vocabulary, it has been observed by another critic that the word 'tone' was the most frequently mentioned, followed by 'light,' then 'smell,' and only then by individual colours and images.[8]

Hoffmann's age was seduced by music. It was to the condition of music, as the purest and most recently liberated of the arts, that all the other arts were aspiring. Just as in 'Kreisler's Musical-Poetical Club' the images are suggested only after the different chords are struck, so it will appear frequently in Hoffmann that pure sound precedes the articulation of words and images, almost to a degree where it might be suggested that the whole of literature and the arts was for him a gigantic reverberation behind a presence of pure sound. Indeed on one occasion he did confess that the synaesthetic experience often arose only after he had had an overwhelming or prolonged association with music.

> Not so much in dreams as in the condition of delirium which precedes falling asleep – particularly when I have been close to music – I find a blending of colours, tones, and odours. It seems to me as if they were all produced through the same beam of light in some mysterious way and were obliged to combine together into a wonderful harmony. The perfume of the dark-red carnation has a strange, magical effect on me; involuntarily I sink into a dream condition and hear then as if from a great distance the deep tones of a clarinet swelling in strength and then dying away again.[9]

It is also noteworthy that in synaesthetic experiences such as those in 'Kreisler's Musical-Poetical Club' it is the modulation of the tonalities that provides continuity, rather than the images they suggest; these are chaotic and follow no logical sequence.

For Hoffmann, the nervous system of music was stretched over the visible, tactile, and olfactory world, reconstituting the elements in dazzling but irrational patterns. But music itself, otherwise invisible, now gains other sense-dimensions so that it begins to take on the appearance of a recognizable though confused cosmology. If the images suggested by Kreisler's attenuated chords were to occur within the context of a rapidly modulating composition, they would produce a phantasmagorical cosmos, much like the world of dreams, irrational, without causality, a cosmos in which scraps of visual, aural, and olfactory sensations spin in an enormous kaleidoscopic cloud.

It is scarcely surprising that Beethoven, as the composer who more than any other in Hoffmann's day pushed the frontiers of harmony to their furthest extremes, should have inspired the most enthusiastic of all Hoffmann's linguistic and descriptive effusions.

If we read again the passages in which Hoffmann is attempting to describe the invisible essence of music, we will see how this invisible essence is given an opaque projection on the screen of the other arts by means of the synaesthetic metaphor.

Look at the sun! It is the triad from which the chords of the stars shower down at our feet to wrap us in their threads of crystallized fire! ('Ritter Gluck')

Rays of light came through the night, and the rays of light were tones which surrounded me with their serene purity. I awoke from my pains and saw a great, clear eye which stared into an organ; and as it stared, tones arose and wound themselves into more shimmering and majestical chords than I had ever thought possible. Melodies poured up and down and I swam in their current and wanted to drown. Then the eye looked at me and raised me up over the raging waves. It was night again. At length two giants stepped up to me in shining armour; the Tonic and the Dominant. They bore me on high with them and the giant eye smiled. 'I know the reason for the longing which fills thy breast. It is the longing for the Third, that tender youth, who now steps up between the two giants. May you hear his sweet voice and until we meet again, may all my melodies be thine.' ('Ritter Gluck')

My eyes closed involuntarily and a burning kiss seemed to be imprinted on my lips. But the kiss was a long-held note of eternal passionate longing. ('Don Juan')

How like a dazzling sunbeam is the splendid theme of the last movement with the rejoicing exultation of the whole orchestra! ('Beethoven's Instrumental Music')

The pages suddenly expanded to giant size and leapt about me, revealing a thousand imitations and variations of the theme, all of which I was forced to play. The notes were alive; they glittered and spun about me. An electric shock travelled through my fingertips to the keys; the spirit which caused it overcame all my thoughts. The whole room was filled with a fragrant vapour in which the candles burned mournfully. Occasionally a nose appeared, or two eyes, but they disappeared again at once. ('Of Kapellmeister Johannes Kreisler's Musical Sorrows')

I saw the stone, and its red veins arose like dark carnations whose perfume became clear and resounding beams leading heavenwards. In the long crescendo of the nightingale's song the beams condensed into the figure of a beautiful woman – and this figure was divine, magnificent music! ('Johannes Kreisler's Lehrbrief')

All these are video-literary descriptions of invisible music. In Hoffmann's day it seemed vitally necessary to *see* musical events, to exchange an eye for an ear. Here is Ludwig Tieck:

> Nevertheless, often the tones seem to be swimming with such striking and individual pictures that it seems to us as if music is assimilated through both the ear and the eye at once. Often you see sirens swimming on the bright mirror of the sea, singing out to you with the sweetest tones. Then you are wandering in a beautiful forest, pierced by sunlight; you wander through dark grottoes decorated with fantastic visions; underground waterfalls ring in your ear and strange lights pass over your head.[10]

There is one remaining question: If music is the most pure, the one truly 'romantic' art, why must it be disclosed through the veil of verbal and visual euphemism?

It seems there are two answers to this question. It is useful to a writer to be able to employ visual imagery, when writing about other sensations, in order to get some glint into his prose. Edgar Allan Poe, for instance, has observed the intensity gained through synaesthetic experience.

> The senses were unusually active, although eccentrically so – assuming often each other's functions at random. The taste and smell were inextricably confounded, and became one sentiment, abnormal and intense.[11]

This intensification of experience was also the sole purpose of the almost grotesque synaesthetic debaucheries of Des Esseintes, the aesthetic hero of Huysmans' novel *A Rebours*, who even sought to establish correspondences between various liqueurs and instruments of the orchestra.

But if a writer adopts one sensation – music – as the root of all other experiences, as is the case with Hoffmann, a different purpose is served by synaesthesia. For Hoffmann, music was so wild and uncontrollable that it needed interpretation to be comprehended. Had not music already turned men mad? It would be difficult to discover a similar conception of music as total lawlessness unless one went back to early Christian times, when the church fathers feared music as 'the songs and dances of Satan.' Certainly this 'fear' of music does not exist immediately prior to Hoffmann's time when, as has been shown, it served merely as a sort of acoustic upholstery for society. This is a new concept of music, or at least a renewed one. Music is the absolute power in the universe. This is what Hoffmann suggests and Schopenhauer later confirms. It is so dynamic, so blazing that it cannot be comprehended by man. If its unbearably wild force is to be apprehended at all it must be apprehended through the screen of a less blinding metaphor first. Music demands its epiphany just as monotheism demanded the figure of Christ as a visible interpreter of the divine kingdom. This metaphor arouses the sympathy of the audience so that man may be raised eventually to an appreciation of the supra-logical revelations of the pure musical cosmos itself. Synaesthesia is the means by which we may read the unintelligible Sanscrit of the language of music, the means by which we may glimpse the ineffable realm which is Kreisler's home.

TWENTY-ONE

The Cosmology Configured

I have drawn attention at the very beginning of this volume to a tendency on the part of the romanticists to sense nature as sound. The romanticists were all ears; for them the whole of nature reverberated like an enormous cosmic orchestra. When Jean Paul advises 'Before a storm set out an aeolian harp but no burning light,' or when he refers to 'echo, the moonlight of sound,'[1] he indicates how susceptible the age had already become to the softening of visible appearances by infusing them with the spirit of music.

Novalis somewhere suggests that there should be music and not-music just as clearly as there is night and day. The prospect of a mute world could strike terror into the heart of a romanticist. This is illustrated in a little-known cantata by Carl Maria von Weber entitled *Der Erste Ton.* The text, by Rochlitz, opens by describing the creation of the world and all its living things; but everything was silent. (A long pause in the music.) Even God found the silence oppressive so he gave each creature a voice with which to articulate the secrets of its heart. Now the world was alive with the sounds of birds and animals, rivers and waterfalls, the whispering wind, the thunder of the storm, and, above all, the voice of man. As the cantata closes, man raises his voice in a majestic tribute to sound: 'O praise the tone! O tone! [B-flat seventh] O tone! [E-flat major; *pianissimo – crescendo – fortissimo – decrescendo – pianissimo.*]

Silence is rarely provoked by the romanticists, and they seem to have had difficulty in conceiving of a soundless world. 'Even before we were men we heard music,' is a strangely romantic saying attributed to Hebel. For Hoffmann, too, music is a reverberation from the profound and secret depths of some *Urzeit* before the creation of the world. Music, he frequently says, is 'not of this world.' Music rings above man, as in the euphony of 'Ritter Gluck.' It touches the earth as an exalted song. Not only man, but trees, birds, water, and animals sense it and imitate its cadences.

It is the sound of the wind as much as it is a Beethoven symphony. Through subtle synaesthetic exercises these resonances are metamorphosed into shapes and appearances which the poet can describe.

For the romanticists this transcendental musical force found its sweetest expression in the beautiful things of nature. This is where Hoffmann came on the scene. In his earliest writings he anthropomorphized the spirit of music so that it became best expressed in the voice of the beloved in song, and she rather than nature became the symbol of fantasized musical perfection.

As we have seen, Hoffmann fell in love no more than twice in his lifetime. In 1794 at the age of eighteen he fell in love with a married woman. In 1811, a thirty-six-year-old married man, he fell in love even more desperately with his fourteen-year-old singing pupil Julia Marc. His previously dry and tidy diary is now broken with one outcry after another of the *souffrant de l'amour*. Julia is frequently pictured in the diary as the tiny drawing of a butterfly. The Jungian scholar Aniela Jaffé has pointed out the significance of this tiny winged creature; Hoffmann has discovered the flights of which his own soul is capable.[2]

The beloved could now be stolen away – as indeed Julia was stolen from Hoffmann – but she would continue to live in the line of her song as both a divine and sensual presence. Jean Paul is merely one of several writers who have shown how these qualities of physical and spiritual beauty could be combined in one muse. Although a Venus may be physically beautiful, it was only with Christianity and the worship of the Madonna that physical beauty was wedded to beauty of the spirit to produce an ideal of womanhood which was total.[3]

The contemplation of divine beauty is its own reward. Beauty of body adds the fire of desire to the beholder; but if the beloved is to remain true as a symbol of musical perfection she can in no way be possessed. This state of equipoise is almost impossible to achieve, but Hoffmann's own two unconsummated love affairs allowed him to sustain it in an unusually effective manner in the lyric sketch, 'Ombra adorata.' There is a very real danger, however, in 'Don Juan' that Donna Anna is too much of a sensual presence, for she fills the author with a passionate insomnia of tormented dreams and sexual desires. As the spirit of music, she had to die in order to save Hoffmann's whole philosophy. For if the love the artist fixes on his beloved is consummated, the whole excitement of longing for the unattainable is destroyed and the goddess is revealed as clay-footed. The satisfied lover does not sing of his beloved. In this sense Hoffmann's 'Don Juan' reveals that he realized the difficulties of perpetuating such a limiting philosophy.

In his notes for a long-projected novel, Carl Maria von Weber was unable to escape this same problem, though he was fully aware of the betrayal of music it implied. The denouement was to have been brief and banal:

CHAPTER THIRTEEN

He goes into the house, finds the room empty, seats himself at the piano, improvises; unnoticed the daughter comes in, stands behind the piano bench and at the end cries out; as if startled from deepest thoughts he turns and sees – Emilia! ... Emilia lays before the composer her favourite compositions, the ones she loves and cherishes above all others; they are his own, which he had published under a pseudonym, and he plays them splendidly, inspired. Emilia is enchanted by them. He can scarcely withhold from confessing that he is their author.

CHAPTER FOURTEEN

He comes daily to their home, improvises, using certain favourite turns of expression so that Emilia soon recognizes him as her composer; new joy and wonder at his modesty ...

CHAPTER SIXTEEN

Emilia ... overcome with love. Boring love scene.[4]

In Hoffmann's work music changes its sex from feminine to masculine after his discovery of Beethoven; and his own creation of Kreisler, which dates from this same period of his life, is further evidence that he needed to find an outlet for a very different kind of music than that in which he had enshrined Julia. This was partly a consequence of the spectacularly assertive power of Beethoven, which quite overcame the pastoral sounds of the Italian love song. But it is also possible to see it as a consequence of a social change in the role of women which, even though Hoffmann has left no explicit comment on the subject, cannot have left him unaffected.

In the eighteenth century woman was kept apart, hidden. The pleasure she gave was provocative rather than fulfilling. Romance was 'flattery, sighs, daring glances, soft handclasps, secret whispers, dangerous proximity, alluring withdrawal.' By the beginning of the nineteenth century woman had begun to be emancipated. In his book on German Romanticism, Oskar Walzel shows how there was a growing desire that woman should now receive an education; they should come spiritually closer to men and enjoy the same privileges that men do.[5] As Schleiermacher had written: 'Let thyself covet the education, art, wisdom, and honour of men.' Women had begun to have an unparalleled freedom. The drama of love was now on the surface; it was no longer concealed behind closed windows. Women were less defenceless. The struggle of love took place in the drawing rooms and salons where frequently women ruled as queens, not as goddesses.

Clearly Hoffmann preferred the eighteenth-century woman. Baroness Seraphina of 'The Legacy' is a suitable muse precisely because she is an isolated figure in a rough masculine society. At the Baltic castle where she is kept prisoner, even the winds howl and the oceans roar with masculine virility. The new woman engages men as an equal; she is not divine, and the whole troubadour concept of adoration ceases. The woman of the nineteenth century continues to be wooed with music but she ceases to be the physical epiphany of the tender art itself. Just at the point in Hoffmann's work where disillusionment might have entered, the personality of Beethoven provided the key to a bold substitution.

In a fine argument Jean Paul tries to demonstrate how anything with sharp and closed outlines is not romantic: 'Romanticism is beauty without bounds – the beautiful infinite.'[6] The ringing of a bell can be romantic, moonlight can be romantic; for each of these suggests a melting into an illimitable expanse of time and space. Of all the arts, music is the most abstract, and for this reason it held an undisputed position as the most romantic. It became symbolic of that state of longing without fulfilment which the Germans described by the word *Sehnsucht*. For the romanticists, incompleteness, yearning, and unfulfilled aspiration often became goals in themselves:

> Only in longing do we find peace. Yes, that is what peace is: when our mind is not distracted by anything from longing and seeking, when it can find nothing higher than its own longing.[7]

Sehnsucht, which is one of Hoffmann's favourite words, could be translated as *desire* as well as *longing*. But this would debilitate its effectiveness. *Desire* carries with it the connotation of moving towards the possession of something. When gratified, desire is discharged. *Longing* cannot be satisfied, for it implies a continuous and inextinguishable current of energy. It was Walter Scott who, in discussing the work of Hoffmann, remarked: 'The imagination of the reader is to be excited if possible, without being gratified.'[8] Hoffmann chose his words carefully to create this effect. Words like 'inexpressible,' 'mysterious,' 'infinite,' are words with an unlimited extension, open on all sides; and Hoffmann employs them in all his musical descriptions.

If music, for Hoffmann, descended from some higher realm to infuse the world, it follows that whoever would experience its quintessence must rise to meet it. It is clear from all his writings that the composer must go up to some higher realm for his inspirations. In this he seems to be assisted by the tones themselves which catch him and raise him aloft. This image of music sweeping down and raising up the listener is encountered over and over again in Hoffmann, and it is by no means limited to him; it is central with the whole romantic movement. Frequently the soul appears not only to be uplifted but literally stolen away from the body and thrown forcibly towards this far-off realm. Thus in Jean Paul's *Hesperus*: 'Higher and higher rose the dragnet of uplifting tones carrying his captive heart aloft.'[9] And in Wackenroder:

> ... it seemed to him as though his soul had suddenly unfurled great wings and he was being raised above the barren earth; the curtain of clouds before the mortal eye diffused and he soared up into radiant heaven.[10]

Throughout his recorded history man has longed to fly. Prefiguring the achievement itself in the twentieth century, this impulse soared to its greatest heights in the imagination during the nineteenth. The romanticist was uplifted and ennobled by the promise of what was, during his time, still only possible in the world of dreams. Now that the desire to fly has been realized, flight has lost its power to stimulate the imagination. Where the nineteenth-century writer uses images and vocabulary to suggest the enormous and impulsive trajectory of flight, the contemporary commentator seems to have retreated to some inner space of the mind, where impressions bore in on the sensibility rather than draw it out. The contemporary critic's words are intensive rather than extensive, implosive rather than explosive: 'intrigued,' 'convinced,' 'overwhelmed,' 'absorbed.'

The most frequent movement in Hoffmann's imagery is upwards, though often the movement is of an oscillating character (up and down, to and fro). Extension horizontally into space is almost unknown; the swing is up and out. For this reason water and air are the most frequently mentioned elements – and fire is occasionally encountered as well. Seldom if ever is earth mentioned, for this is anti-dynamic, therefore undesirable. And of all the elements air (sky, heavens, clouds) is by far the most frequently mentioned and therefore the most closely implicated with music.

Only one thing dwells above music in the cosmos: truth. Indeed the two are related, for truth can only be attained by the creative artist who, refusing to be beguiled by the world of dreams into which he is drawn, maintains his presence of mind (*Besonnenheit*), and forces his way up to

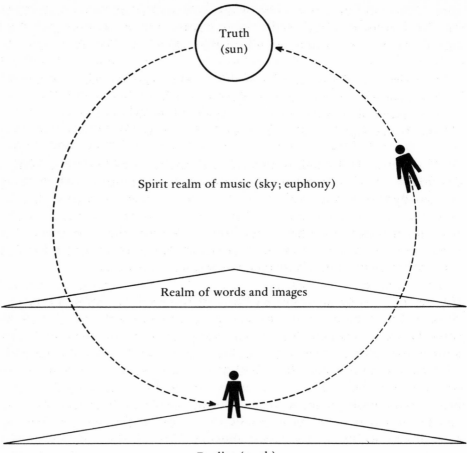

the pinnacle; the insights thus gained are cast into the concrete form of the inspired composition.

Hoffmann's musical cosmology is, therefore, highly graphic and might be presented in the form of the above schema. The highest point in the trajectory of musical experience is attained only by the composer at the apex of inspiration. The music lover is left hovering in a state of suspension, remote alike from his point of departure in the real world and from his visionary goal. It is a world of magnetic fluidity in which the unattainable becomes in itself the highest ideal.

The movement of this state is oscillatory. The images Hoffmann and the others employ are almost always dynamic; they bend, sway, flash. The descriptions vibrate with a hallucinatory ecstasy that is frequently incoherent. This world of the incoherent dream would today be given the name of 'the unconscious.' The artist, then, has the task of informing us of the far-off realm of our own unconscious mind. Aniela Jaffé has written:

> Hoffmann gives the unconscious and its fleeting, apparently meaningless and contemptible presentation in dreams the same value as the world of the sun, stars, and earth. This discovery of the spirit as unbounded nature was not his alone, but belongs to the decisive experience of all romanticists.[11]

Of all music Hoffmann responded with the most enthusiasm to that of Beethoven. Here the conflicts, the abrupt changes of disposition, the exaggerated dynamics, the explosions of sound, all seem to suggest that the even flow of the conscious mind is being interrupted and challenged by deep disturbances. Beethoven was the composer who most effectively challenged the banalities of the real world. He accomplished this at the price of distancing himself further and further from society.

The distance which began to separate the artist from society replaced another form of social distance which was beginning to wither. In the past there had been an enormous social distance separating the prince from his subjects and it was not until the eighteenth century that the ropes which kept the aristocracy apart from the lower classes at dances and concerts in Germany began to come down. With Hoffmann, the musician replaced the prince as a superior being and as the social distance between the classes began to diminish, so much greater became the distance between the artist and society. When Kreisler is improvising at the Röderleins' tea party, society disappears into the vapour of oblivion: 'Occasionally a nose appeared, or two eyes, but they disappeared again at once.' In this way an aristocracy of the soul was established, a coterie of special individuals whose spiritual nobility placed them above the pedestrianism of the real world.

One of Hoffmann's most decisive achievements as a critic was to force on public consciousness the distinction between those who lived for music and those for whom it was merely a diversion. Hoffmann is quite uncompromising in presenting the true artist as a divine luminary. Nowhere does Hoffmann give us a portrait of the ordinary or déclassé musician; his musicians are men of genius or, pushing the spirit past human endurance, of madness. As the spirit of music itself, Johannes Kreisler is the prototype. To Kreisler the world is an 'eternal, inexplicable misunderstanding,' and he lives nourished by music alone. All his attempts to communicate with society are awkward and unrewarding. In the end he, like Beethoven, carries music to a solitary height where it can no longer be disfigured by those around him.

Hoffmann gives us Kreisler and the public at opposite poles and makes no attempt to unify them in a higher synthesis. Had not Jean Paul, in his introduction to the *Fantasiestücke*, warned Hoffmann that his *Kunstliebe* could easily lead to *Menschenhass*? There is something unfinished and unpleasant about Hoffmann's aesthetic philosophy and, while his elevation of the artist is genuine, his denunciation of the philistine is equivocal. He mocks at their dullness, but secretly envies their economic efficiency. An example of this unresolved dichotomy was his friendship with Hippel, whose life, so different from his own, was outwardly successful and rewarding. Another example was his choice of the Mozartian name Amadeus for his artistic work, while for his legal duties he retained the name Theodor in order to preserve his social standing. Hoffmann attempts to force society to recognize the noble vocation of the artist by a hubristic emphasis on the distance separating him from society. However, the grim and sardonic humour that keeps Hoffmann's Kreisler writings alive does not cover up the central sociological problem.

Despite the gravity of the opposition between the artist and society, Hoffmann's general optimism about music is unrestrained. He venerates its past achievements, rejoices in the new dimensions Beethoven has opened up for it, and looks forward expectantly to the future. It is worth noting that by contrast with later romanticists, Hoffmann's whole conception of music is free of melancholy and despair. For the later poet Lenau, the music of Beethoven had become a 'sweet sensation of death'; and in a tortured letter to Hofrätin Reinsbeck Lenau wrote: 'Do you know that sweet despair into which Beethoven carries us?'[12] Hoffmann could never have written that. For Lenau, also, there was certainly an impulsive terror in the music of Beethoven, a frightful knowledge that man is here struggling with the forces of his own destiny and everything stands to be won or lost in the struggle. Hoffmann can only marvel at the protean courage of the composer in combat; he cannot sympathize with his setbacks and misfortunes. Thus Hoffmann, on the brink of the romantic movement, was in the envious position of having been able to regard romanticism as a lifegiving rejuvenation, quite innocent of its destiny as a perilously evil force in the later sentimental forms of expression.

E.T.A. Hoffmann has been our window on the birth of romanticism. Through him we have tried to train our lenses of perception on the subject without recourse to paraphrases from intermediary figures. Hoffmann has here spoken for himself. Like all movements romanticism defines itself in its works; and every age owes it to itself to re-examine the works of the past and try to expose areas of shadow to a new light. This is not always easy. It will be difficult to appreciate the values of overworked vocabulary and unfashionable metaphor. The romanticist's vision of music appreciation as a vividly pictorial flight may seem strangely extravagant today. But these are merely figures of speech, designed to prepare us for initiation to music's incomprehensibly pure and unbearable message. The state of ecstasy achieved with tones cannot be duplicated with words; it can only be intimated, and Hoffmann's writings are an attempt, perhaps the bravest attempt yet made by any critic, to intimate it, for the whole nervous system of his art is fused to that of music itself. As such, his work exemplifies that truest function of criticism which Schumann was later to proclaim: 'The highest criticism is that which leaves an impression identical with the one called forth by the very thing criticized.'[13]

Notes on the Translations

Hoffmann has been translated into English on many occasions, but no systematic attempt has ever been made to translate the bulk of the musical writings. Some of the tales in which music plays a leading role have been translated numerous times, though others have appeared too specialized to attract the translators' interest. Such was the case, for example with 'Don Juan,' no published translation of which existed before 1945, though half-a-dozen translations are now in print. The equally fine 'Ritter Gluck' did not appear in English until 1969, when it was translated by Leonard J. Kent and Elizabeth C. Knight for their collection *Selected Writings of Hoffmann* (2 vols, Chicago, 1969). The same collection contains the first English translation of *Kater Murr.* The field is still open, however, for a more effective translation of the novel. Most of the *Kreisleriana* has never been translated, nor has the extensive body of the music criticism.

It is not easy to render Hoffmann into English without a certain Tennysonianness of speech making an appearance. I have sought merely to keep this under control by abbreviating some of his sentences, permitting only three adjectives at a time to modify any noun, and in the very odd case, adopting more extreme measures to redeem sentences in which the author seems to have completely lost the nerve of his thought. Hoffmann never indented his paragraphs in manuscript and was careless about punctuation. I have taken the liberty, therefore, of breaking the body of the text into shorter sentences and paragraphs than is customary in the German original.

In Hoffmann's style the same overworked vocabulary undergoes minor internal shuffles so that, for instance, the 'ominous feeling of longing' will reappear as 'the feeling of ominous longing.' This opens up questions which only someone with greater knowledge of semantics than I can go into; so I have taken liberties at times to standardize some of these expressions in order that their leitmotif character may be more clearly established. Nor has it been my aim to cover Hoffmann's muse with sand by apologizing for the inadequacies of the English language and punctuating tricky bits of text with the *Urtext* German in square brackets.

CHAPTER 3: RITTER GLUCK
Source: *Werke* 1: 23-32

A literal translation of the original title of this story – 'Ritter Gluck' – would be *Chevalier Gluck* or *Sir Christoph*. Hoffmann scholars disagree on the story's exact date of composition. Although Ellinger assigns it to the Bamberg period, Hans von Müller thinks it was written in Glogau, before the author's arrival in Bamberg. At any rate, it was Hoffmann's first published work of fiction. He sent it to Friedrich Rochlitz, editor of the *Allgemeine Musikalische Zeitung*, on 12 January 1809 together with a note introducing it:

> I am taking the liberty of sending a little story which narrates a real event in Berlin, with the hope that it may prove suitable for the *Musikalische Zeitung*. I have seen similar things in the magazine before; for example, the most interesting account of a madman who could improvise in such a wonderful manner on the clavier.

'Ritter Gluck' was published in the *Allgemeine Musikalische Zeitung* in March 1809. Hoffmann referred to the story as music criticism, and while by strict standards it is not, one may be amazed after reading the story to realize how much commentary on Gluck's music has been introduced without obscuring or diverting the narrative. Hoffmann knew Gluck's music well; and it is interesting that he worked into the story an account of an actual performance of *Armida* in Berlin on 19 February 1808. We may deduce that Gluck's music was on the wane by this time from a review by Hoffmann of Gluck's *Iphigenia in Aulis*, dating from 1810, where he says bitterly:

> As the reviewer went through the piano edition of this work he was gripped by a feeling of grief, for he was convinced once again that the composers of our time, be it as a result of a mistaken attitude to art, or be it through plain imbecility, have abandoned the true *opera seria*, and thus have lost completely the key to the heights that such a wedding of poetry and music can bring to the stage. (*Schriften zur Musik* edited by Friedrich Schnapp, Munich 1963, 61-2)

CHAPTER 5: BARONESS SERAPHINA
Source: *Werke* 3: 182-5

'Das Majorat,' from which the section I have entitled 'Baroness Seraphina' is taken, has been translated in its entirety under different titles. At least two good translations exist in English. Christopher Lazare has entitled it 'The Legacy' in his collection *The Tales of Hoffmann* (London 1946). J.M. Cohen entitles it 'The Deed of Entail' in *Tales from Hoffmann* (London 1951).

CHAPTER 7: OMBRA ADORATA
Source: *Werke* 1: 40-3

On 25 August 1812 Hoffmann entered the words *Ombra adorata* into his diary. Whether he wrote the sketch at this time or not until December of that year after Julia Marc's marriage is not known; but it is clear that the sketch was intended as a homage to her. It was later taken up as part of the collection of *Kreisleriana* fragments. I have been able to locate no previous translation of 'Ombra adorata.'

CHAPTER 9: DON JUAN
Source: *Werke* 1: 72-83

Hoffmann uses the German rather than the Italian title for Mozart's opera. The manuscript of his own 'Don Juan' story was sent to Härtel on 27 January 1813 for consideration for the *Allgemeine Musikalische Zeitung*, and it appeared in that publication on 31 March 1813.

'Don Juan' was written at a time of intense personal tension (Julia Marc had just been married to a Hamburg merchant) and professional upheaval (the Bamberg Theatre was sinking and Hoffmann had been suspended from the variety of executive positions he held there). The author was forced to request Härtel in an accompanying letter to send him 25 thalers as the magazine was, for the moment, the only source of income left to him. On the edge of Hoffmann's letter Härtel jotted 'will send it to him' and we know from Hoffmann's diary that it was received.

According to Hoffmann's Bamberg friend Kunz, Julia Marc was strongly identified in the mind of the author with Donna Anna. If we allow this, it is not unreasonable to assume that Hoffmann identified himself with Don Giovanni and Julia's fiancée with the frigid lover Don Ottavio. (See Hans Dahmen *E.T.A. Hoffmanns Weltanschauung* Marburg 1929, 71.)

The 'travelling enthusiast' is Hoffmann himself. The name of the travelling enthusiast's closest friend is Theodore. Theodore is also one of Hoffmann's own names. This splitting of the personality into two friends is an example of the 'double' complex frequently found in Hoffmann's writings; and it comes up later in Schumann as well, in his *Davidsbündler* group.

The first translation of 'Don Juan' (under the Mozart title 'Don Giovanni') was that by Sabilla Novello, made in the 1860s but unpublished until 1956. (See 'Mozart and Hoffmann's "Don Giovanni" – An Unpublished Translation of Hoffmann's Novelle,' in John Andrews, ed. *Proceedings of the Leeds Philosophical and Literary Society* (Literary and Historical Section) vol 8, part 1, May 1956.) Although it lacks verbal felicities, Sabilla's translation does not lack prudery, and contains a number of exciting euphemisms. The line which describes Donna Anna's kiss as a 'long-held note of eternal passionate longing' is omitted entirely. Altogether too daring.

Oddly enough the first published translation of 'Don Juan' did not appear until 1945, this being the translation by Abraham Loft in *The Musical Quarterly* (31, 1945: 504-16). However, since that time it has been retranslated numerous times and has begun to appear in all the anthologies.

CHAPTER 11: BEETHOVEN'S INSTRUMENTAL MUSIC
Source: *Werke* 1: 48-55

The essay 'Beethoven's Instrumental Music' was compiled by Hoffmann from two reviews he had written for the *Allgemeine Musikalische Zeitung* of the fifth symphony and the two piano trios, opus 70, which originally appeared in the magazine in July 1810 and March 1813 respectively. The revised essay became part of the *Kreisleriana* sequence of the *Fantasiestücke in Callots Manier*, hence the inclusion of Johannes Kreisler's name. In this version it has become by far Hoffmann's most celebrated piece of music criticism and has appeared previously in an abbreviated English version in Oliver Strunk's *Source Readings in Music History* (New York 1950, 775-81).

CHAPTER 13: ANCIENT AND MODERN CHURCH MUSIC
Source: *Werke* 6: 148-56

The core of the essay 'Ancient and Modern Church Music' comes from Hoffmann's review of Beethoven's Mass in C, which appeared in the *Allgemeine Musikalische Zeitung* in July 1813. The extensive analytical portions of the original review were removed and the central argument was considerably expanded when Hoffmann reprinted the work in his *Serapionsbrü-der* collection. The work exists in English only in a gauche translation entitled *Serapion Brethren* by Major Alex. Ewing, in two volumes (London 1886).

CHAPTERS 15, 17, 19:
OF KAPELLMEISTER JOHANNES KREISLER'S MUSICAL SORROWS;
REFLECTIONS ON THE HIGH VALUE OF MUSIC;
KREISLER'S MUSICAL-POETICAL CLUB
Source: *Werke* 1: 35-40, 43-8, 280-3

'Johannes Kreislers, des Kapellmeisters musikalische Leiden' originally appeared in the *Allgemeine Musikalische Zeitung* on 26 September 1810. 'Gedanken über den hohen Wert der Musik' appeared in the same publication on 29 July 1812. 'Kreislers musikalisch-poetischer Klub' did not appear until the *Fantasiestücke* collection of 1815, where, together with the other pieces, it formed part of the *Kreisleriana*. So far as I have been able to determine, this important cycle of writings has never been translated into English.

E. T. A. Hoffmann as Composer

You have no idea how it tortures me to go against my resolution and desire. My studies proceed slowly and sadly. I must force myself to become a lawyer.

These are the words Hoffmann wrote to his friend Hippel on 1 May 1795 after he had decided to pursue law instead of music as a profession. But it was a resolution he was unable to keep, for a large portion of his life was devoted exclusively to music and at no time does he appear to have been totally without music of some kind. Though the current of his life was unstable and the exuberance of his creative faculties was intensely varied, music remained the continuous thread that bound his existence together. Up to his thirty-third year his chief artistic productions were his compositions, and although his activity as a composer diminished sharply after the discovery of his literary talents, he continued to write occasional compositions up to 1820, two years before his death.

This book has in no way been a study of Hoffmann as a composer. But the inevitable question must have occurred frequently to the reader interested in Hoffmann's writings about music: what was Hoffmann's own music like? And he deserves some kind of answer to this question, especially since I have tried to present Hoffmann's cosmology of music not merely as the vagary of a literary man for whom music meant a great deal, but as an authoritative expression by one who understood the birth of romantic music from the intimate point of view of a participant.

There is no doubt that Hoffmann wanted above all things to be a great composer. It is a repeated confession to his friends. But his talent seems to have been easily adapted to different forms of expression, and one is amazed on reading his diaries to discover how quickly his energies could be transferred from one medium to another. His talent was also combustive; there are no barren periods in his life. From his diaries we know that he worked fastidiously at his compositions but was assisted by a considerable fluency of expression. Considering the many kinds of activity in which he indulged, he may be considered a prolific composer.

The most complete and recent list of his compositions is that given by Hans Ehinger in *E.T.A. Hoffmann als Musiker und Musikschriftsteller* (Olten and Cologne 1954, 214-21). From this list we can see that he wrote no fewer than eight operas and *Singspiele: Die Maske*; *Scherz, List und Rache*; *Die lustigen Musikanten*; *Der Kanonikus von Mailand*; *Liebe und Eifersucht*; *Der Trank der Unsterblichkeit*; *Aurora*, and *Undine*. Of these the last two operas are the most accomplished, and of the two *Undine* is undeniably the finest. In addition to these works, there is a large quantity of miscellaneous stage and ballet music; the Mass in D major and the *Miserere* in B-flat minor, both of these scored for soloists, mixed chorus, organ, and orchestra; *Sechs geistliche Chöre* for a cappella chorus; several groups of *canzonettas* and other assorted vocal works such as arias and hunting songs; the Symphony in E-flat; four piano sonatas; a piano trio with strings; a quintet for harp and strings; and numerous other pieces of incidental orchestral and chamber music.

Much of this music is still in manuscript, the largest collection being that in the Deutsche Staatsbibliothek in Berlin. An ambitious attempt was made in 1922 by Gustav Becking to publish the *Musikalische Werke* but the edition (Kistner und Siegel, Leipzig) was discontinued after three volumes appeared. The works published were: *Vier Sonaten für Pianoforte*, *Quintett für Harfe oder Pianoforte und Streichquartett*, and *Trio für Klavier, Violine und Violoncello* (as parts one and two of volume two) and *Sechs geistliche Chöre a cappella*. A piano edition of the important opera *Undine* was published by Hans Pfitzner in 1906 (Peters Edition, Leipzig). Numerous other Hoffmann compositions, or fragments of compositions, have been published in the twentieth century, among the more important of which are: the *Agnus Dei* from the Mass in D, the hymns 'Ave maris stella' and 'O sanctissima,' and the duet 'Ah che mi manca l'anima' in Hans von Müller's *Das Kreislerbuch* (Leipzig 1902); *Türkische Musik* in *Die Musik* (vol 11, supplement to no 18, June 1912); *Trio für Klavier, Violine und Violoncello* in *Zeitschrift für Musikwissenschaft* (vol 2, no 1, 1919); *Sonate und Andante für Klavier* (Drei Masken Verlag, Munich 1921); the text and musical selections from *Die Maske*, edited by Friedrich Schnapp (Berlin 1923); a duet from *Aurora* in *Zeitschrift für Musikwissenschaft* (4: 550-2); the prelude to the second act of the same work in a piano edition in Paul Greeff's book *E.T.A. Hoffmann als Musiker* (Köln und Krefeld 1948); *Nachtgesang* in *Mitteilung der E.T.A. Hoffmann-Gesellschaft* (no 11, 1964). In 1971 the firm of Otto Harrassowitz of Wiesbaden announced an ambitious plan to bring out twelve volumes of Hoffmann's music under the title *Ausgewählte musikalische Werke*, edited by Georg von Dadelsen. In that year the first volume appeared, consisting of the first act of *Undine*. Other works to be included are the stage works *Die lustigen Musikanten, Liebe und Eifersucht, Das Kreuz an der Ostsee*; the Mass in D major, the *Miserere* in B-flat minor, the Symphony in E-flat major and numerous other chamber and choral compositions.

It has been difficult for critics to dissociate Hoffmann the author from Hoffmann the composer. As a result, exaggerated claims have frequently been made for the music, chiefly by literary people whose musical opinions are often untrustworthy. When, for instance, Berlioz disparagingly referred to Hoffmann's music (without, incidentally, having heard any of it) as 'writer's music,' it was not a musician who sprang to its defence but Hoffmann's French translator Champfleury, who pronounced, rather irresponsibly, that there was more melody in the first of Hoffmann's *Sei Duettini Italiani* than in Berlioz's combined output.

Anyone expecting to find Hoffmann's music infused with the same turbulent and adventurous spirit that characterizes his literary compositions will be disappointed. This disappointment, it may be noted, has been apparent all along with Hoffmann's admirers. Hieronymus Truhn, who in 1839 arranged the first posthumous concert of Hoffmann's music, wrote of the experience in *Der Freihafen* (3, 1839: 79):

> Whoever opens a Hoffmann score expecting to be greeted by the ghost-like spirits that haunt the *Phantasie* and *Nachtstücke* will be terribly disappointed. His music never approaches the pulsing fury of Weber, Marschner, or Lindpainter, or the tragedy of Loewe's ballads. Rather it perpetuates – even *Undine* – the spirit of the classical masters, of Mozart and Cherubini, and is always respectful of the rules of pleasant harmony and formal beauty. Hoffmann the poet and Hoffmann the composer are two completely different persons.

Those who have tried to assess Hoffmann's compositions independently of his literary achievement have always been forced to the conclusion that with the possible exception of the opera *Undine*, which was somewhat influential in the history of music, the level of achievement in general, while as high perhaps as that of composers such as Cramer, Pleyel, Reicha, or Hummel, was certainly no higher. Hoffmann's compositions seem not to have been very widely circulated and we know that he experienced much difficulty in getting them accepted for publication, as illustrated by Nägeli's refusal of his 'Grosse Fantasie für das Klavier.' Aside from a few hunting songs for men's chorus, only two of his works were published during his own lifetime, the *Tre Canzonette Italiane* (1807-8) and the *Sei Duettini Italiani* (1812). One of the few reviews of Hoffmann's music by a contemporary is this anonymous review of his *Tre Canzonette* which appeared in the *Allgemeine Musikalische Zeitung* on 23 June 1808.

> Men who not only are good composers but also understand the art of singing as does Herr Hoffmann, music director at Bamberg, gain for themselves a tribute from all understanding souls for little compositions like those being reviewed here, in which this talent is stimulated and developed. From this statement it will be obvious that the reviewer has found his task uncommonly pleasant. All three pieces, but chiefly the second and the third, have simple, flowing, and pleasing melodies which are nevertheless in no way insipid or empty. These melodies are interlaced carefully without becoming difficult, affected or unnatural; and the third piece possesses a quite special charm with its naïve, rather comical tone. The accompaniment is neither empty nor overlaid; it supports both the singers and the mood of the whole, just as it should in this kind of song ... What more could we expect of these little blooms strewn in our path?

Little blooms then, pleasant and accomplished, but in no way startling.

Hoffmann's love of Italian song is evidenced in many of his stories. In 'The Legacy' Baroness Seraphina sings songs by Abbé Steffani. In 'The Fermata' the two Italian singers inspire the author so much with their duets that he delivers up to flames his own attempts at writing toccatas and fugues as being the work of a contrapuntal fossil. The heroine of 'Ombra adorata' sings an aria Crescentini's opera *Romeo and Juliet.*

Hoffmann's own *canzonettas*, duets, and arias are much influenced by the style of these Italians. They also show affinities to the Berlin School of song writing, with its masters Reichardt and Zelter. There is, in fact, some speculation as to whether Hoffmann may have at one time actually studied with Reichardt. As indicated in chapter six, this attachment to the romantic song style was a natural enthusiasm for one who believed music to be a tangible symbol of the beloved. Even after he had ceased most of his compositional activity he continued to view these works with great affection and mentioned them as favourites of Kreisler and Julia Benzon in *Kater Murr*. But Hoffmann also possessed a remarkable ability for self-criticism and caricature, and it may be observed that the very same kind of song literature is held up to ridicule in *Kater Murr* through the buffoonery of the cats. There is no denying that Hoffmann's greatest failing as a composer was his melodic poverty, and perhaps this accounted for his continual praise of melody as the highest attribute of music. One of Hoffmann's most perceptive critics (Paul Margis in *E.T.A. Hoffmann: Eine psychographische Individualanalyse* Leipzig 1911, 98) has noticed a simi-

Opening of the last of the *Tre Canzonette Italiane*

lar melodic deficiency in Hoffmann's few poems, for the rhyming is found to be gauche and contrived.

In attempting to discover the influences in Hoffmann's music, one must bear in mind that music crept slowly and haphazardly across Europe at his time. It was, for example, not until four years after their publication that Beethoven's fifth and sixth symphonies were reviewed by Hoffmann for the *Allgemeine Musikalische Zeitung*, and even then it is debatable whether the reviewer had ever heard them performed. Despite his championship of Beethoven, Hoffmann's own music was less influenced by this master than one could have wished. The Beethoven influence is there, and it continued

Opening of the *De profundis*, the second of the *Sechs geistliche Chöre a cappella*

to grow in the more mature works, but a much more dominant and pervasive influence is that of Haydn, Mozart, and the classical school. Above all, Mozart was his model. Friedrich Rochlitz has narrated in his *Für Freunde der Tonkunst* (Leipzig 1830, 2: 15-16) how Hoffmann, in setting about to write a *Requiem* mass, imitated Mozart as carefully as possible:

> It is the same length as the Mozart work, conceived in the same way, and as far as Hoffmann was able, composed in the same style. How close it comes to the original after which it was worked!

Next to the influence of Mozart and Beethoven, that of Cherubini and the Gluck school (Spontini) is felt. In the choral works, as may be expected from the argument of 'Ancient and Modern Church Music,' there is evidence of influence from the religious music of the Italian baroque, particularly from Durante, Lotti, and Leo. Hoffmann had had a good chance to hear this music, as well as that of Palestrina, in the cloistral churches of Plock. These influences are particularly strong in the *Sechs geistliche Chöre a cappella*, though this in no way spoils the beauty and obvious sincerity of the work, one of Hoffmann's most successful.

Despite the derivative quality of his work, Hoffmann was a composer of integrity, for he seldom descended to produce potboilers for the popular market. Only once or twice was he guilty of this: the composition *Die Schlacht bei Leipzig* obviously caters to a public demand for battle symphonies – a demand which even Beethoven was unable to withstand – though, significantly, Hoffmann's isolated exercise in this *Schlachtsinfonie* genre was signed with the pseudonym Arnulph Vollweiller. Other than this, Hoffmann's intentions, like his models, were beyond reproach.

The *Miserere* is the largest of the choral works and is in many ways the most accomplished. Although it owes much to Mozart it is less slavishly imitative of this master than other works, and one critic (Edgar Istel in *Die Blütezeit der musikalischen Romantik in Deutschland* Berlin 1921) goes so far as to call it 'absolutely original. Particularly fine is the way in which, at the beginning of the five-part chorus Hoffmann looks back to the first movement, takes up its themes and works them out on fresh lines.'

Hoffmann's precocious admiration for J.S. Bach has been pointed out in chapter sixteen. A stylistic influence of the Bach era is noticeable in many of his compositions where extended contrapuntal interludes intrude between lyric sections, occasionally, unfortunately, in a mechanical fashion. This is the case in particular in the piano sonatas where these contrapuntal excursions, while skilful in themselves and unusual for the period, clash ineffectually with the lyrical sections.

Indisputably, Hoffmann's greatest single compositional achievement was his opera *Undine*, practically the last piece of music he wrote. *Undine* was the only work by Hoffmann that was influential for the future. The plot of the opera adheres closely to de la Motte Fouqué's celebrated *Märchen*. The opera was performed at the Royal Theatre in Berlin on 3 August 1816 and was repeated thirteen more times before the disastrous fire that burned the theatre down together with all the costumes and sets for the production.

The composer Carl Maria von Weber attended several of the performances and wrote an enthusiastic letter to his fiancée telling her how he had rushed from the theatre after hearing the work for the first time to thank and congratulate the composer. Weber's review of *Undine* appeared in the *Allgemeine Musikalische Zeitung*, on 19 March 1817, and it was enthusiastic:

The whole work is one of the most ingenious that our time has given us. It is a magnificent product of an intimate familiarity with the subject brought about by a profound reflection and calculation of the effects of all the materials of art; and it is marked as a fine work by its beautiful and intimate melodic conception.

Weber, however, had two minor complaints: 'the predilection for little short figures which tend to lack variety and obscure the melody' and 'the partiality for ... diminished-seventh chords' – a valid criticism, though Weber was scarcely the one to point it out.

One interesting feature of the opera – perhaps what Weber was referring to as the 'short figures' – was the use of the recurring themes to identify characters or situations, a principle Weber was later to employ himself, and one which was to be fully developed into the leitmotif principle by another Hoffmann admirer, Richard Wagner.

The orchestration of *Undine* is most effective. One observes in Kühleborn's aria an uncommon use of the deep woodwinds in the accompaniment – a notable feature of Weber's operas also. The use of *pianissimo* brass in the opera is unique for the time, and the divided strings – particularly the celli – make for an effectively rich and ominous colour. The score is, in fact, outstanding for its orchestral colour, especially if one compares it with other works such as Spohr's much more timidly scored *Faust* of the same year, or even Lortzing's *Undine* of 1845.

Let Hans Pfitzner, who edited the work, pass final comment:

> The overture and the large ensemble numbers have been put down with a confident hand and testify to someone well-acquainted with musical form. Very occasionally one encounters sloppy voice-leading, an unintentional coarseness, or something that one might venture to call tastelessness ... Those who see Hoffmann only as a conjurer of devilish pranks will be greatly surprised by the melodic content of the opera, for many of the songs could be taken for pure Mozart ... And even if *Undine* could not be brought completely back to life, it continues to play a role backstage in music history, perhaps a greater role than generally suspected, and presents itself in such an ingenious and professional garb that it could be displayed in the best of circles. (Hans Pfitzner: *E.T.A. Hoffmanns 'Undine'* in *Vom musikalischen Drama* 2nd edition, Munich and Leipzig 1920)

German critics are still disputing precisely when German romantic opera came into existence. There are those who attribute its birth to Weber with his *Der Freischütz*; but the majority place its beginning several years earlier with *Undine*. If not a perfect expression of romanticism in opera, *Undine* certainly played no small part in inspiring Weber to exploit fully the themes it suggested so clearly.

As the whole mosaic of nineteenth-century music begins to fall into place and the critic has the benefit of an overview, the true highlights of the period stand out and the rest is relegated to incidental detail and shadow. For every true artist there are a hundred superfluities and only time has the power to disengage them. Ultimately the Beethovens and the Schuberts stand out in unflattering relief from the Hummels and the Hoffmanns.

Dannreuther, writing at the end of the nineteenth century, has the picture spread before him, and holding up Hoffmann to Beethoven he finds him slightly ridiculous, merely a gifted amateur. But such a conclusion is valid only when one takes a long view of history. To move in close on the age is to observe Hoffmann as a musician very much on the inside, plotting along with others a stormy and combustible future for the arts. That his own role in this plot was not as a composer but as a critic and writer was Hoffmann's own deepest regret.

E. T. A. Hoffmann's Legacy

In the introduction to a French translation of Hoffmann's tales in 1874, Théophile Gautier wrote: 'Hoffmann is popular in France, more popular than in Germany.' The French critics picked up Hoffmann soon after his death and compared him favourably with Pascal, Diderot, Rousseau, even Homer; and French writers soon began to cultivate the *genre Hoffmannesque*. But Hoffmann has also left a strong impression on world literature. His mark is evident in the work of Hans Christian Andersen, in Gogol and Dostoevski, in Hawthorne, Carlyle, and most conspicuously in the mystery and detective stories of Poe.

Equally strong is the impression Hoffmann's writings have made on musicians. An interesting study could be made of the precise ways in which the fictitious figure of Johannes Kreisler affected the behaviour of real composers such as Schumann, Berlioz, Wagner, or Wolf. They surrendered themselves more than a little to the image of this dispossessed genius and cultivated his subtle and fiendish philosophy to a point at least where Oscar Wilde's aphorism about nature imitating art begins to take on meaning. Brahms, too, payed homage to Kreisler by signing his first compositions Johannes Kreisler, Junior, and, as we have seen, for years he kept a notebook entitled *Des jungen Kreislers Schatzkästlein* in which he copied out his favourite sayings about music.

Many of Hoffmann's stories have suggested subjects for opera and ballet. The story of Tchaikowsky's *Nutcracker* ballet is that of Hoffmann's 'Nussknacker und Mausekönig,' and the story of Delibes' *Coppélia* is taken from 'Der Sandmann.' Busoni's opera *Die Brautwahl* is based on Hoffmann's tale of that name, and Hindemith's opera *Cardillac* is based on 'Das Fräulein von Scuderi.' Perhaps the most celebrated of the Hoffmann-inspired compositions is Offenbach's *Les Contes d'Hoffmann*. In 1851 Jules Barbier and Michel Carré had published *Les Contes d'Hoffmann*, 'drame

fantastique en cinq actes.' They had displayed great skill in binding together elements from 'Der Sandmann,' 'Das verlorene Spiegelbild,' and
'Rat Krespel,' placing the whole in the familiar setting of the 'Lutter and
Wegner' wine room; and in 1881 Offenbach took this drama as the basis
for his opera text.

Of all musicians, none were more caught in the Hoffmann spell than
Schumann and Wagner. On 3 May 1838 Schumann wrote: 'Spent three
wonderful spring days waiting for a letter from Clara; then composed the
Kreisleriana in four days. Entirely new worlds are opening up for me.' The
Kreisleriana piano cycle (opus 16) attempts to suggest some of the many
moods of Kreisler, and Schumann regarded it as one of his finest youthful
works. To Clara Wieck he wrote: 'Do you sometimes play my *Kreisleriana*?
Some of the pages contain a truly savage love.' Schumann claimed to have
discovered the person Hoffmann had used as a model for Johannes Kreisler; he was a dilapidated musician named Johann Ludwig Böthmer (see
Robert Schumanns Jugendbriefe Leipzig 1885, 254) but this assertion is
quite unfounded.

From Hoffmann's writings on music Schumann inherited a sense of passionate subjective criticism and the technique of approaching a work simultaneously on many levels. When Schumann began his work as a critic in
1831 with the celebrated article on Chopin's opus 2, he had already invented the principal personalities of his *Davidsbündler*: Eusebius, Florestan, and Master Raro. This technique of criticism through discussion had
already been well developed, above all by Hoffmann in his *Serapionsbrüder*. Here we have the author's personality split into a number of sharply
defined characters, each of whom could present a different point of view.
The principal characters of the Serapion's brotherhood are Lothar, the
realist, Cyprian, the total romanticist and mystic, Ottmar, the sceptic, and
Theodore who, as a composer, is the most lyrical and impassioned of the
group. The figures of Schumann's *Davidsbündler* are similarly contrasted:
Florestan is impulsive, passionate, humourless; Eusebius is dreamy and reflective; while Master Raro appears as the reasonable mediator between
these extremes. In both cases these figures are merely projections of the
author's own personality and reflect intense contradictions within the
mind, contradictions which suggested to Hoffmann a future of insanity for
his Kreisler, contradictions which led Schumann literally to this state.

Hoffmann's influence over Wagner was equally decisive, if less concentrated. Although the two artists never met, while Hoffmann was in Leipzig in 1813 he had played through the score of *Undine* on the piano for
Adolph Wagner, the uncle of the composer. Richard Wagner seems to have
come under Hoffmann's influence as early as 1827 when he was about

fourteen years old. He later narrated how reading stories such as 'Ritter Gluck' had actually inspired him to compose:

> I was then in my sixteenth year, and on fire with the maddest mysticism, chiefly from perusing Hoffmann's works. I had visions by day in semi-slumber in which the tonic, third, and dominant seemed to take on a living form and revealed a mighty significance to me. But the notes I wrote down were stark with folly. ('Autobiographische Skizze' in *Gesammelte Schriften und Dichtungen* Leipzig 1907, 1: 6)

Wagner later learned to derive a more profitable kind of inspiration from Hoffmann by employing the tales as a source for opera libretti. Both *Tannhäuser* and *Meistersinger* borrow extensive ideas from Hoffmann tales, the former from 'Der Kampf der Sänger' and the latter from 'Meister Martin der Küfner.' In his autobiography Wagner acknowledged textual indebtedness for *Tannhäuser* to both Hoffmann and Ludwig Tieck:

> If all that I regarded as essentially German had hitherto drawn me with ever-increasing force and compelled me to its eager pursuit, I here found it suddenly presented to me in the simple outlines of a legend, based upon the old and well-known ballad of 'Tannhäuser.' True, its elements were already familiar to me from Tieck's version in his *Phantasus*. But his conception of the subject had flung me back into the fantastic regions created in my mind at an earlier period by Hoffmann, and I should certainly never have been tempted to exact the framework of a dramatic work from his elaborate story. The point in this popular pamphlet which had so much weight with me was that it brought 'Tannhäuser,' if only by a passing hint, into touch with 'The Minstrel's War on the Wartburg.' I had some knowledge of this also from Hoffmann's account in his *Serapionsbrüder*. But I felt that the writer had only grasped the old legend in a distorted form, and therefore endeavoured to gain a closer acquaintance with the true aspect of this attractive story. (*My Life* London 1911, 260)

We have no recorded utterance by Wagner that he consciously employed the plot of 'Meister Martin' for his *Meistersinger* and indeed only the bare outlines of Hoffmann's story have been preserved. The setting of 'Meister Martin' is sixteenth-century Nuremberg; the plot concerns the fate of a beautiful girl who can be won in marriage by the suitor meeting certain specific conditions imposed by her father, the master cooper, Martin. The public singing is only an incidental detail in the Hoffmann story, but Wagner, for obvious reasons, expanded it to form the central theme of his drama.

Wagner also drew a third libretto idea from Hoffmann. This was the *Bergwerke zu Falun*, which he produced not for himself but for the composer Dessauer. He describes the undertaking:

> ... Dessauer obtained the promise of a ... commission, and he now offered me two hundred francs to provide him with a ... plot, and one congenial to his hypochondriacal temperament.
>
> To meet this wish I ransacked my brain for recollection of Hoffmann, and quickly decided to work up his 'Bergwerke zu Falun.' The moulding of this fascinating and marvellous material succeeded as admirably as I could wish. Dessauer also felt convinced that the topic was worth his while to set to music. (*My Life* 261)

Passing attention should also be drawn to Wagner's stories 'Die Pilgerfahrt zu Beethoven' and 'Ein Ende in Paris,' both of which are purely Hoffmannesque tales.

Hoffmann's influence over composers has perhaps exhausted itself today. If he continues to live in music history it will be primarily for the valuable record he provided of the musical society of his own day, and for his lofty musical ideals which found their best expression in the figure of Johannes Kreisler. Hoffmann's legacy extends over the whole of the romantic era, but beyond this it could scarcely be expected to travel.

Notes

CHAPTER ONE

1 *Flegeljahre* quoted from Johannes Brahms *Des jungen Kreislers Schatzkästlein* Berlin 1909, entry 364
2 *Franz Sternbalds Wanderungen: Eine altdeutsche Geschichte* 1798; see *Ludwig Tiecks Schriften* 28 vols, Berlin 1828-54, 16: 84
3 Jean Paul *Vorschule der Ästhetik, Werke* Munich 1960, 5: 92
4 *Die Automate, Werke* 6: 95
5 *A.W. Schlegels Werke* Leipzig 1846-7, 9: 13
6 August Schlegel first coined this colourful phrase, later picked up by many others, including Goethe.
7 See *Heinrich von Kleists Werke* 5 vols, Leipzig and Vienna 1904-5, 5: 429
8 See *Ludwig Tiecks Schriften* 16: 243
9 *Novalis Werke* Munich 1969, 527
10 Friedrich von Schelling *Philosophie der Kunst* in *Werke* Berlin 1845, 5: 382
11 *System des transcendentalischen Idealismus* ibid 4: 627
12 *Philosophie der Kunst* ibid 5: 369
13 Robert Schumann quoted from Oliver Strunk *Source Readings in Music History* New York 1950, 827
14 Artur Schopenhauer *Die Welt als Wille und Vorstellung* Leipzig 1819, 1: 340

CHAPTER TWO

1 Immanuel Kant *Anthropologie, Werke* Frankfurt am Main 1964, 6: 400, note
2 Details of musical life in Königsberg, including the newspaper clippings, come from Hermann Güttler *Königsberger Musikkultur im 18. Jahrhundert* Kassel 1925. Güttler shows that by 1776, for example, concerts had become weekly affairs and were given on Sundays. A subscription list of ticket holders to attend Friedrich Ludwig Benda's comic opera *Louise* (1791) ran to 320 names. With reference to the 1785 newspaper announcement, it should be known that ladies escorted by gentlemen were admitted to concerts without charge, as were visitors and travellers – a fact also noted by Carl Maria von Weber in his *Ideen zu einer musikalischen Topographie Deutschlands* 1811.

It is probable that the music of J.S. Bach was quite well known in Königsberg in the eighteenth century, due to the presence there of Carl Gottlieb Richter (1728-1809), a Berliner who had come from C.P.E. Bach's circle to Königsberg in 1761. To gather from descriptions in *Kater Murr*, which are probably autobiographical, Hoffmann (Kreisler) made the acquaintance of J.S. Bach's music at an early age, and his decisive respect for Bach would seem to date from childhood. Hoffmann himself studied the organ with the Königsberg organist Christian Podbielski (1740-92).

3 *E.T.A. Hoffmanns Briefwechsel* edited by Hans von Müller and Friedrich Schnapp, 3 vols, Munich 1967-9, 1: 62

4 See Hippel's *Erinnerungen an Hoffmann* published in Julius Eduard Hitzig *Aus Hoffmanns Leben und Nachlass* 2 vols, Berlin 1823.

5 *E.T.A. Hoffmann im persönlichen und brieflichen Verkehr* edited by Hans von Müller, Berlin 1912, 1: 26-7

6 Letter to Hippel, 28 February 1804, *Briefwechsel* 1: 182

7 The essay was entitled 'Sendschreiben eines Klostergeistlichen an seinen Freund in der Hauptstadt.' It was published in Kotzebue's magazine, *Der Freimüthige*, 9 September 1803.

8 This is part of Hitzig's description of Warsaw. See his *E.T.A. Hoffmanns Leben und Nachlass*, revised and enlarged edition, 5 vols, Stuttgart 1839, 3: 231-3.

9 Letter to Hippel, 23 December 1808, *Briefwechsel* 1: 254

10 Friedrich Rochlitz *Für Freunde der Tonkunst* Leipzig 1830, 2: 18-21

11 Baron Max Maria von Weber *Carl Maria von Weber: The Life of an Artist* translated by J. Palgrave Simpson, 2 vols, London 1865, 1: 190-1. On 3 March 1811, Hoffmann noted in his diary: 'Made the acquaintance of the composer Carl Maria von Weber,' and on the following day he wrote: 'Spent a very pleasant evening – Weber.'

12 Julius Eduard Hitzig *E.T.A. Hoffmanns Leben und Nachlass* 5: 18-20

13 Carl Friedrich Kunz [Z. Funck] *Aus dem Leben zweier Dichter* Leipzig 1836, 1: 1-3. Carl Friedrich Kunz, a Bamberg wine merchant and proprietor of a book store, was one of Hoffmann's closest friends in Bamberg, though it would appear they had a falling out later in life. Kunz was to prove himself an unworthy confidant and after Hoffmann's death sought to exploit his friendship with the author, even to the point of possibly forging correspondence and other documentation.

14 For much of the material of this inquiry section I am indebted to Paul Margis's exhaustive study *E.T.A. Hoffmann: Eine psychographische Individualanalyse* Leipzig 1911. It should be pointed out parenthetically that the information concerning Hoffmann's sense of pitch comes from the review of the *première* of Weber's *Freischütz*, long thought to be by Hoffmann, but now seriously questioned. See Wolfgang Kron *Die angeblichen Freischütz-Kritiken E.T.A. Hoffmanns* Munich 1957.

15 Rochlitz also testifies that Hoffmann was especially good at improvisation. When the Danish poet Adam Oehlenschläger visited Berlin he met Hoffmann at a literary gathering, which he described thus: 'It was a very enjoyable evening; for among other things Fouqué had recited while Hoffmann had seated himself at the piano and accompanied the narration, depicting all the shocking, warlike, tender and moving things with tones, and doing it splendidly' (Adam Oehlenschläger *Briefe in die Heimat, auf einer Reise durch Deutschland und Frankreich* translated from Danish by Georg Lotz, Altona 1820, 2: 244).

16 *Werke* 1: 61

17 The diary entries come from *E.T.A. Hoffmanns Tagebücher und literarische Entwürfe* edited by Hans von Müller, Berlin 1915, vol 1.

18 Ibid, diary entries for 5 and 16 February 1811, 6 January 1811, 25 February 1811, 8 March 1811, and 17 January 1812
19 Carl Friedrich Kunz [Z. Funck] *Aus dem Leben zweier Dichter* Leipzig 1836, 1: 15
20 *E.T.A. Hoffmanns Tagebücher*, diary entry for 18 February 1811
21 Ibid, diary entry for 9 May 1813
22 Letter to Kunz, 20 July 1813, *Briefwechsel* 1: 399
23 *E.T.A. Hoffmanns Tagebücher,* diary entries for 1809
24 Thomas Carlyle's translation of 'Der goldene Topf' may be found in *Tales from Hoffmann* translated by various hands and edited by J.M. Cohen, London 1951.

CHAPTER THREE

1 Notes on the translations are given in appendix A.
2 A light opera by Friedrich Heinrich Himmel (1765-1814)

CHAPTER FOUR

1 Novalis *Werke und Briefe* Munich 1953, 439
2 Franz Koch's harmonica concert is described in *Hesperus* in considerable detail. See Jean Paul *Werke* Munich 1960, 1: 944 ff. An English translation of this section can be found in Oliver Strunk *Source Readings in Music History* New York 1950, 769-74.
3 *Vorschule der Ästhetik, Werke* Munich 1960, 5: 88. See also Strunk *Source Readings* 746.
4 Hoffmann's attack on the fabricators of the Mozart story occurs in the 'Höchst zerstreute Gedanken' portion of the *Kreisleriana, Werke* 1: 57.
5 *Das Euphon* was also a musical instrument invented by Ghadni in 1799 in which tones were sounded by means of glass tubes, though Hoffmann, who writes *der Euphon*, can scarcely have had this in mind here.
6 *Der Jubelsenior (Vierter Offizieller Bericht)* in Jean Paul *Werke* 4: 495

CHAPTER SIX

1 *Franz Sternbalds Wanderungen, Ludwig Tiecks Schriften* Berlin 1828-54, 16: 411-12
2 *E.T.A. Hoffmann im persönlichen und brieflichen Verkehr* edited by Hans von Müller, Berlin 1912, 1: 143. The attribution of the song 'Forget Me Not' (*Vergissmeinnicht*) to Mozart is incorrect.
3 *Lebensansichten des Katers Murr* in *Werke* 9: 144
4 *Friedrich Hölderlins Sämtliche Werke u. Briefe* edited by Franz Zinkernagel, 5 vols, Leipzig 1914-26, 2: 72, 75
5 *Werke* 1: 302
6 Ibid 309

CHAPTER EIGHT

1 Hoffmann provided no title for this story, but his German editors have been unanimous in according it this title. It has been translated into English many times under a variety of titles: 'Councillor Krespel' by J.M. Cohen (*Eight Tales of Hoffmann* London 1952) and 'Antonia's Song' by Christopher Lazare (*Tales of Hoffmann* New York 1959). Another popular English title is 'The Cremona Violin.'

2 Leo Weinstein *The Metamorphosis of Don Juan* Stanford 1959, 67
3 Tirso de Molina *Obras* Barcelona 1968, 555
4 Eulenburg edition of *Don Giovanni* edited by Alfred Einstein, introduction, xi. To what extent Mozart's *Don Giovanni* does or does not possess the demonic qualities Hoffmann saw in it may be pursued in the following publications: Georg Ellinger *E.T.A. Hoffmann: Sein Leben und Werke* Hamburg and Leipzig 1894, 83f.; Otto Jahn *W.A. Mozart* Leipzig 1891, 2: 432; C. Benn *Mozart on the Stage* London 1946, 72-3. On Schröder-Devrient and others who performed Donna Anna in accordance with Hoffmann's conception see L. Rellstab *Musikalische Beurtheilungen, Jahr 1827, 1831, 1832, 1836, Gesammelte Schriften, Neue Ausg.* vol 20, 1861. It has been alleged that Mozart indicated a demonic feeling by using trombones to accompany the Commendatore, as trombones were employed almost exclusively in religious music at the time. However, this does not seem to alter the character of the whole opera sufficiently, nor does it really seem to correspond with what Hoffmann had in mind.
5 For Kierkegaard's penetrating discussion of *Don Giovanni* see *Either/Or* translated by David F. Swenson and Lillian Marvin Swenson, New York 1959, vol 1, 'The Immediate Stages of the Erotic or the Musical Erotic.'

CHAPTER NINE

1 Hoffmann means the eighth bar.

CHAPTER TEN

1 See Paul Bekker *Richard Wagner, His Life in His Work* London and Toronto 1931, 292
2 Quoted from Alfred Einstein *Music in the Romantic Era* New York 1947, 79
3 Karl Ditters von Dittersdorf *Autobiography* London 1896, 252
4 *E.T.A. Hoffmanns Tagebücher und literarische Entwürfe* edited by Hans von Müller, Berlin 1915, vol 1
5 Quoted from Alfred Einstein *Music in the Romantic Era* 79
6 S. Kierkegaard *Either/Or* translated by David F. Swenson and Lillian Marvin Swenson, New York 1959, 1: 49
7 For the complete picture of Beethoven as he emerges from the Goethe-Zelter correspondence see J. Pulver 'Beethoven in the Goethe-Zelter Correspondence' *Music and Letters* vol 17, no 2, April 1936. Grillparzer's most detailed account of Beethoven's alleged crimes against music occurs in 'Beethovens nachteilige Wirkungen auf die Kunstwelt, ungeachtet seines hohen, nicht genug zu schätzenden Wertes' *Sämtliche Werke* Vienna 1909 etc., part 2, 9: 171.
8 J.F. Reichardt *Briefe eines aufmerksamen Reisenden* quoted from Oliver Strunk *Source Readings in Music History* New York 1950, 700, note
9 J.F. Reichardt *Briefe geschrieben auf einer Reise nach Wien* quoted from Strunk *Source Readings* 728-30
10 *Schriften zur Musik* edited by Friedrich Schnapp, Munich 1963, 19
11 J.F. Reichardt, quoted from Strunk *Source Readings* 738
12 *Allgemeine Musikalische Zeitung* 12 April 1809, 434-5

CHAPTER ELEVEN

1 Hoffmann obviously had in mind in this paragraph symphonies such as Dittersdorf's programmatic Ovid symphonies (twelve in all) or his other quasi-programmatic works such as *Il combattimento delle umane passione*, etc.

impressive fictional musician, Joseph Berglinger. The two creations have much in common. However, Kreisler is much more fully developed than Berglinger, and as a hero he is both more credible and more dynamic. No age could have adopted the studious and sentimental Berglinger as its archetype.

In his obiturary of Hoffmann (*Allgemeine Musikalische Zeitung* 9 October 1822) Rochlitz claimed it was he who had originally suggested the creation of Kreisler to Hoffmann, when the latter had first offered his services as a critic in 1809. But as Hewett-Thayer has demonstrated, this does not square with the facts. See Harvey W. Hewett-Thayer *Hoffmann: Author of the Tales* Princeton 1948, 276, note.

6 See Hitzig *Aus Hoffmanns Leben und Nachlass* Berlin 1823
7 See volume two of *Selected Writing of E.T.A. Hoffmann* translated by L.J. Kent and E.C. Knight, Chicago 1969.
8 *Werke* 9: 77
9 Ibid 1: 277
10 Karl Philipp Moritz quoted from Marcel Brion *Schumann and the Romantic Age* London 1956, 271
11 Oswald Spengler *Untergang des Abendlandes* Munich 1921, 1: 383

CHAPTER SIXTEEN

1 See Ronald Taylor *Hoffmann* London 1963, 33.
2 See 'Bach Through the Ages' by Alfred Einstein in *Music and Letters* vol 16, no 3, July 1935, 231-7.
3 Here is part of Rochlitz's description: 'Mozart came to Leipzig. I was with him often and witnessed his behaviour towards Bach's works. That inspired me. I modestly gathered up all Bach's music I could find and eagerly set about it. It should have succeeded; I had all the optimism of an adolescent; but it did not succeed, for the adolescent soon learns to temper his optimism. I took Bach's many-voiced compositions before me, but they seemed to be totally chaotic and in my haste I saw nothing in them ...' (*Allgemeine Musikalische Zeitung* April 1803, 513). In all fairness to Rochlitz it should be added that he did eventually come to respect Bach and to glimpse his greatness. But another contemporary, Carl Maria von Weber, never came to appreciate Bach and regarded him as no more than a musical charlatan.
4 Little of the choral music had been published, none of the cantatas and passions, none of the concerti, in reality nothing but a few organ works, some chorales, and *The Musical Offering*. See Ernst Ludwig Gerber *Historisch-biographisches Lexikon der Tonkünstler* Leipzig 1790-2, 1: 91-2. Gerber also shows that Bach's more illustrious son, Carl Philipp Emanuel, had fifty-five works in print by the same date.
5 *Werke* 1: 56
6 Ibid
7 E. Buchner *Das Neueste von Gestern* Munich 1912, 2: 81 translated by W.H. Bruford in *Germany in the Eighteenth Century* Cambridge 1935, 91
8 'Nachricht von einem gebildeten jungen Mann' *Werke* 1: 283
9 From Carl Maria von Weber's projected novel *The Life of an Artist* quoted in James D. Haar *Gleanings from Germany* London 1839
10 *Werke* 1: 291-2
11 Karl Ditters von Dittersdorf *Autobiography* London 1896, 297
12 Baron Max Maria von Weber *Carl Maria von Weber: The Life of an Artist* translated by J. Palgrave Simpson, 2 vols, London 1865, 1: 56

13 *E.T.A. Hoffmanns Briefwechsel* edited by Hans von Müller and Friedrich Schnapp, Munich 1967-9, 1: 257
14 *Werke* 9: 179

CHAPTER SEVENTEEN

1 Tubal-cain, inventor of brass and iron, was the brother of Jubal, the inventor of the harp and organ (Genesis 4: 22). Hoffmann is being ironical with his suggestion that Tubal-cain, rather than his brother, invented music.

CHAPTER EIGHTEEN

1 See 'Brief des Barons Wallborn an den Kapellmeister Kreisler' *Werke* 1: 276.
2 *Herzensergiessungen eines kunstliebenden Klosterbruders* in *W.H. Wackenroders Werke und Briefe* Jena 1910, 1: 131
3 Ibid 136
4 Marcel Brion *Schumann and the Romantic Age* London 1956, 9
5 Observe the reaction to this chord in the following translation.

CHAPTER TWENTY

1 *Werke* 1: 278
2 See Moritz Katz *Die Schilderung des musikalischen Eindrucks bei Schumann, Hoffmann und Tieck* (doc. diss.) Leipzig 1910.
3 *A.W. Schlegels Werke* Leipzig 1846-7, 9: 13
4 Karl von Eckartshausen *Aufschlüsse zur Magie aus geprüften Erfahrungen über verborgene philosophische Wissenschaften und verdeckte Geheimnisse der Natur* Munich 1791, 1: 336-9
5 The material concerning Schubart comes from Paul Greeff *E.T.A. Hoffmann als Musiker und Musikschriftsteller* Cologne and Krefeld 1948, 105-6.
6 The subject may be pursued in a more general way in Hugo Riemann's *Grundriss der Musikwissenschaft* Leipzig 1908, 75.
7 Table from Heinz-Richard Stock *Die optischen Synästhesien bei E.T.A. Hoffmann* (doc. diss.) Munich 1914
8 Paul Margis 'Die Synästhesien bei E.T.A. Hoffmann' in *Zeitschrift für Ästhetik und Allgemeine Kunstwissenschaft* Stuttgart 1910, 5: 91-9
9 *Werke* 1: 56. I have substituted 'clarinet' in the translation for the word 'basset horn' in the original.
10 'Phantasien über die Kunst,' Ludwig Tieck's continuation of Wackenroder's Berglinger story, *Herzensergiessungen eines kunstliebenden Klosterbruders* in *W.H. Wackenroders Werke und Briefe* Jena 1910, 1: 306-7
11 Edgar Allan Poe 'Colloquy of Monos and Una' in *Complete Works* New York 1965, 4: 206

CHAPTER TWENTY ONE

1 Quoted from Johannes Brahms *Des jungen Kreislers Schatzkästlein* Berlin 1909, entries 380 and 363

2　See Aniela Jaffé *Bilden und Symbole aus E.T.A. Hoffmanns Märchen* in C.G. Jung *Gestaltung des Unbewussten* Zurich 1950, 266 ff.

3　See Jean Paul *Vorschule der Ästhetik, Werke* Munich 1960, 5: 229 ff.

4　Carl Maria von Weber 'Tonkünstlers Leben' *Sämtliche Schriften* Berlin and Leipzig 1908, 437-510

5　See Oskar Walzel *Die romantische Schule* Berlin 1928, translated as *German Romanticism* by A.E. Lussky, New York 1932.

6　Jean Paul *Vorschule der Ästhetik, Werke* Munich 1960, 5: 88

7　Friedrich Schlegel *Lucinde*, in *Entwicklungsreihen (Reihe Romantik)* edited by P. Kenckhohn, Leipzig 1931, 4: 226

8　*The Miscellaneous Prose Works of Sir Walter Scott* London 1835, 2: 273

9　Jean Paul *Werke* Munich 1960, 1: 948

10　*Herzensergiessungen eines kunstliebenden Klosterbruders* in *W.H. Wackenroders Werke und Briefe*, Jena 1910, 1: 130

11　Aniela Jaffé *Bilden und Symbole* 227

12　Quotations from R.H. Thomas 'From Lenau and Beethoven' *Music and Letters* vol 18, no 4, October 1937, 474

13　Robert Schumann quoted from Oliver Strunk *Source Readings in Music History* New York 1950, 743

Index

Note: Hoffmann's literary works are indexed according to their English titles, where these have been used in the text. Incidental or rarely consulted works are indexed according to their original titles, as are Hoffmann's musical compositions.

E.T.A. HOFFMANN AND MUSIC

R. MURRAY SCHAFER

E.T.A. Hoffmann (1776-1822) was a man of diversified talents – an artist, composer, conductor, critic, jurist, and writer. Although he is best known for his stories, he was a music critic and composer for years before he wrote his celebrated *Tales*. Hoffmann has long been considered an extremely important force in the shaping of musical romanticism, yet this volume is the first adequate documentation of his influence. Because much of the primary material upon which the study is based has not previously been available in English, the author has chosen an unusual but especially appropriate format, in which translations of Hoffmann's writings and Professor Schafer's critical commentary alternate. This book not only fills a unique gap in the history of the romantic movement by showing the effect of Hoffmann's writings on the early phases of musical romanticism in Germany, but also presents an over-all picture of romanticism in its incipient years.

R. MURRAY SCHAFER, a composer and specialist in music education, is professor in the Department of Communication Studies at Simon Fraser University.